Praise for *Love and Struggle*

"Warning: this is not your daddy's New Left heroic adventure memoir, nor is it your conventional right-turn mea culpa. Dave Gilbert has written an honest, self-critical, sometimes painful, sometimes humorous reflection on what he learned over the course of three decades of activism. His journey from democrat to revolutionary was filled with mistakes and miscalculations, as well as extraordinary insights and revelations. Speaking to a new generation of activists, Gilbert reminds us that speeches and demonstrations alone do not make change, and the 'good fight' of the 1960s and '70s was a global fight—a bold act of solidarity with the world's oppressed."
  —Robin D.G. Kelley, author of *Freedom Dreams: The Black Radical Imagination*

"David Gilbert's story is a tale of consciousness, counterculture, and action during the generation of revolution, love, and hope. A tale of the best and worst of America, of struggle and love, and of hope and repression."
  —Zack de la Rocha, rapper, poet, activist, Rage Against the Machine vocalist

"Required reading for anyone interested in the history of radical movements in this country. An honest, vivid portrait of a life spent passionately fighting for justice. In telling his story, Gilbert also reveals the history of Left struggles in the 1960s and '70s, and imparts important lessons for today's activists.
  —Jordan Flaherty, author of *Floodlines: Community and Resistance from Katrina to the Jena Six*

"This story is from a true freedom fighter, a warrior against U.S. imperialism and for peace and justice."
  —Roxanne Dunbar-Ortiz, author of *Outlaw Woman: A Memoir of the War Years, 1960–75*

"When Malcolm X said John Brown was his standard for white activism, he could have easily meant David Gilbert. He is our generation's John Brown. His support of Black liberation as a method of freeing the world is to be studied, appreciated, and applied."
  —Jared A. Ball, associate professor of communication studies at Morgan State University, author of *I Mix What I Like! A Mixtape Manifesto*

"David Gilbert's memoir is a gift to the future. His story brings together three generations of social justice movements. The book is more than a fascinating history of an incredible life; it is an example of political praxis. Gilbert combines humor and humility, analysis and adventure, as he shows what it means to live one's life in pursuit of freedom. Brimming with insight and optimism, *Love and Struggle* shows the way."
  —Dan Berger, author of *Outlaws in America: The Weather Underground and the Politics of Solidarity*

"David Gilbert has written a rigorously honest, analytic memoir that grapples with the many dimensions of his history as a revolutionary anti-imperialist. Responding to a request from his son to write a book that reflects on his personal experiences, David is unafraid to examine his mistakes and shortcomings, especially regarding sexism and racism, while affirming the revolutionary principles that have guided him throughout his adult life. For thirty years, David has engaged in a dynamic conversation across the walls about radical history and the path forward. *Love and Struggle* is a compelling contribution to that critical dialogue."
—Diana Block, activist, author of *Arm the Spirit: A Woman's Journey Underground and Back*

"David Gilbert was there when it all jumped off: from the Civil Rights movement, to the emergence of Black Power, to the movement against the U.S. war in Vietnam and the subsequent years of resistance against the genocidal policies our government was carrying out in our name. This starkly honest history—told from the prison cell where David has spent thirty years and where, if nothing changes, he will spend seventy-five to life—is infused with the sharp intelligence of a scholar and the courage of a man of conscience. It is full of hope, even as it recounts, with brave honesty, too many losses and hard lessons learned."
—Laura Whitehorn, activist, former political prisoner

"Like many of his contemporaries, David Gilbert gambled his life on a vision of a more just and generous world. His particular bet cost him the last three decades in prison, and whether or not you agree with his youthful decision, you can be the beneficiary of his years of deep thought, reflection, and analysis on the reality we all share. I urge you to read it."
—Peter Coyote, actor, author of *Sleeping Where I Fall*

"After suffering thirty years of hard time in several of America's most brutal dungeons, after enduring separation and isolation and loss, after braving a decades-long campaign of demonization and misinformation orchestrated from the pinnacles of power, David Gilbert speaks up with hope and a simple clarity that belies his circumstances. This is a unique and necessary voice forged in the growing American gulag, the underbelly of the 'land of the free,' offering a focused and unassailable critique as well as a vision of a world that could be but is not yet—a place of peace and love, joy and justice. Gilbert's humanity, dignity, and integrity are entirely intact, his fierce intelligence full up, his sense of urgency unchanged. Anyone who wants to understand the sorry state we are in and hopes to participate in finding a more hopeful path forward should read this passionate and compelling book."
—Bill Ayers, author of *Fugitive Days* and *Teaching Toward Freedom*

"This book should stimulate learning from our political prisoners, but more importantly it challenges us to work to free them, and in doing so take the best of our history forward."
—Susan Rosenberg, author of *An American Radical: Political Prisoner in My Own Country*

"David Gilbert's revolutionary spirit vibrates after thirty years in prison. His wisdom and love have empowered him to withstand and positively transform personal and political difficulties throughout the decades and still remain a loving and courageous human being and teacher. Most importantly, the reader cannot escape a dialogue with the heart and a constant reexamination of what is real and human about love and struggle. Gilbert's understanding of mistakes made in the name of liberation serves as a valuable lesson and inspiration. This is a book of hope kindled in the love and struggle of the world's people."
—Alicia and Lucy Rodriguez, former Puerto Rican political prisoners

Love and Struggle

My Life in SDS, the Weather Underground, and Beyond

David Gilbert

Love and Struggle: My Life in SDS, the Weather Underground, and Beyond
David Gilbert

© PM Press 2012
All rights reserved. No part of this book may be transmitted by any means without permission in writing from the publisher
PO Box 23912
Oakland, CA 94623
www.pmpress.org

Cover by John Yates
Interior design by Jonathan BHR

ISBN: 978-1-60486-319-2
Library of Congress Control Number: 2011927953
10 9 8 7 6 5 4 3 2 1

Printed in the USA on recycled paper, by the employee owners of Thomson-Shore in Dexter, Michigan.
www.thomsonshore.com

CONTENTS

—To today's activists and organizers—

"Love is an action, never simply a feeling."

bell hooks

"Mask no difficulties, mistakes, failures. Claim no easy victories... Our experience has shown us that in the general framework of daily struggle this battle against ourselves, this struggle against our own weaknesses... is the most difficult of all."

Amílcar Cabral

{ An Appreciation by Boots Riley }

In college, the 1960s and '70s were the stuff of legend. For me and my friends, debating political stances for hours at a time, it seemed mandatory to name-check Marx, Malcolm, Mao, Lenin, and of course the Panthers. (Even if you weren't so sure of what you were talking about. I was definitely guilty of this!)

You also had to begin a sentence at some point, to seem credible, with: "In the '60s, they used to…" The 1960s, in our minds, were an exciting time, one in which we all wished we could have played a part. A time, we imagined, when you had but to intone the word "rally" and thousands would magically appear, fired up and ready to occupy a building or battle the police.

We critiqued, with praise and derision, organizations and figures that seemed almost from an alternate universe. "When Huey got that letter where the FBI forged Eldridge's name on it, he should have… When the Weathermen did that Days of Rage shit, it was…"

It was, and still is, so easy to sit back in awe of what our heroes did, or to talk about what we would have done instead. Usually, this sort of thinking was not enough to make us organize for ourselves. It was kind of like reading a book about playing piano, and then debating what we had read without ever touching a piano. It takes a certain discipline and initiative to actually sit in front of the keys and try to play.

David Gilbert is a player. Like the Panthers of old, he and his comrades in Weather heard the symphony of revolutionary thought and action from around the world, and instead of simply applauding or critiquing, climbed down out of the balcony, jumped up on the stage of history, and banged out a tune.

Right now, we have access to information about current struggles and atrocities at our fingertips. Thousands of blogs pontificate on the latest political occurrence. You can be in Oakland or St. Louis and see video of the protest that happened in Bangladesh two hours ago. But this access to information is almost meaningless without the organization or initiative to take action upon it.

David Gilbert cuts through the mystique of what it takes to build an organization, call for action, and take action. This new book of his is not some glorified "I was there" fantasy reading as autobiography. Gilbert cares about the people he struggled with, the causes for which he fought.

The actions taken were so bold, the intentions so optimistic, and in some cases, the consequences so devastating, that the reader will not be able to help but get caught up in the romantic fervor.

We need more of that fervor today. David calls it "love for the people." It is the source of the intense feeling of hope that lights up these pages as he tells his story. Hope for a just world. And that feeling of hope was only able to emerge, in the 1960s, from a sense of power. A sense that within one's reach, within one's community, there was the power to change the world.

What instills that feeling of power to change the world in a populace? Exposing the truth? Unveiling statistics? Making sure you have a correct analysis of the world? Showing that there is power in numbers via victorious campaigns for material changes? Many would argue that it is a combination of all these things and more. Some would make their argument with words. Others would make their argument by organizing. Others by taking action in the laboratory of social upheaval.

I make music that calls for many of the same things David Gilbert and his comrades called for. It is my attempt to communicate my interpretation of the world. I use words, rhythms, and melodies to spark ideas that might cause someone to form or join an organization that may have an actual chance of changing the world. This is a book about someone who, with others, communicated their interpretation of the world—and of the need to change the world—by simply getting out there and changing the world. No complicated, roundabout, message-hidden-in-the-art-to-the-point-that-it's-almost-irrelevant bullshit for them. They took action.

I will probably not go to prison simply because of my music. That's ironic, because some of the best players, past and present, are in prison today. Like David Gilbert.

> Activist artist Boots Riley is best known as the leader of The Coup, which *Billboard* magazine declared "the best hip-hop act of the past decade." Riley also teamed with Tom Morello of Rage Against the Machine to form the revolutionary new group Street Sweeper Social Club. Recently he has been a vital voice of the Occupy movement.

{ INTRODUCTION }

"**H**onestly, Dad, I'm not enthusiastic about *No Surrender*. I mean, you have some good stuff there, but it's almost all analytical. People relate much better to personal experiences. I wish you'd write about yours, about what life in prison is like."

That's my son, Chesa, and he's talking about the book that just came out with some of my essays and book reviews. It's July 2004, he's twenty-three, and we're on a family reunion visit at Clinton Correctional Facility. (In a reform won after the 1971 Attica rebellion, New York State allows periodic forty-four-hour visits from immediate family in small trailer homes on the prison grounds. Chesa has been coming on these "trailer visits" since he was five, and they've played a wonderful role in strengthening our bond and enriching our relationship.)

The idea of a memoir is not a new suggestion to me. Since I came "upstate" in 1983, fellow prisoners have repeatedly encouraged me to write my "life story," but I've never had the slightest desire to do so. Everyone's life, if well told, is interesting; but I always said I wanted to live my life rather than write about it, and the memoir as a form always felt too self-involved, and often too self-justifying, for me.

But this challenge is different. Beyond my natural desire to be responsive to my son, there's new context. Since the 2003 release of the Sam Green and Bill Siegel film *The Weather Underground*, I've received a steady stream of letters from young activists who admire the WUO's deep commitment to fundamental social change. These lively and engaged letters are filled with questions trying to learn from my generation's experiences. I consider these correspondences my top priority; but there is only so much one can say in a letter, and only so many dialogues one can carry on at a time. For a number of reasons, I'm not yet ready to write about prison, as Chesa urged. But a memoir about my movement experiences has become appealing as a way to respond more fully and widely to the issues young activists have been raising with me.

This book is not at all a comprehensive history of SDS and the WUO (the best such account can be found in Dan Berger's *Outlaws of America*). Nor does it tell my life story. For one thing, there have been far more major influences on me, wonderful people, than I could even mention, let alone adequately describe. Because the experiences briefly recounted here can't begin to do the individuals involved justice, I generally avoid giving real or full names unless I'm discussing public events or the person has given me permission.

There are many pitfalls to writing memoirs. Memory can get hazy, and honesty is a constant struggle. There is the danger of pontificating with latter-day wisdom or, alternatively, of living the feelings of the moment in a way that justifies errors. The reader will decide how well I do. My fondest hope for this effort is that it can be of use in the ongoing struggle.

David Gilbert, July 4, 2010

{BEGINNINGS}

Whack. "*Talk, motherfucker, talk!*"

(*How the hell did I end up here—handcuffed and getting worked over in the back of a police car?*)

POW. "*Who else was involved and where are they headed?*"

(*Good, at least some of the comrades got away.*)

Whomp. "*Tell us.*"

(*Cops always go for the balls; that used to happen when I got jumped at demonstrations too. Sure, it's a sensitive spot, but if you see it coming you can usually protect with your legs and thighs. So why is it their favorite target, some hang-up about emasculation?*)

Whack. "*Talk if you know what's good for you, goddamn it!*"

(*Surprising that they're hitting me in the face too. Aren't they worried about visible signs of the beating? Are they so enraged that they're not thinking? Or do they feel that the car crash that ended the chase gives them cover for any bruises?*)

…It's October 20, 1981. The little drama of my "interrogation" follows the much bigger one of a Brink's armored car robbery that went terribly wrong: Unexpected gunshots at the scene; someone who just happens to be looking out a rear window at an otherwise deserted and obscure spot sees the sloppy switch of vehicles; the escape truck gets caught at a red light, by the entrance to the NY Thruway, as police come in to set up a roadblock; a shootout; a car chase on unfamiliar streets; a crash, relatively mild but enough to stop the car, as our Honda can't quite negotiate a sudden right-angle turn. Maybe at that point revolutionary ideals call for a shootout, but I don't have a gun and wouldn't be effective if I did. So it is capture instead. The time is late afternoon. I don't remember exactly, maybe four-thirty or five…

The beating continues in the station. Now I'm up against the wall, with my hands cuffed behind my back. But my adrenaline must be flowing, because it seems like I can see the punches start long before they land, enough time at least to cross my legs when they're going for my nuts and to bob and weave a bit, so they don't hit quite as directly when going for my head. Can't do much about the body shots. With all the adrenaline, I feel the impact but not the pain—that won't come until a day or two later.

Someone brings grim news: a wounded officer has just died. Now I know this is as serious as it can get. The cops in the room, understandably, are livid. I'm also thinking about consequences. For someone who's defied the law for many years, I'm surprisingly ignorant of its specifics. I'm thinking now that I could be charged with "accessory to murder" and guessing that could mean something like seven to ten years in prison.

Now a cop bursts in with a shotgun, while another shouts, "Don't shoot! Don't shoot!" The barrel is jammed into my neck, right under the Adam's apple. "Talk, goddamn it! Who else was involved? Where are they headed?" (They wouldn't really splatter my brains against the station wall; that would be too much of a scandal, right?) In any case, talking is not an option for me. When I say nothing, he slams the barrel across my face, opening a half-circle cut on my left cheek.

No one plays "good cop" until the FBI guy comes. He's in a suit, calm and rational. "You can get the death penalty for this." (I don't think New York State has a death penalty.) "The first one who talks is going to get a big break." (The first? No one will rat.)

The interrogation, beatings, and psychological warfare go on well into the night. My main thought is how to get through this with the minimum damage. No spitfire bravado from me; I'm certainly no tough guy, and I try my best not to inflame them any further. But it's also important to be firm because any sign of wavering encourages them to ratchet up the pressure. So my only response—to all of this, for hours—is "I want to see a lawyer." I figure they may have some concerns about messing up their legal case by denying me access.

At one point I make a mistake. The pressure is great about where those who escaped may have headed, and I say, "Well, you have my ID," and they go rushing off to check the address. It's a phony ID that has nothing to do with any place I've lived or operated, and I figure that they have it anyway. But then it occurs to me: What if by a bizarre quirk of fate a comrade goes to that neighborhood—I don't know where people hang out—and the heat from my remark leads to his or her getting spotted? (Fortunately, nothing came of this.) As an experienced revolutionary I should know: never tell them anything, no matter how innocuous it may seem.

As tense as things are, I'm spared any anxiety at all about whether to talk. That's a bedrock principle, one based on the reality that, however bad a situation is, ratting throws others into that same cauldron. So my focus is completely on bobbing and weaving—physically and psychologically—trying to minimize the damage I sustain. It's not even defiance or resolve; it's just that talking is never even an option that enters my mind. Perhaps that foundation gives some firmness to my refusal, even if it's devoid of bravado. It also helps that I'm not feeling any physical pain. As I will later learn, from what happens to two of the Black comrades, there is a big difference between beatings, even with death threats, and systematic torture. The latter involves maximizing the pain and anguish that the victim feels.

At around ten-thirty the interrogation finally ends as I'm taken out to be fingerprinted. Kathy (Boudin) and I, each sur-rounded by cops, get a glimpse of each other in the hall, and we exchange a longing look, which in that fleeting moment speaks volumes: most of all, our anguish about our year-old son, who is at childcare with a neighbor; also a recognition of the seriousness of our situation, and an affirmation of our love.

How the hell did I end up in such dire straits?

Missing the Wink

America is a democracy "with liberty and justice for all," based on the principle that "all men are created equal…with certain unalienable rights, that among these are Life, Liberty, and the Pursuit of Happiness." That's what they taught me, and it sounded beautiful. Still does. I fervently embraced these ideals and fully accepted them as the reality in our country. I thought that everyone had the same benefits and opportunities I had in upper middle-class Brookline, Massachusetts: a secure, comfortable home; food, clothing, and medical care; a good public school system, where the vast majority went on to college; an expectation that each of us would end up making a good living in a profession that afforded considerable self-esteem. Somehow I missed the wink that the "all" referred only to white males with money. When the myths were later exploded by the eruption of the civil rights movement, I became deeply upset. The entire impetus for my becoming politically conscious and active was to get America to live up to its ideals of democracy for all.

How could I have been so stupid or, to put it more charitably, naïve? Beyond the typical childish assumption that the whole world is an extension of one's immediate experience, I was especially susceptible to such idealism due to my family upbringing. Bea and Sam Gilbert were not only devoted and loving parents, but also decent and ethical people. They weren't Left or radical by any means—in the first presidential election that I followed, in 1952, they voted for the Republican, Dwight Eisenhower. And they were very patriotic toward a country that offered children of immigrants great opportunities. Each of my four grandparents had fled the anti-Semitism of a different Eastern European country, and my parents had lived the often-told but still inspiring story of immigrants who grew up in poverty. They had jobs at an early age, and my father worked his way through night school to become an engineer. I still remember some of the family stresses from not being able to make ends meet—until I was five, in 1949, when my dad got a good-paying job as production manager for Hasbro Toy Company.

Their main moral influence on me came from the ethical lives they lived. They weren't self-righteous toward others, and they practiced what they preached to their children, from not smoking to the importance of community service. My dad was "Mister Boy Scouts" in our neighborhood, a scoutmaster for many years and also the director of our temple's youth league for teenagers. My mom was both a den mother for Cub Scouts and the leader of the local Girl Scout troop. Their attraction to scouting was not to the more militarist aspect but instead was rooted in a love of nature and a wish to provide positive activities for kids. When our rabbi complained that weekend camping trips kept the scouts away from services, my father responded, "They're closer to God in the woods than in the temple." In fact, they started taking me camping when I was just one year old. A true son of both my parents, I went on to become an Eagle Scout and also to win the highest religious medal for Jewish scouts, the Ner Tamid. Religion was a foundation in our household, too, not as a rigid set of ritual prescriptions but rather as a core of ethical teachings summed up by the "Golden Rule": Do unto others as you would have them do unto you.

While not at all activists, my parents taught me, unambiguously, that racism is wrong, that all people should be treated with respect. These values grew out of their experiences being Jewish following the Holocaust. My very first piece of creative writing, when I was ten or eleven, described the wonderfully accomplished and worthwhile life of a man named Carl, and ended with: "But none of the above ever happened because Carl was killed, as a young boy, in a concentration camp." The message I heard loud and clear was that racism, all racism, is the greatest evil of all. This sensibility was central to my later readiness to respond so full-heartedly to the emergence of the civil rights movement. Three other factors also played important roles: religious bigotry, proto-feminist sisters, and rock 'n' roll.

As a kid, religion was important to me because it offered a set of ethical teachings and a purpose in life beyond crass self-interest. I worried about the many friends who didn't abide by the dos and don'ts, and I was upset by the blatant hypocrites who piously went to services each Saturday and then conned and cheated in business dealings all week. But it was finally religious bigotry that drove me out of the temple.

Brookline, almost all white, had three main social strata that broadly correlated with religious background. A small enclave of upper-crust Protestants lived in mansions. The mainstay of the population was upper middle-class, small business owners and professionals, and Jewish. There was also a more working-class, predominantly Catholic neighborhood, which filled the bulk of Brookline's quota for the military draft. The rich kids went to private schools, so I had little contact with them. But there were a number of Catholic kids in the public schools, and several of them became my friends.

The Hebrew School teacher who was in charge of the youth services, Mr. Ross, was a bigot. Both in classes and at our services, he railed that Catholic doctrine was ludicrous. "How could God possibly be born of woman?" and "How can one God be three?" and on and on and on. I didn't want to hear it. They had their religious belief, and I had mine, but my Catholic friends weren't idiots to be constantly put down. When I was thirteen, some months after my Bar Mitzvah, I was at a service when Mr. Ross started one of his rants. I whispered my complaints to the friend sitting next to me. While Mr. Ross didn't hear what I said, he bridled at the disruption: "Anyone who doesn't like the way I run the services can leave." I didn't yet have the courage or confidence to stand up to him, to speak out, but I wasn't going to sit there while he attacked my friends. So I thought about it for a couple of minutes and then walked out. That was it for me, and I never went back to organized religion.

My parents argued, quite reasonably, that it was a shame that Mr. Ross was bigoted, but he didn't represent Judaism. But I guess that by the age of thirteen I already had a strong stubborn streak. In any case, there was too much hypocrisy and narrow-mindedness in all religions for me. I would try to live up to the ethical ideals, but not be beholden to any religious authority. I guess I was becoming a bit of a rebel too—largely due to the influence of my big sisters.

As the youngest of three children and the only boy, I undoubtedly got preferential treatment (years later my mother told me that with each successive child she became more confident and relaxed), but it didn't feel that way because my sisters teased me mercilessly, even if still lovingly. Ruth was six years old than me, and Brenda three and a half. They were my mentors, and I admired them. Since Brenda was closer in age, she played with me more, and she was one of the best athletes on the block. I remember our neighborhood football games and her ability to run right through my attempted tackles. In that situation I looked up to her literally as well as figuratively.

Ruth, and especially Brenda, were more rebellious than I was, and they did their best to make sure that my goody-two-shoes devotion to morality did not lead to my growing up to be a stuffed shirt. They instilled in me that great American value of always rooting for the underdog. Long before any political consciousness, we sided with the Indians on TV instead of the cowboys, even though they always lost; and we always found playing them, or the robbers against the cops, more interesting and fun. We didn't watch much TV or have a lot of elaborate toys. My sisters were very creative, and the way we played was to invent our own games and to act out various fantasy stories.

I'm not sure why they were rebels, but I suspect it had to do with their early feminist consciousness before the reemergence of the women's movement, before the "second wave." My parents firmly believed that the girls should be educated and have the ability to have successful careers, but that encouragement to achieve was encased within the traditional message that their prime goal was marriage and children. The professional degrees were in case their husbands died. But to my sisters, this was an impossible mixed message: on one hand to excel, and on the other to catch a husband—at a time when men were turned off by smart, challenging women. In retrospect, I feel the stress from this tension engendered their strained relationships to our mom and dad—who in so many ways were wonderful parents.

But for me, it meant that in the late 1950s, as I moved into adolescence, I was steeped in their indignation and insistence on women's rights.

This was before Betty Friedan's *The Feminine Mystique* was published. The book they relied on to teach me was Ashley Montagu's *The Natural Superiority of Women*. Some of it was kind of crude, in the war-of-the-sexes mode, but a lot was refreshingly iconoclastic, and my admiration for my sisters meant that I took it all seriously. Their frustrations with the way society limited women also led, I believe, to the general identification with the underdog, which they so deeply imbedded in me.

My sisters also introduced me to popular music. In the early 1950s, Ruth was a big Eddie Fisher fan, which was a bit risqué relative to my parents' devotion to classical music. But then Brenda brought me, at the age of ten, right into the birth of rock 'n' roll in 1954. I remember listening with rapt excitement to "Rock Around the Clock," "Silhouettes on the Shade," and "A Rose and a Baby Ruth." Brenda was crazy about Elvis, and she enlisted me to call into radio stations to request "Love Me Tender." My loyalty to her made me an Elvis fan too, but Chuck Berry and The Coasters stirred me even more. Their songs had a more exciting beat, and I delighted in Berry's saying openly that school was a drag and his telling Beethoven to "roll over." The sexual innuendos were thrilling too. For me, and I suspect for many in my generation, our love of rock 'n' roll played an important role in our ability to identify with the Black struggle as it erupted.

Illusions Replaced by a Dream

A model citizen in training, I carefully studied each candidate's program and itched for my twenty-first birthday and the right to vote. My illusions were shattered in February 1960, with the sit-ins in Greensboro, North Carolina. A group of Black students sat down to order at a Woolworth's lunch counter that was for "whites only," and they were denied service. At subsequent sit-ins racist mobs spat on the protesters, dumped food on their heads, and beat them. I saw it on the news. I couldn't believe it—and I couldn't accept it.

The modern civil rights movement had started over four years earlier, on December 1, 1955, when Rosa Parks refused to give her seat on a public bus to a white man, setting off the famous and ultimately successful Montgomery Bus Boycott. There were many dramatic campaigns and incidents that followed. But it wasn't until I was fifteen that I was ready to follow and focus on such events—and to begin to feel they affected me because of my ardent desire to live in a democracy.

It wasn't long before I learned that segregated lunch counters were just the surface—that Black people throughout the South weren't allowed to vote, usually lived in poverty, and were terrorized with brutal violence for "insolence," for "not knowing their place." The first time I spoke up in any way, about a year later, was to write an article supporting civil rights for my high school newspaper, the *Sagamore*.

My oldest sister, Ruth, had become an activist at Radcliff, and was soon on picket lines against Woolworth's in Boston because of their segregated lunch counters in the South, one of the first such civil rights actions in the North. As Ruth became more radical, she and our father got into some bitter, screaming arguments. There was obviously some psychological dynamic beyond the political differences involved. In any case, I wasn't knowledgeable or articulate enough to join the debate. I hated her contempt toward our dad (which didn't save me from moments of gross arrogance toward our folks a few years later) but tended to agree with her more on the issues. While Ruth and I were on different pages emotionally (she considered me stodgy and conservative), she was my first source of Left literature. It was actually pretty tame stuff—the *Progressive* and the *New Republic*—but it opened a new world to me, to see anything that challenged official government positions and presented some of the facts that didn't make it into the mainstream media. It was exhilarating.

My reading exposed me to a wider range of issues. I was outraged to learn that our government was paying farmers billions of dollars *not* to grow food, while people, especially children, around the world were going hungry—the epitome of an irrational and inhumane policy. When John Kennedy was elected president in 1960, with his image of youthful vigor and idealism, I formulated a plan and dedicated myself to realizing it. Each year the president met with about a dozen outstanding Boy Scouts or

Explorers (the scouting program for teens), with each region selecting one representative. I worked to be the one from New England. I was already an Eagle Scout and a senior patrol leader and had attended a few national scouting events. The other prerequisite was the top religious award, and I quickly fulfilled the requirements and got my Ner Tamid.

If and when selected, I was going to find a moment and say this to the president I admired: "How can we pay farmers not to grow food when people are starving? I know we have to support the farmers, but couldn't the government encourage them to grow all they can and then buy it all at the support price to distribute to the hungry?" Obviously I was a bit naïve about the logic of capitalism; adequate food or housing at the bottom would ease demand up and down the line, thereby lowering prices and cutting into profits. And I didn't even have an inkling of the deeper reasons why these countries were no longer growing enough food for themselves. My simple proposal would never happen, but I didn't get to learn that lesson in 1961 because I wasn't selected as New England's scouting representative.

From both reading and current events, I started to learn that the U.S. was not about democracy internationally either. In fact, our government supported and even installed a raft of brutal dictators. How could that happen? My very superficial analysis was that business interests had somehow managed to corrupt our State Department's true mission. An article in the *Progressive* described how the U.S. had plucked Ngo Dinh Diem from a Catholic monastery in Ossining, New York, and made him president of South Vietnam, at the head of a hated regime. At the same time, a friend who had had a Vietnamese exchange student living at his house told me that she—from an aristocratic background and certainly no Communist—had said that Ho Chi Minh was considered the George Washington of their country. I was still staunchly anti-Communist, but democracy, people's right to choose their own leaders, came first. Besides, the level of repression to maintain the unpopular Diem in power was unacceptable. In 1961, I wrote an article for the *Sagamore* saying that America was in danger of getting drawn into a major civil war in South

Vietnam, and on the wrong side at that. It's hard to imagine now, but back then it was simply unheard of to question "our" foreign policy. In response to my article, a good friend's father, an MD, threatened to fill out a form to have me committed to a mental hospital.

What moved me from writing to activism was Martin Luther King Jr. I don't remember the exact time and place, but the first time I saw him speak on TV this ripple went through my chest. My heart leapt to his idealism, responding with: "That's what it means to be human, to care about people, to lead a moral and engaged life!" My first demonstration was a picket line protesting segregated (and, more to the point, inferior) education for Black children in Boston. To my surprise, my father was very upset when he found out. My folks were sympathetic to civil rights but opposed to my activism. My father claimed that, if I was seen on TV, it could hurt him with Hasbro's business affiliates in Tennessee. I suspect that it was more his fear that I could get arrested and ruin my prospects for a professional career. In any case, I wasn't yet active enough for our differences to come to a head. I obeyed my parents' order not to go to a demonstration for the last time in 1963, when I was in college and living in New York City. As a result I missed the historic civil rights March on Washington where Martin Luther King Jr. gave his stirring "I have a dream" speech.

As I talked with adults in Brookline and challenged their denials of discrimination, I saw that there was a vicious cycle strangling equality. When I asked why Black families didn't live in our community, the answer was that they didn't have the jobs to afford the houses. Why didn't they have the jobs? It was that they weren't educated. Why didn't they have a good education? They lived in poor neighborhoods. So I decided the only way to proceed was to take on the complete cycle, to work on jobs, housing, and education together. And where were the employers, realtors, and educators? They almost all went to churches and synagogues in communities like mine. So I formulated a plan: I would go to every denominational head for the greater Boston area and get them to sponsor a program for all their congregations that educated parishioners about the need to work for equality, and how to do so, in all of these key areas.

Of course we would need anti-racist educators, so I went to the NAACP (National Association for the Advancement of Colored People), the largest and most prestigious civil rights organization. It was my first trip to an activist office, and I remember the intensity, too much work for too few staff, the dedication. I also remember my arrogance, my unconscious racism in fighting racism, in being so sure that I, with no experience, had the breakthrough idea that would turn things around, that implementing my plan should be their top priority. As busy as he was, their president, Tom Atkins, acceded to my persistence and took time out to listen to my idea. He was skeptical (and in reality my plan was a waste of his time) but graciously agreed to provide the instructors if I could set up the sessions.

I then wrote to every denominational head in greater Boston, and ended up meeting with a couple of them. I went to these meetings clean-cut and scrubbed, in my Explorer Scout blazer and tie. And the results were that they would tell me what a fine young man I was, but would offer nothing concrete in terms of implementing the program. One or two said they would get back to me, but as the months dragged on, no one did. I guess I was supposed to be satisfied with the personal praise, but instead I was extremely frustrated that this program didn't get off the ground, that this eminently reasonable plan for working within the system got nowhere. Evidently the religious leaders I spoke to, who wouldn't publicly condone the evil of racism, didn't want the controversy and possible backlash of bringing civil rights to their congregations. Perhaps with enough time and persistence I could have found someone, somewhere, to get one local program going. My hope had been for the churches to adopt the program and give it to the NAACP to run, because I would soon be leaving Boston to start college in New York City.

{ THE 1960S AND THE MAKING }
OF A REVOLUTIONARY

Wow! I never thought that freshman orientation at Columbia would be like this. These skits to introduce us to the various student organizations and activities are all about one thing: SEX. It's like you're expected to go up to the first Barnard girl you see and rip open her blouse. But now the dean is addressing us with a serious impassioned plea: "Whatever you do, don't go into Harlem, especially with a Columbia sweatshirt on!"

That clinches it for Steve and me. The next night we cut the regular program and go to Harlem (although without our Columbia sweatshirts). To us it's like stepping into another country, with a language we barely understand. The streets are alive, teeming the people out socializing at night. A few folks are kind of reeling as they walk; I guess they're high. There's an animated card game on the stoop across the street; and on the corner four young guys are singing doo-wop, and it sounds great.

The next morning Steve and I head down to Wall St., and we're amazed by the long, sleek limousines. Rapping with one of the chauffeurs we learn what the limo is worth. The price would cover four years at Columbia, an education the youths we had seen in Harlem could never afford.

Columbia and the Black Struggle

My first voluntary act after arriving at Columbia University was to join the local CORE (Congress of Racial Equality) chapter. That was in the fall of 1962. CORE was the most militant northern-based civil rights group of that time (by the late '60s CORE completely changed its leadership and direction, promoting an "anti-crime" program). They were sponsoring the electrifying "freedom rides" of the day. Integrated groups were riding the bus lines into the South, demanding that the federal government desegregate interstate travel. They were brutally attacked by Ku Klux Klanners (and it was later revealed that FBI agents participated in some of those attacks). I didn't have the courage or commitment to volunteer to go on a freedom ride, but I wanted to lend my support to these efforts.

The guy sitting at the table on Low Plaza introduced himself as the chairman of the chapter. I remember thinking, but not saying, "What's wrong with these activists? Why can't they pick a good old American title like 'president'? 'Chairman' sounds like it's from the Soviet Union." That's how strong anti-Communism was, coming out of the 1950s. And it was used as a bludgeon against any social stirrings against the system. Before long I got involved in CU CORE's campaign to support the university's cafeteria workers, mainly Black and Latino/a, who were trying to form a union. I wasn't part of NY CORE's attempt to block entrance to the 1964 World's Fair in Queens. I was stunned by their audacity and tried to defend their action against the hostile reaction on campus.

In those days, there were a number of liberal, do-good projects emanating out of Columbia. Most of the programs brought ghetto kids to the university for tutoring. We used to joke—with incipient consciousness that something was seriously wrong—that the programs were designed to mold Harlem Blacks to think like Brooklyn Jews. However, one of the projects had the position that learning took place best in the child's own environment. That's the one I chose. So, in 1964, I was going into Harlem once or twice a week to tutor.

Despite my civil rights consciousness, I was still shocked by the level of oppression that I saw. A friend's uncle died because of lack of access to basic medical care; some buildings didn't have heat during the winter; police intimidated and abused people. At first, in my naïveté, I was running to the Human Rights Commission every month, but I soon learned that that route did not change a thing.

If the experience had been only of the starkness of oppression, I might have remained a militant liberal. But I saw the other side, too, the strength of Black people and the vibrancy of the culture they developed in the face of those hardships. There was a much greater sense of community, of the extended family, of helping each other out, of openness and expression of human feelings, than anything I had experienced in Brookline or at

Columbia. I don't mean to romanticize Black culture; the strains from oppression were there, too: violence, drugs, absent fathers. But there was a strength from their resistance and a basic humanism that really struck me.

This experience helped me understand that Black people could run their own communities far better than any outside force—including well-meaning liberals like myself—could run it for them. I was in transition from a liberal, who wanted to "uplift" the oppressed (to make them more like me), to a radical who realized that oppressed people themselves must become the arbiters of their own destiny. The other side of becoming a radical was realizing that things were far from ideal in the society I came from. I did not want to pass on to my children a society wracked by racism and unjust wars, where the almighty dollar was valued far above human beings. Joining with the Black struggle for human rights was a key to achieving a more humane society for white people also.

The understanding of U.S. society was much more advanced in Harlem than at the Political Science Department at Columbia. I was still tutoring when the U.S. started bombing North Vietnam. Actually, the first bombing was in August 1964, with the famed Tonkin Gulf Resolution. This was an initial flurry to prepare public opinion and establish a "legal" justification for an undeclared war. The sustained bombing did not begin until February 24, 1965, shortly after Johnson's election as the "peace" candidate. I had, by fortuitous circumstances, been part of the minute percentage of people in the U.S. who knew that our government had imposed an unpopular dictator on South Vietnam. So, on a February day in 1965, I was tense, brooding about the new bombing campaign as I rode the subway into Harlem. The families who would have me tutor their kids were far from the most militant. When I got to the door, the child's mother could see from my face that I was terribly upset. "Dave, what's the matter?" "I can't believe it. Our government is bombing people on the other side of the globe for no good reason." At that point, she had never heard of Vietnam nor did she know the background, but her response was immediate: "Bombing people for no good reason, huh? Must be colored people who live there." She made the connection in a very direct way, opening my eyes even though I had been working on both fronts, civil rights and peace, for some four years. I was still blinded by defining our system as a "democracy" with some faults, while she understood it as, in its essence, a racist and exploitative system.

The basic connection between Black liberation here and national liberation struggles throughout the Third World was developed and expressed in its most crystalline and powerful form by Malcolm X. At a time when "well-meaning liberals" were cautioning Blacks that they were a 10 percent minority that might provoke a white backlash, Malcolm demonstrated that Black people were part of the vast majority in the world, oppressed peoples. At a time when most Americans didn't yet know the war in Vietnam was going on, Malcolm already saw that the U.S. would be defeated there. Some analysts feel that as soon as Malcolm X traveled to Africa and directly connected the Black struggle here to Third World struggles abroad, the CIA signed his death warrant, even if the immediate executioners were from the Nation of Islam. Within a year of those travels, he was assassinated. (Many of his speeches can be found in *Malcolm X Speaks*, Grove Press.)

On February 18, 1965, Malcolm spoke to a capacity audience in the Barnard gymnasium. Of course I was there, although with mixed feelings. I felt favorably toward him because I supported Black militancy, but his nationalism made me uneasy—would I be rejected just because I was white? What role did we have in the struggle?

It is rare that a mere speech has lasting impact on one's consciousness. But seeing Malcolm speak was one of the formative experiences of my life. I had never encountered such a clear exposition of social reality. He explained that the division in the world wasn't between Black and white but rather between the oppressed, who were mostly people of color, and the oppressors who were mostly white. He also put forward a positive role for whites—but not within the Black struggle. Our role was to fight the system and organize within our own communities. Three days later, he was dead.

Assault on a Black-Jewish Alliance

On that day at Barnard, the most persistent questions from the audience were about "Black anti-Semitism." This charge both surprised and upset me. I certainly hadn't experienced any bias during my work in Harlem. I felt that the tension expressed was being used to evade fundamental issues of white supremacy in America. These blinders were being used to shut out the sunlight of Malcolm's lucid exposition of social reality.

The history and development of this highly charged controversy is worth an essay in itself. Here, I just want to indicate that this charge of "Black anti-Semitism" did not arise as a spontaneous response to some general position in the Black movement. It had been developed and promoted in a conscious fashion. As early as 1963, Norman Podhoretz wrote an article (for *Commentary*, I believe) arguing that Black anti-Semitism was a major problem. At the time, he had a certain "Left" cover for his charge. Later, Podhoretz came out as a stalwart among the "neoconservatives" who prepared the intellectual groundwork for much of Ronald Reagan's program. Regardless of whether or not Podhoretz was working directly with a government agency in the mid-1960s, his argument was part of a conscious counterinsurgency effort to destroy Jewish support— which was considerable at the time—for the civil rights movement.

The year 1967 brought the issue of Zionism into the open. With the Six-Day War, the state of Israel stood in much clearer relief as an enemy of Third World people. The Student Nonviolent Coordinating Committee (SNCC), the most militant of the civil rights organizations, and some other Black organizations came out, quite justly, in opposition to Israel's war of conquest at that time. So did Students for a Democratic Society (SDS), the radical student group based mostly in the North, but the furor and backlash was overwhelmingly against the Black movement. I experienced the reality of Zionism as a form of racism in a very painful and personal way: a few close friends from the movement—and most painfully for me, my oldest sister—vehemently turned against both the Palestinians and SNCC, seemingly overnight. With other activists I knew,

Zionism worked as a right-wing influence more subtlety over time. For myself and many other Jews in the movement, the bedrock lesson from the Holocaust was to passionately oppose all forms of racism; we could never join in the oppression of another people.

Black Education

A major theme in the 1960s was the Black struggle for decent education. It was a struggle that dated back to the laws against slaves learning to read. After the Civil War, the two main demands from Black people were for land and free education (see W.E.B. DuBois, *Black Reconstruction*).

The dominant approach in the early 1960s was to fight for school integration. The white schools had the best-trained teachers, the best resources, and far more money. Rev. Milton Galamison led a popular movement to integrate the New York City schools that included a march of thousands to the Board of Education in 1964. I remember the exhilaration of crossing the Brooklyn Bridge among such a large and spirited group of people. The city was adamant against school integration, and the movement was defeated for the time being.

After "Black Power" became a popular slogan, people tried a new strategy, community control. The idea was for the Black community to supervise its schools to ensure that their children received a relevant, respectful, and quality education in their own neighborhoods. Despite strong community support, this program was smashed through the combination of a frontal attack led by the teachers' union (UFT) and a sophisticated co-optation effort to create essentially powerless community boards led by the Ford Foundation. In 1968, during the height of the struggle, the UFT called a teachers' strike in direct opposition to community control. During the strike, a number of teachers, including some led by my close friend, Columbia SDS graduate Ted Gold, broke into the locked schools to help teach freedom classes.

The city, having blocked school integration, also smashed the community control movement. The system, as it had for 350 years, again proved adamantly opposed to Black people getting a decent education. Of course these demands, if won, would have also helped to create a higher quality of education for many white children—both through the struggle to improve the educational system in general and through providing us with a truer, fuller history of this country and a broader understanding of the world.

Black Power

The tutoring session ran late and night has already fallen as I walk to the subway. The street is unusually empty and eerily quiet. Suddenly there's a loud crash, sounds of glass breaking, and angry shouts. A crowd surges around the corner, mainly young Black men, with their eyes darting up and down the block like they're looking for a target. Is this the beginning of a second Harlem riot? I'm the only white person around, and I nervously scan the array of faces, trying to find one of my friends who can tell them that I'm a good guy, I'm on their side. But I don't see anyone I know, and it doesn't matter, as they sweep past me, heading down the street...

Once my tension drains away, I wake up. Smiling, I appreciate the way the dream worked through my anxieties; whatever's happening, it's not all about me, one way or the other. That frees me to evaluate the dramatic new slogan politically—and it's starting to make a lot of sense.

When the slogan "Black Power" erupted in the summer of 1966, it sent shock waves throughout the country. First shouted by a SNCC fieldworker, Willie Ricks, it became publicized and developed by Stokely Carmichael. Actually, the concept is much older. Richard Wright, for example, wrote a book in 1954 entitled *Black Power*, inspired by the struggles for independence in Africa. But the slogan became a breakthrough in 1966 because it expressed the necessity of moving to a higher level of clarity and struggle.

I supported the slogan, but, like many white activists, I was also afraid of it. Whites had a lot of power within the civil rights movement. Whether consciously or not, white educational background and prestige in society were manipulated to gain disproportional control, while the development of Black leadership was being stifled. Whites had something to protect. It was comfortable to be at the peak of a morally prestigious movement for change while Black people were taking most of the casualties in the struggle. On the other hand, the challenge of anti-racist organizing within our own communities was difficult to take on. Also, behind the "Black Power" slogan was a struggle around nonviolence. Most whites in the movement tended to be ideologically committed to nonviolence. The young Black fieldworkers of SNCC had seen too many Blacks murdered; many began to advocate armed self-defense. The name was soon changed so that the "N" of SNCC stood for "National" rather than "Nonviolent."

Despite my initial defensiveness, "Black Power" made fundamental sense to me on many levels. First, it expressed the basic reality that Black people had to develop their own leadership and set the terms of their own liberation. Second, it challenged us to organize a revolutionary consciousness within the white community, thus focusing us on our primary responsibility. "Black Power" also taught an important political lesson: the need was not, as we had thought, to "shake the moral conscience of America." Those in power knew very well what they were doing. The point, rather, was to shift or overturn who had power—from the small elite on top to the vast majority underneath them. So the "Black Power" slogan also became a fountainhead for the development of a revolutionary tendency within the white student movement.

Several Black organizations tried to put the teachings of Malcolm X and the electricity of "Black Power" into programmatic form: the Revolutionary Action Movement (RAM) in 1964, SNCC in 1966, the Black Panther Party (BPP) in 1966, the Republic of New Afrika (RNA) in 1968, and others. The Panthers were the most widely known and in the sharpest confrontation with the police. All these groups were revolutionary nationalists. The "nationalism" meant, most basically, that Black people must direct their own struggle and that the goal was to achieve control of their own communities, land, and other means of livelihood. The "revolutionary" meant that this could not be achieved without a struggle, including most likely armed struggle, and that independence had to serve the interests of the most oppressed sectors of the nation, not those of a new Black bourgeoisie. These groups also tended to identify with and support national liberation struggles in the Third World. It was around this time that people changed the spelling of "black" (simply a racial designation) to "Black," with the capitalization underscoring their claim to nationhood, just as French or Chinese is capitalized.

As with previous periods of history, Black nationalism inspired a high tide of militancy, including dozens of "riots," actually uprisings, that rocked the U.S. in 1964–72. I was in shock watching, on TV, as the National Guard and police shot down Black citizens in Newark, Watts (Los Angeles), Detroit, and other cities. The headlines always screamed "Negro Violence!" but almost all of the nearly 250 persons killed and tens of thousands wounded were Black, usually shot for allegedly looting. Even without getting into the way that many of the stores had been looting the community for years, how could the authorities justify killing a human being for grabbing a TV? But this thought was never raised in mainstream America. I couldn't believe it! Clearly the system valued even petty property over Black lives. Despite the human costs, these rebellions brought the struggle to a new level, and the U.S. government faced the daunting prospect of fighting a two-front war: in Vietnam and at home.

Internationalism

My focus in this section on the impact of the Black struggle artificially separates out the other major reality that moved us to activism and pushed us in a revolutionary direction: Vietnam. Before turning to the war, I want to use some of Malcolm X's analysis to draw out how international and domestic developments influence each other. There's no question that the emergence of the African independence movements after World War II, achieving their first success with Ghana in 1957, and with ten African countries achieving independence in 1960 alone, provided tremendous inspiration for the rebirth of the civil rights struggle within the U.S.

Additionally, I believe, events in Africa had a big impact on the ruling class. The U.S. emerged out of the wreckage of World War II as the premiere imperialist power. They felt that Third World theaters of exploitation previously controlled by various European powers should now be fields for U.S. penetration and domination, and the nation's "anti-colonial" history and image provided a good opening in what would have to be a postcolonial age. In reality, the U.S. held outright colonies, including Puerto Rico and Hawaii. On an even bigger scale, the U.S. had been the early leader, especially relative to Latin America, in "neocolonialism"— avoiding direct rule, which generates opposition, but instead making sure that the regimes in those countries were compliant clients that guarantee the most favorable terms for U.S. businesses and the extraction of raw materials.

When the civil rights movement reemerged, the U.S., playing on its anti-colonial image, did not want to tarnish its relationships with emerging African nations with the blatant racism of the Jim Crow South. It's my opinion that the Eisenhower administration encouraged the Supreme Court to render the favorable decision in the famous *Brown v. The Board of Education* case of 1954, to put forward a more palatable public face to Africa; that result in turn gave hope to other challenges to segregation. As often happens, the rulers underestimated people of color, underestimated the depth of oppression and anger, and therefore didn't anticipate the demands for qualitative change that would explode and rock America from 1955 to 1975.

Naturally, it wasn't just the Black struggle. As the realities of racist America became exposed and as struggle against it became more possible, strong radical movements emerged among Puerto Ricans, Chicano/as, Native Americans, and Asian Americans. For example, the Chicano/a Brown Berets formed in 1968, and the Puerto Rican Young Lords Party emerged in 1969. These were rich and powerful struggles in their own right that added to the understanding that the U.S. was an empire based on the conquest and internal colonization of these peoples and on virulent racism. But for me, in New York City in the 1960s, my awakening came mainly in relationship to the Black struggle.

Just as African independence inspired civil rights within the U.S., the struggles against racism led to greater sympathy with and support for national liberation movements abroad. In my opinion, the main reason for the decisive difference in public response to the wars in Korea and in Vietnam was the civil rights struggle that arose in between them. That movement cracked open to whites in the U.S. the reality that people of color were human beings too, whose lives matter, and that the U.S. was far from perfect as a purveyor of democracy. Indeed, the scope and militancy of resistance to the Vietnam War may well represent an unprecedented level of opposition *from within an imperial power*. The war in Vietnam became the piston driving an accelerating movement and a growing radicalism among white youth.

Vietnam

I'm heartsick as I watch President Johnson, or "LBJ," on national TV. He's announcing a major and murderous escalation of the war, now ordering systematic bombings of the North and sending another two hundred thousand troops to the South. He says that these measures are needed to uphold the Geneva Accords, the prevailing international law for Vietnam, which require independent, separate North and South Vietnams. That account doesn't square with my sense of what the Accords were about, so I head out to the Columbia School of International Affairs to find the actual text.

The Accords couldn't be more explicit: the north and south of Vietnam are in no way intended to be permanent political entities; they are simply military disengagement and regrouping zones until elections to reunify the country, scheduled for 1956.

The difference isn't a question of arcane legal interpretations: LBJ's justification is a black-and-white lie. Given what's at stake with this escalation and how easy it is to check, I expect to see banner headlines: "LBJ Lies to Launch a War!" But the next day there isn't a peep in the mainstream media.

It may be unprecedented in human history that a people at such a colossal disadvantage in terms of military technology and economic power actually *won* a war. The main reason was the incredible depth of organization and mobilization of their people, based on a long history of resisting invasions; international solidarity, including the U.S. anti-war movement, also played an important role. Winning the war has not, so far, enabled the Vietnamese to, as Ho Chi Minh had predicted, "rebuild the country ten times more beautiful than before." The wholesale destruction of human life and the environment wreaked by the U.S. war machine continues to take a toll, along with the limits of national liberation in general to achieve full development and equality.

But the Vietnamese did win a stirring victory for independence and caused a giant setback to the U.S. project of world domination, so much so that for the following decades a principal, and perhaps the primary, strategy of the U.S. ruling class has been to get the public past "the Vietnam syndrome," past their reluctance to get involved in invasions of Third World countries. The political ability to launch such aggression is crucial: you cannot run an economy based on the brutal plunder of the entire Third World without having the power to stop those countries who try to opt out. Since the defeat in Vietnam, a succession of U.S. administrations have engineered a series of invasions designed to have minimal U.S. casualties: Grenada, Panama, the first Gulf War. And they've developed a set of new rationales—such as "human rights" in dismembering Yugoslavia, "terrorism" in Afghanistan, and "weapons of mass destruction" in the second war on Iraq—all designed to win public support for military interventions or, as the senior President Bush openly proclaimed, to "kick the Vietnam syndrome." But they are still a long way from the freedom of action they enjoyed back in 1964. Their occupation of Iraq, starting in 2003, proved to be another major setback to imperial impunity, as does the costly quagmire in Afghanistan.

Vietnam first became a public issue here with the Gulf of Tonkin incident in August 1964; but secret and illegal military intervention went back to the early 1950s, as the U.S. provided 80 percent of the financing for France's war to reconquer its former colony—reconquest because the Vietnamese had resisted the Japanese occupation during World War II and then declared independence at the end of that conflict. The French were defeated in 1954. Under the Geneva Accords that ended that conflict, the U.S. was allowed to send a maximum of 685 military advisers to southern Vietnam. Soon, they numbered in the thousands and were illegally involved in combat operations. But even that wasn't enough to keep the hated client regime in the south in power; an escalation was needed beyond what could be kept secret.

In August 1964, President Johnson announced that a small North Vietnamese patrol boat had wantonly attacked and fired torpedoes at a U.S. destroyer, the *Maddox*, in the Tonkin Gulf. This "aggression" required a response, and Congress passed a resolution authorizing the president to use force. That resolution was a legally insufficient surrogate for the constitutionally required declaration of war, but served as the basis for years of escalations and mass murder.

At the time, the handful of us who knew something about Vietnam were exceedingly skeptical. Why would a little boat attack a destroyer? And had the U.S. ship penetrated the North's side of the Gulf? We thought the incident was probably a deliberate provocation; for questioning our government's version, we were considered "the lunatic fringe." Four decades later, the release of government documents has revealed that it wasn't a provocation—rather;, it was a complete fabrication: no torpedoes had been fired at the *Maddox*.

The Tonkin Gulf resolution was followed by the bombing of North Vietnam—seen then as a one-shot retaliation. In fact, I was, very reluctantly, roped in by the Young Democrats at Columbia to canvassing for

LBJ in the 1964 election—as the peace candidate. He promised no wider war, while the Republican, Barry Goldwater, was seen as a warmonger.

Once Johnson was safely reelected as the peace candidate, the all-out war began, rationalized by his fraudulent account of the Geneva Accords. We later printed up copies of the relevant sections of the Accords and distributed them on campus. The context for the regrouping zones had been to allow the defeated French colonial troops to withdraw safely. The 1956 elections to reunify the country never happened. As historical research confirmed, the United States blocked them because CIA intelligence showed that Ho Chi Minh would win overwhelmingly.

Today a carefully constructed narrative paints the media of the time as anti-war and blames it for staying the military's hand in Vietnam. This myth is as accurate as LBJ's rendition of the Geneva Accords. Back then the media didn't question the government's foreign policy and they never reported the years of U.S. violations of the Geneva Accords with excessive "advisers" and the combat role they played. I remember news footage of the later-revered CBS anchor, Walter Cronkite, which was nothing more than a propaganda film, filled with disinformation, justifying U.S. intervention. Only after the U.S. started to lose militarily, after it was being discredited internationally, after a burgeoning anti-war movement was tearing the country apart, and after segments of the ruling class considered it more strategic to cut their losses, did elements of the media publish critical information on the war. The reason so much effort has gone into constructing the myth of the liberal anti-war media is that today's aggressors want to wipe out the idea that the U.S. was defeated militarily, and whip the media back into shape as a pure propaganda organ.

So, in February 1965, outraged by this aggression and heartsick about the lives it was costing, I waited for one of the liberal groups on campus to organize against the war; I was ready to be the first to sign up. I waited and waited for a month, and nothing happened. The most likely organization seemed to be Action, an affiliate of the National Student Association. I had talks with their chairman, who seemed interested but kept stalling. A couple of years later it was revealed that the NSA was heavily infiltrated and manipulated by the CIA. Some of their "assets" went to international meetings and then turned over to the CIA the names of foreign student radicals, who were later eliminated by the repressive governments they opposed.

The May 2nd Movement (M2M) had held an anti-war demonstration in the city and had a presence on campus. They were a youth group set up by the Progressive Labor Party, the same PL that four years later, in a flip-flop not unusual among sectarian groups, tried to lead the student movement away from anti-war activism. PL, which was Maoist and was seen as flamboyant and extreme, could not reach many students at Columbia. I went to and supported their actions, but finally (in those days, a month seemed like a long time) got together some friends and formed the Independent Committee on Vietnam (ICV) at Columbia. The "Independent" meant both of the government and of "Communist" groups. While I was already communistic with a small "c" (as I was a small-d democrat) in terms of supporting the ideals of community and sharing the wealth, I was still anti-Communist in terms of the powers and parties that had that name. But there was also a valid concern in letting a broad spectrum of people know that our organization wouldn't be manipulated by a disciplined sect. On the other hand, some liberals wanted us to exclude individual Communists and set ourselves up as a competitor to M2M. But I already had a sense of how anti-Communism was used to squelch radical opposition, and in any case exclusion seemed anti-democratic. So I was careful to support and coordinate with M2M activities, and make sure that members of PL and the Socialist Workers Party (SWP) were welcomed into the ICV. In this period there was a broad enough sweep of new activists that sectarian takeover of the organization was not a major concern.

Even before the ICV was off the ground, I worked with some professors and graduate students in the anthropology department, following the example of the University of Michigan, to organize the second "teach-in" on Vietnam, as part of a wave that then swept across campuses nationwide. The "teach-in" was a terrific format to draw students who knew little about Vietnam into discussing and learning about the war. Combining debates with proponents of the government's position, and workshops on Vietnamese history and U.S. interventions against democracy in the Third World, the teach-ins were a wonderfully vital way to get people thinking and involved.

The ICV set up literature tables on the main plaza on campus, and we'd be out there all day discussing and debating with those who stopped by. It was an amazingly dynamic time, a savory stew of debate and new ideas. At first, almost everyone who came by our tables was hostile to our lack of "patriotism," but many were already somewhat wary of the war. Within two years, the vast majority of students at Columbia opposed it, but I don't want to give the wrong impression that our great arguments immediately turned people around. It is rare indeed that someone will give up a presupposition in the course of a discussion. Ideas don't change that quickly, and ego makes it hard for most of us to readily admit we are wrong. Organizers who expect instant conversions will become overbearing and end up disillusioned. Instead, our educational work planted seeds and helped people see there were alterative interpretations and sources of information, so that once events developed to create more stress—the war intensified and the military draft expanded—people had a way to see that something was wrong, instead of just becoming more fervent about escalations to "win."

Since the U.S. press simply touted the government's line, the ICV set up teams, with various language skills, to scour the international press. Of course no "Communist" source would be considered credible, but even the European press was better than ours. A key source for us was *Le Monde*. The French, as a defeated imperial power, had a lot more sense of Vietnamese history. Mel Baron, an older student in the School of General Studies, led in this work. The years he had lived in Algeria had not only left him fluent in French but also made him a firsthand witness to the horrors of colonial wars.

Education without activism doesn't get you very far. Fortunately a national organization, Students for a Democratic Society, had called for a march on Washington against the war for April 17, 1965. Their broader Left politics and understanding of U.S. foreign policy as anti-democratic had led them to call for such a demonstration back in December, before the systematic bombing campaign had started. So they were in position, with something concrete for us to do, when interest in the war mushroomed. The ICV's first project was to bring people to the march.

As exciting as the organizing work was, it somehow dawned on me that no matter how big this demonstration turned out to be, it wouldn't end the war; that was going to take a much more developed movement. So we decided beforehand to plan our next organizational and educational activities. We had the meetings and events already scheduled, so that we could pass out flyers to everyone on the buses. Similarly, before each major educational activity, we tried to have the next demonstration or action already planned so that we could encourage people to participate. We tried to maintain this mutually reinforcing rhythm throughout our work. It took another ten years—and tremendous struggles—for the war to end. With more understanding of history, I can now see that, as properly impatient as we were, ten years is a blink of the eye compared to what it usually takes to achieve major changes.

Even in this early period and during Easter vacation, when many students had returned to their families, we filled a convoy of buses with 650 protesters. It was exhilarating to join 20,000 marchers in D.C.—for then an unheard-of number of people to protest foreign policy. The speeches weren't that great, but the size and energy of the gathering was a rush.

There was another dimension of excitement for me: my first movement love affair. I'd fallen head over heels for Melissa, SDS's New York coordinator for the march. A Black woman my age, she was already a skilled organizer, providing me valuable political leadership—and, while not at all pretentious, she had movie-star looks. To my surprise, other white male campus leaders in the city thought they could and should order her around, but Melissa and I connected strongly around common work and mutual respect. How intensely romantic it was to make love at four thirty in the morning, just before we departed for her to go downtown and lead the citywide trains and for me to head up to the Columbia buses for the march. But I was a very inexperienced and inept lover; and then, at the national council (NC) meeting following the march, the national SDS leaders in Melissa's circles were totally indifferent to me as a neophyte. Later, when we were crashing at night on an apartment floor with about ten other people, it never even occurred to me that couples would still make love. Anyway, I was in way over my head, and the affair, while sweet (and which ended amicably) didn't last long.

National SDS

The NC, although difficult, had a positive result. The leaders of national SDS had seen the march as a one-shot deal, assuming that the organization would now return to its community-organizing projects. While I supported those, a few of us newcomers to SDS had an urgent sense that the campuses were ready to take off around the war. I argued that it wasn't an either/or situation; if we organized around the war, the influx of new members would also provide volunteers for the community-organizing projects. As a compromise, the NC agreed that SDS would participate in local mobilizations against the war in October. As with education and action, the movement also had to learn to develop a rhythm between national and local demonstrations. That same weekend, I went to a planning session with principled pacifists opposing the war, such as Bob Paris of SNCC, Dave Dellinger, and Staughton Lynd. These meetings and the fall actions gave birth to what later became "The Mobe," the National Mobilization Against the War.

Local Action

Soon after returning from D.C., we carried out a valuable early example of civil disobedience against university complicity with the war machine. This action was initiated by the civil rights group CORE, which planned to repeat an action done the preceding year, when a few of them sat-in to disrupt a Naval ROTC (Reserve Officers Training Corps) ceremony. Now we had a large ICV contingent to offer support. The administration moved the ceremony inside, and when we marched to the door we were locked out, so people jammed up in the doorway and refused to disperse. The university called in the police, who started to pull people away, one by one. I'd been in the front of the march, so I was against the door and the last one the police reached. Back then, I wore a jacket and tie to demonstrations to show how clean-cut and respectable we were. The cops twisted the tie around my neck, choking me, until, fortunately, it broke. They dragged me away and threw me down, ripping my jacket almost in half. As I hit the ground in this tug-of-war, I was thinking, "OK, you guys won, you got us away from the door." Then I saw the cop's foot headed for my balls. I quickly rolled and caught the kick on my thigh. But I was so angry that, in one motion, I kept rolling to my feet and ran back to the door, and most of the other protesters followed.

Afterward, Columbia threatened to suspend the "ringleaders," but we were able to rally a lot of support. Still, there were many complications in that process. Some liberals wanted us to reduce all organizing to defense of the right to dissent; but we maintained a balance, building a coalition on those terms while continuing to speak out against having the military on campus. And there was a tendency for students to get pumped up about how they had been subject to "police brutality." The conduct of the police was an issue, but I knew from my civil rights work that our bruises were minor compared to what was done routinely in Harlem. I tried to make our experience a starting point to raise consciousness about the far more severe problem of police brutality against people of color.

With summer coming, we set up committees to bring the anti-war message to several communities in the city. The initiative came from folks with an Old-Left background that made them more conscious of class. For me, this project was a welcome alternative to the elitist contempt some students had for those less educated. We didn't have instant success; as I remember it, only one of the communities developed its own self-sustaining committee. But it was positive work for us, learning more about working with people's needs and helping to nurture anti-war sentiments outside the university.

One experience in particular stands out. We were speaking on a street corner in Flatbush, Brooklyn. A few men in their thirties joined the crowd, but their faces twisted with discomfort and anger as the speaker from the Catholic Worker organization spoke about racist atrocities against Koreans during that war. These guys, who said they were Korean War vets, rushed our little soap box and knocked the speaker down. It was not an all-out brawl, but the threat was clear. The event organizer then asked me to speak next. To diffuse tensions, I went back to 111 B.C. Our antagonists at first couldn't see what I was getting at, but that was the year the Vietnamese resisted a Chinese invasion. By the time I got through the 2,000 years of history, the point was obvious: the Vietnamese would never accede to foreign conquest.

Later I joked about the value of my exceedingly boring (or, as I put it back then, "soporific") speeches. But something on the faces of those vets upset me. If the charge of abuses had been false, they could have spoken out against it, with their authority from experience. Their level of turmoil and quick move to violence to suppress the issue made me feel that they had done or seen things that still haunted them. For the first time, I realized that those who harm others often have guilty consciences as well as gripping fears that their victims will retaliate. The working-class guys sent off to fight imperial wars were themselves heavily damaged by the horrors.

Class, and especially the role of soldiers, was a major theme for the anti-war movement. The service deferment given to college students meant that those drafted into killing and dying in Vietnam were overwhelmingly poor, "minority," and working-class. Some anti-war sectors saw the GIs as brutes, but those of us with a deeper analysis of the social system understood the class oppression involved—that the GIs were being used as cannon fodder in a war that served the interests of those who ruled over us. Both draft resistance and GI rebellions became powerful aspects of the anti-war movement.

Within a couple of years, the anti-war movement got into draft resistance, helping young men either evade or flee (to Canada or underground) the draft, and thousands did. We also supported GI resistance to the war—initially with GI coffeehouses situated near military bases, where the soldiers could come to get some cultural respite, literature, and legal and moral support. Desertions peaked at eighty-nine thousand in 1971. (The old Chevrolet that my parents had given me a few years earlier was conveniently "lost," but, by agreement, not reported until well after it was abandoned by a soldier who successfully went AWOL.)

As the anti-war movement grew, resistance by the troops in Vietnam became critical. It was spearheaded by Black GIs, who understood the racist character of the war, but it spread throughout the ranks. These soldiers became some of the most poignant and eloquent anti-war voices, and the Vietnam Veterans Against the War (VVAW) became one of the most effective organizations on the home front. In Vietnam, soldiers' resistance made the army much less effective. Many a gung-ho or racist officer was shot or hit from behind by a fragmentation grenade. The Pentagon, undoubtedly underreporting such discrediting events, tallied 209 "fraggings" in Vietnam in 1970 alone.

"Hey, Hey, LBJ, How Many Kids Did You Kill Today?"

My turning point from ardent protest to throwing my whole life into stopping the war can be marked with an issue of *Ramparts*. While most of the alternative media were small papers in black and white, this was a magazine with color photos. While we knew about the napalm bombs the U.S. was dropping (designed to stick to and severely burn flesh), it was different to see its effects. On January 1, 1967, *Ramparts* published a series of color photos of Vietnamese children and babies burned by napalm. The mainstream media had completely censored out any such pictures. The emotional impact was overwhelming, and I've never gotten those pictures out of my mind. The human horror and suffering was totally devastating. Later we heard accounts of massacres of civilians and of the common use of torture during interrogations—all the logical outgrowths of a war of occupation. But the napalm was enough; from then on for me, as for many of us, it was *all out* to end the war.

By 1971, majority opinion in the U.S. had swung against the war, although most still disapproved of the protesters. Millions of people in the U.S. had actively demonstrated against the war, and hundreds of thousands had consciously broken the law in some way. Public opinion surveys showed that one-third of college students considered themselves "far-left" and nearly three million thought a revolution was necessary. Many of us who had started out seeing the war as a mistake now understood it as the logical outgrowth of an imperialist system. While we began as protesters, during free time from school or jobs, we were now full-time activists dedicated to a fundamental transformation of society.

In the course of the war, the U.S. dropped seven million tons of bombs on Vietnam, more than twice the amount dropped on Europe and Asia in World War II. Even the tiny percentage that didn't explode, that lay buried in the ground, are causing danger and death for farmers today. The U.S.'s massive use of twenty million gallons of the poisonous Agent Orange not only created ecocide in regions of Vietnam but also continued to cause a high rate of heartbreaking birth defects long after the war. Some fifty-eight thousand Americans and over three million Vietnamese, mainly civilians, along with another million in Laos and Cambodia were killed; and many times that number were maimed or made homeless. By 1975, Vietnam had maintained its independence and faced the struggle to rebuild; U.S. imperialism was exposed and set back as never before; national liberation and revolution was sweeping the Third World; and a generation of American youth had been radicalized.

Strike!

There were many different trends in the white student movement. Some activists argued that we could only organize people around their "immediate needs," such as student power. Others argued that we should go to the working class and organize them around their "immediate needs," such as a shorter workweek and higher wages. But reality showed that people were most motivated to move around the issues reflecting the general crises in society—the war, the Black struggle. The most advanced and militant struggles were those that synthesized these two issues. When that connection could be related to the concrete realities of the institutions or communities where we lived, there were good conditions for sustained, militant struggle. These were some of the conditions that produced the famous Columbia strike of 1968.

I won't try to tell the history of the strike here (there is a factually accurate account in the book *Up Against the Ivy Wall* by the 1968 staff of the *Columbia Spectator*). I just want to highlight a few key moments for me. The strike cannot be understood solely in terms of events and developments on campus; we were very much catapulted forward by world events. The Tet offensive in Vietnam—the turning point in the war because it showed that the U.S. could not win—started in February of 1968. Martin Luther King Jr. was assassinated on April 4, which was followed by Black uprisings in more than a hundred cities across the country. These events provided both the urgency and the inspiration for a higher level of struggle. The Columbia strike began in late April.

The burning issues in society also had very specific expression at Columbia. While the administration initially lied outright, SDS researcher Bob Feldman found documentary proof that the university was doing war research as part of the Institute for Defense Analyses. Also, Columbia, which we already knew to be one of the main slumlords of the city (the old Columbia fight song, "Who Owns New York?" is meant quite literally) moved to take over scarce parkland in Harlem to build a school gym. Community people actively protested this rip-off. Students, in addition to taking a stand on the great issues of the day, were saying something about what kind of institution we wanted to be part of. We could not be free, grow, and acquire the knowledge we needed in a structure based on oppressing other people. We demanded that Columbia stand on the side of humanity.

The Columbia strike was an event of tremendous importance for our movement. Even though Black students, less than 1 percent of the student body, felt isolated at Columbia at the time, they took the lead in seizing Hamilton Hall. Spurred on by their actions, large numbers of white people participated in shutting down a major institution, in solidarity with Third World peoples, especially Vietnam and Harlem. This development was significant enough for ruling-class elements to do their best to defeat and deflect it. Strike leaders and many participants were kicked out of school, the press grossly distorted the goals and methods of the strike, and the Ford Foundation moved in as a "friend" of the students—the same Ford Foundation that later that year moved to co-opt the Black community control of schools movement. They funded a group called "Students for a Restructured University" (SRU), which argued that the real issue of the strike was student participation in the decisions of the university. The Ford Foundation was willing to let us have all sorts of "democracy" within this elite, white institution as long as it could sever us from solidarity with national liberation struggles. SRU then became a base to try to create a liberal vs. radical split among the strikers over the questions of militancy and on the centrality of the demands around war research and the gym.

This contradiction inherent in a white, upper-class form of "democracy," which, after all, had been the basis of the American Revolution, produced an amusing personal anecdote from the strike. As an alumnus who knew many professors (I'd graduated from Columbia College in 1966 and was still relating to the SDS chapter while a graduate student at the downtown New School for Social Research), I was sent as a strike representative to a faculty assembly meeting. Given the tumultuous events, I hadn't gotten a chance to sleep the night before. Most of the faculty was hostile to the strike, which threatened their bread and butter. Some of the slicker professors set a trap for us based on our commitment to, but confusion around, democracy. They had surveys showing that, while about two-thirds of the students supported us on the issues, a comparable majority would vote against the strike as a tactic, probably because in the large and diverse university community many students were not aware of our long series of prestrike efforts to get Columbia to stop the gym and the war research.

A professor asked me, "Would the strikers abide by a democratic vote of the entire university as to whether to end the strike?" Torn between their definition of "democracy" and the fundamental principles of the strike, I stammered out an answer: "We believe in democracy, we will abide by the results of a vote…uh, as long as the people of Vietnam and Harlem can vote too, since it is their lives that are most affected by these decisions." My statement was later cited by the Columbia alumni magazine as a prime example of the "irrationality" of the strikers.

The confrontation with business-as-usual provided a context for changing consciousness. By the time the strike was over, a majority of CU students either participated in (25 percent) or supported (31 percent) the strike, while 43 percent actively or passively opposed it.

The solidarity we expressed was warmly received in Harlem and their response helped save the strike. While we held several buildings, the main one occupied by SDS was the administration building, Low Hall, where several documents that compromised Columbia University President Grayson Kirk were found. At one point, the right-wing students decided to starve out the strikers by blockading Low Hall, preventing supporters on campus from bringing food. When the word went out about the blockade, people in Harlem organized a march that came up and broke through to bring food to the strikers. Fourteen years later, in Rockland County Jail, I discovered that one of my Brink's codefendants had been part of that Harlem contingent.

A bizarre sideshow to the strike is worth recounting because of later developments: the role of the now notorious Lyndon LaRouche. At the time he was working as a stock analyst on Wall St. and went by the name of "Lynne Marcus"; he said it stood for Lenin and Marx. He latched onto and developed a cult-like following among a small sector of the Columbia SDS chapter—the kids who had been part of the Maoist Progressive Labor Party but got kicked out for joining the militancy of the strike. PL's basic politics of selling out the Black struggle to appeal to white workers left these ex-members vulnerable to LaRouche's appeal. They brought him to our freedom school, where he argued the following position: The teachers' strike being organized for the fall (where the main issue was *opposition* to Black and Latino/a community control of schools) could be the beginning of a workers' general strike that would bring down capitalism. Columbia SDS should drop all its other work and put our full efforts into supporting the teachers' union and building it into a general strike. In other words, he invoked Marxist rhetoric to divert us from one of the most dramatic actions in solidarity with national liberation to supporting the racist actions of an elite, white union.

Mark Rudd, the chairman of Columbia SDS and main leader of the strike, quickly recognized the dangers. He arranged a debate between us and them: Mark would take on their main person on campus, Tony Papert, about movement strategy, and he asked me to oppose LaRouche on economic analysis, since I was one of the few among us who had studied Marxian political economy and tried to apply it to current developments.

This was the summer of 1968, and LaRouche predicted that the U.S. economy would collapse into another Great Depression in six to eighteen months. This impending cataclysm was the reason we had to immediately mobilize a general strike of city workers. In contrast, I argued that there were deep problems in the U.S. economy but also many countervailing measures in place, so a slow and more variegated development of economic difficulties was more likely, resulting in stresses that couldn't be calculated with a mathematical formula but instead would be fought out in the social and political arenas. I was able to provide detailed economic data on changes in the level of consumption and the rate of profit that showed LaRouche's model of a quickly collapsing financial bubble was not in play at that time. I don't know how well people followed that debate, but there was a sense of relief that LaRouche's economic theories were not sound and did not compel acceptance of his strategy. Much more importantly, Mark homed in on the racist implications of shifting the Columbia strike into support for the teachers' union.

Discredited by that debate, it wasn't long before the LaRouchites came out as open fascists, using axe handles to attack and break up Left meetings. Over the ensuing decades they went through many transformations, always having the money to put out large printings of their various glossy publications; in some periods they reverted to seemingly left-wing rhetoric in order to organize people into believing right-wing conspiracy theories. They were almost unique on the Right for trying to organize Black people. Decades later I again encountered their dirty work when they became the main source for the "AIDS conspiracy" theories circulating in prison, which were used to convince Black youth that AIDS prevention measures were irrelevant.

Women: Relationships

Why is Corrine headed across the quadrangle in my direction? I hope this doesn't turn into a scene. It's spring of 1965 and I'm sitting in a shaded corner of the campus, enjoying a rare moment of solitude in between classes and staffing the ICV table. Corrine wants to know where things stand with us; why haven't I said anything about getting together? I cringe at how "clinging" she is. Why should there be any such expectations, just because we slept together a couple of nights ago? Of course I had been the one who was so set on making love; her initial sense had been to go slower, to first let a relationship develop. But once I "scored," my interest had ebbed; it was "conquest" that drove me, not love or even sexual pleasure. So my response is, more or less, "whatever," and she bursts into tears. I hate to see her cry, but what can I do? I'm not going to let anyone fence me in. She gets the message from my coldness and walks away...and never has anything to do with me again. But in a way she's still with me because it's a scene, along with a few others like it, that replays and replays in my mind.

As a campus anti-war leader, I got to meet many bright, idealistic women. Columbia College was male-only back then, but the university included Barnard College for women, as well as the coed General Studies and graduate schools. Not only did I have a certain status as a leader, but the background of the thoroughly male-supremacist culture gave me another unfair advantage: as many women told me years later, most movement men simply didn't listen to or credit women's ideas at all. Against that dark backdrop, even limited enlightenment could look like quite a bright spot. Given how my sisters raised me, I knew that I could learn a lot from women, although how well my understanding held up after sexual "conquest" was another matter.

My ethics prohibited me from directly lying to a woman; I would never say I was intent on a committed relationship or that I was in love when I wasn't. But de facto I was taking advantage of a bifurcated and unequal culture, where women viewed sex more in terms of relationships while men saw it simply as scoring. So, a woman might respond to my coming on sexually, especially given my political role, as a beginning to something more serious, whereas I would tend to quickly lose interest. Such a scoring mentality doesn't even lead to the best sex, let alone more meaningful relationships. In addition, usually the terms were so male-centered that there was little understanding or attention to sex being satisfying for her—and if it wasn't, she was to blame. (It wasn't until 1970 that feminist Ann Koedt published "The Myth of the Vaginal Orgasm.")

My sex mania at the time isn't surprising. Being raised in a repressive culture where such things weren't even discussed made sex, once available, even more mysterious, more craved at any price, more a thing in itself. This explosion of interest came in a male-dominant context, where young men were extremely averse to being "tied down" by any commitments. There wasn't yet a feminist movement, so many women experienced their problems in relationships as their individual failings. The pervasive homophobia made lesbianism almost invisible as a possible alternative to depending on men for love.

It's not at all that I've now come to the conservative view of saving sex for marriage. It's natural and healthy for people to be open and experimental sexually well before they may decide on a long-term committed relationship, and there was a liberating aspect to overthrowing the repressive, often harmful attitudes of the day. In some of my relationships, we had a mutual understanding on the level of commitment, with a lively sexual chemistry on top of a comfortable friendship. But too often I let the woman believe there was a lot more there. My scoring mentality ended up hurting people in situations where they were emotionally vulnerable. In retrospect, given the era, I can understand the context for my cavalier attitudes—but it is still hard to accept that the hurt on Corinne's face didn't break through my male conditioning. And not incidentally, her consequent need to avoid me meant that the Vietnam Committee lost a valuable member.

Naturally, radical women tried to challenge and change the terms. This happened in the clearest way for me after I met Naomi Jaffe in 1966. It was my first semester of graduate work at the New School for Social Research, but by this point school was just a "gig" for me, a place to have a community and subsistence economic support while I functioned as a full-time political organizer. So I was sitting in the back of a large sociology class, pretty alienated by the terms of the discussion, when Naomi spoke up. I was immediately and simultaneously taken by the radical insight in what she had to say, and by how good she looked to me. I was never brash enough to approach a woman without an introduction, but meeting her proved effortless when we both attended the first meeting to form an SDS chapter at the New School. Since we both lived on the Lower East Side, we sometimes headed back together after nighttime SDS meetings.

Naomi didn't show any particular attraction to me, so I accepted and benefited from a working relationship, which only slowly (months being a long time in this heady period) ripened into our becoming lovers. As I learned, my best relationships started as strong friendships first. In this situation, we were doing some great work together, including organizing a student strike against the war at New School as an example for campuses across the country. Naomi was a first-class Left intellectual, and we fed off each other's ideas. It was exciting to combine sexual passion with radical organizing and challenging theoretical work.

But this love affair is not the romantic "happy ending" to my male chauvinism and immaturity. While I was attracted to her brilliance—and for her there was the excitement of a movement man responding to her work—there was also a competitiveness that surfaced soon after we became lovers. Her ideas were good, but I just assumed, and I maneuvered so that others would see, that my analysis was better, more important to moving things forward. This process led to an unequal exchange, where she supported and enhanced my efforts while I depreciated hers. The other contradiction was a new form of the old issue of commitment. Perhaps there was a two-way problem in that Naomi's view of our settling down together was unrealistic given our youth and the turmoil of the day. But that's something couples can discuss and negotiate. I was, without admitting it to myself, terrified of serious commitment; instead of openly grappling with these issues, I created distance by sexual promiscuity, rationalized under the slogan of "free love." Free love had a liberating aspect and some women embraced it as a way of reclaiming women's agency and pleasure in a society that had polarized their choices to either Madonna or whore. But my promiscuity was much more a continuation of the old cavalier attitude, much more a way to keep Naomi feeling off balance, disempowered and at a distance. Once again, I was causing considerable hurt to a good person, and to someone who was loving and supportive to me.

While each person and relationship is different, my pattern continued through two more serious relationships: I would become enamored of a brilliant and very attractive woman. She initially would be excited by the rare synthesis of romance with a passion for political ideas and action. After we became lovers, I would subtly undercut her work and create emotional distance. Again, these patterns are not surprising in this prefeminist era; again, my failure to break through them—my inability to respond to the hurt I caused as well as to the potential for a greater growth from a more equal interaction—is rueful. The strength in these situations was the common political work. There was enough shared, enough mutual respect, and enough generosity on their part that usually I was able to maintain valuable friendships after breaking up. Naomi and I are very close friends today. We, as I have with another lover from this period, have been able to discuss these issues. I'm struck that these women, while clear in their criticisms of me, don't view themselves as victims; they also hold themselves responsible for not doing more to either change the terms or end it quickly.

The rise of a women's liberation movement set the basis for major changes in values and in power. In the frantic prelude to going underground, during the fall of 1969, the Weather collectives engaged in incessant "criticism/self-criticism" that was usually misused to tear people down. Naomi led six Weather women in sitting me down for a session, but this one was, in contrast, amazingly constructive. As firm as the women were about my intolerably cavalier attitudes, about the ways I undercut women who loved me, the session also offered a hopeful sense that I was worth struggling with, that there was a potential revolutionary there even if encased in and marred by thick layers of male chauvinism. For four years I had successfully bobbed and weaved when individuals had raised these issues with me. Now there was something about their collective strength and the new context where feminist politics mattered that got me to stop and listen. I felt the ways I had hurt people, the ways I had undercut their strengths and contributions as revolutionaries, the ways I had stunted my own growth by not learning more from women.

This brief summary sounds too much like an epiphany. Of course, I wasn't magically past my male chauvinism. There would be future issues and struggles. But the collective criticism was, I feel today, a breakthrough where women's feelings and views came across to me with great strength, where the reality of my hurting people dawned on me, where the determination and possibility for more equal and mutually enriching terms became more tangible. Of course this personal change had a lot to do with the context of the political struggles about women's liberation.

Women: Politics

Our SDS chapter is having a meeting to discuss some kind of strategic impasse, but we're floundering. Lily gets to speak and makes some really good suggestions, provides the skeleton that

could be fleshed out to a good program. But the next five speakers
don't mention her or what she said, as they continue to meander.
Then a male graduate student, considered brilliant, paraphrases
Lily, undoubtedly not even conscious that he got his great ideas
from her. All of a sudden, everyone responds and we're on our
way. Later, when I ask Lily about it, she just shrugs and says,
"Sure, it always happens that way. I'm just glad we could move
things forward."

Women were central and critical to the early anti-war movement, not only as consistent workers but also as initiators and strategists. But in those days almost all the visible leaders and speakers were male. Typically, one organizational office was held by a woman—secretary. In the first year of the Independent Committee on Vietnam, ours was the dedicated and well-organized Christine, who was a member of the Socialist Workers Party. Shortly before elections for the following year, I proposed to Christine that we switch places, that she become chair and I would be secretary. She firmly demurred, without stating her reasons. Was it personal shyness? Or a belief that the men in the ICV wouldn't accept her? Or, most likely, that the Socialist Workers Party line at the time was to avoid the appearance of directly running the broad-based Vietnam Committees?

It's a good thing that my profeminist but somewhat flip suggestion wasn't implemented, as SWP came to play an increasingly negative role over the next couple of years. The anti-war movement was going through an organic development of seeing the war in Vietnam as part of a broader foreign policy. This impetus became stronger after the U.S. invaded the Dominican Republic on April 24, 1965, to *prevent* the return of the democratically elected president, Juan Bosch. Many activists felt we needed to begin talking about U.S. business interests and the military-industrial complex, and also the right of self-determination throughout the Third World. But the Marxist/Trotskyist SWP wanted to limit discussion to Vietnam, and even there the focus was "Bring the Troops Home," with little said about Vietnamese casualties and rights. It wasn't simply that they had a conservative view of an anti-war movement, but also that they felt that those who began to see a fuller picture should become recruits for the SWP. Similarly, they were intent on keeping protest within the limits set by the police, while horror at the war was pushing many young people toward militancy. We had the anomaly within the ICV of the SWP joining the Young Democrat types in voting against the rest of us, who were eager to build a more radical anti-war movement. For this reason, the initiative, energy, and popular following soon shifted from ICV to the SDS chapter, which linked civil rights and foreign policy and began to confront and disrupt CIA and military recruiters on campus.

Besides, even if Christine had become the head of the ICV, this token gesture would have accomplished little. The problem of sexism within the New Left went a lot deeper. It would take independent power for women, struggles to change men's consciousness, and qualitative developments in politics and program to make a real difference.

By 1967, women started to demand to be heard. The modern women's movement, the second wave of feminism (the first wave culminated in women's right to vote in 1920) in many ways sprang out of the early civil rights movement. (Sara Evans provides an excellent account in *The Personal Is Political*.) Once racism was exposed and the lie of "equal rights" cracked open, other people, including women, began to articulate how they were oppressed and their need to fight—especially after "The Position of Women in SNCC" was raised as an explicit issue in November 1964 and the concept of women's liberation began percolating into SDS in the spring of 1967. Soon after, independent radical feminist organizations formed, such as WITCH (Women's International Terrorist Conspiracy from Hell)—Naomi was a member—and a little later, Redstockings. But what should have been a natural birth within SDS proved to be very traumatic.

SDS's first women's liberation caucus was held in June 1967, at the SDS National Convention (NC) in Ann Arbor, Michigan. The way the workshop was put on the agenda was almost accidental, during the planning session at the spring meeting of the National Council (also

"NC"). (The quarterly council meetings, where each chapter could have a representative for each twenty members, set interim policy. The annual conventions set overall policy for the year: here chapters could send a representative for every five members, but in practice the conventions were open to anyone who came.) Someone was at the blackboard writing down a list of topics. Betty, very bright and extremely shy, was sitting next to me and whispered, "We should have one on women's liberation." So I raised my hand and made the proposal, and it was added to the list without any discussion or thought about its political significance.

Naomi and I went to this NC together, and she was clearly excited by what was happening in the workshop. Even those of us not attending the sessions could feel the electricity in the mix as we walked by the circle of women sitting on the lawn.

As with all workshops, their chair presented a report to the plenary, but when Marilyn Buck took the stage to do so, all hell broke loose. Men hooted and whistled from the floor, threw paper planes at Marilyn, and shouted such gems as, "I'll liberate you with my cock." It was more than upsetting. SDS was supposed to always side with the oppressed; even with a "new" issue, it was hard to understand why SDS men wouldn't sympathize, or at least *listen*. The circus response revealed the depth of sexism within SDS.

Marilyn was amazing in the dignified and determined way she chaired that session. She never lowered herself to respond in kind to the catcalls and insults hurled at her, but neither did she retreat an inch in the face of the attack. While there was vociferous opposition, many other people spoke in favor of the proposal, mainly women but also a couple of men. I had my hand raised but didn't get called on. The report was completed and accepted. Women's liberation had breached the sexist ramparts of the New Left.

Both politics and practices about sexism were now on the agenda and went on to play a rarely noted role in the dramatic split of SDS that destroyed the organization in 1969. The fault line was primarily between Progressive Labor Party's effort, with their claim that "all nationalism is reactionary," to get SDS to make a U-turn away from solidarity with Vietnam and the Panthers, and those of us, including Weather, who upheld the Revolutionary Youth Movement (RYM) strategy, with solidarity with national liberation as the cutting edge. But there was also a difference about how to analyze and fight sexism. PL, like many old-line Marxist groups, saw class as the fundamental contradiction, with problems like racism and sexism as secondary. They agreed that the Left should oppose "male chauvinism" which defined the problem mainly in the realm of ideas and culture, and not as a fundamental structural problem that included oppression within the working class and the Left. Women who insisted on independent forms of organization as a power base were accused of being "divisive." In contrast, influenced by the women's movement, we were beginning to call the problem "male supremacy," a systematic power structure whose origins preceded capitalism and played a central role in shaping society. Women had the right, and even the need, for autonomous caucuses, and it was the men who opposed that who were divisive. Unfortunately our line in this regard was much better than our practice.

The June 1969 SDS National Convention was the most intense factional battle imaginable, where the very meaning and life of the premier radical organization among whites was at stake. Every issue, from the naming of workshops to the order of the agenda, was an arena for tactical advantage and fought over intensely. PL had the strength of packing the meeting; we had the prestige coming from an alliance with the still-widely-revered Black Panthers. We looked forward to their address to the convention as the point that would turn the tide.

The Panther spokesman started out great, but when he was asked about women's liberation, he dismissed it as "pussy power." Pandemonium broke out on the floor as PL seized the opportunity and started to scream "Smash male chauvinism!" It's not surprising that the BPP, like all Left organizations of the day, was still rife with sexism. But the struggles against that were being led by women of color and could not and would not be imposed by groups of the white Left which themselves were sexist. Delegates immediately lined up at the mike for a chance to speak. Like virtually everyone else, I was responding to the situation in terms of the all-consuming faction fight. When I saw Naomi Jaffe approach the mike, I said to myself, with a sigh of relief, "Great, one of our people will get to speak and put PL in its place." To my surprise, Naomi's voice rang out across the tumultuous hall with, "We will not allow women's liberation to be used as a political football!" What a dramatic moment and powerful lesson: women's oppression and politics were too important to be reduced to a weapon in a faction fight—even a historic one by her/our side. It was only with later discussion that I understood the second aspect, her refusal to excuse our side's shortcomings on women.

Our line about "male supremacy" notwithstanding, our practice and politics were atrocious in many ways. While many of us supported caucuses *within* the Left, we tended to have contempt for those who formed an independent women's movement. And men were using "free love" as a tool to make women sexually available rather than as an opening to let love and equality flourish. Our political program about women's issues was reduced to extolling women guerrillas in the Third World and urging women here to become fighters. Doing so was an important role and contribution of women, but limiting our focus to armed struggle was not only a negation of the many other crucial battles against patriarchy but also tended to promote a macho concept of struggle, in which the humanistic basis for our militancy got lost.

Only later did I learn from Naomi and others what a difficult, almost schizophrenic period it was for them: politically "at home" neither in the anti-imperialist Left, with its still rampant sexism, or the predominantly white women's movement, which distanced itself from frontline national liberation struggles and gravitated toward defining women's issues from a white and often middle-class perspective. Some individuals, like the outspoken Black feminist Flo Kennedy, and a few scattered organizing efforts worked in both arenas, but in most ways the two broad movements were on separate, often divergent tracks.

Anti-imperialist men, with our crass sexism, have a major share of the responsibility for this setback of historic proportions: the failure at that time to forge a strong alliance and synergy between anti-imperialism and feminism. Such an alliance would have made both sides' politics more revolutionary and humane, with the Left developing a fuller program around women, and feminists becoming a major force to move an oppressed sector of whites toward anti-racism. In a way it should have come naturally, considering that three-fourths of the women of the world are people of color and more than half of those ravaged by imperialism are women. But capitalism has always been masterful at fostering divisions among the oppressed, and people all too readily play into that trap. For Naomi and other feminist anti-imperialists this painful tear started to heal only once they could connect with the leadership of women of color in beginning to put these two struggles together. (For some outstanding writings from the women of color movement see Cherrie Moraga and Gloria Anzaldua's *This Bridge Called my Back*, which includes the trailblazing "Combahee River Statement," and Barbara Smith's *The Truth That Never Hurts*. An important early precursor was ex-SNCC worker Fran Beal with her 1969 essay, "Double Jeopardy: To Be Black and Female," that later led to her newsletter that also included class, *Triple Jeopardy*.)

Sex, Drugs, and Rock 'n' Roll

> "Blonde on Blonde *is coming out today! I'll have it by tonight, so come down to my place; we'll light up a joint and play the album all night till we can make out every word.*"

You might not think that invitation came from a sophisticated graduate student, but that's the way it was back in 1966 when every new Dylan album was a major cultural event, especially for the more political edge of youth culture, reflecting the continental divide between the Old and New Lefts. Bob Dylan emerged in the early 1960s as a brilliant folksinger, with insightful political lyrics. I remember seeing him on TV in 1963, singing "Only a Pawn in Their Game," about the murderer of civil rights leader Medgar Evers. I was awed by how Dylan both expressed the poignancy of losing the beloved Evers and sharply analyzed the way poor whites are used as the violent enforcers for systematic racism.

Then, at the Newport Folk Festival of 1965, Dylan went electric, and reportedly the folk purists booed him. Old-Left cultural critics lambasted him for "selling out." In contrast, young activists like myself felt electrified because we already loved rock 'n' roll: its energy, its dissonance against a staid and repressed society. While Dylan's lyrics were now less explicitly political, they did a better job of articulating the alienation young people felt in a society whose multiple heaps of consumer goods buried the human soul. A couple of years later, our political analysis caught up to see the potential of rock to help create a conducive cultural climate for a much broader youth rebellion.

The exuberance and sense of revolution in the air that came with the cultural upheavals of the 1960s was exhilarating—even if my view today is tempered with an awareness of both the sexism and the tremendous damage drugs have done. Still, coming out of the social conservatism of the 1950s, with its sexual and gender repression, when the government was always right and serious dissent was automatically discredited as "Communist," youth culture was like a giant plow, breaking up that hard, caked ground to open up fertile soil for all kinds of new life. A world of many splendid colors burst out of the preceding drab background, opening up space for a wide range of nonconformity. The flowers of creativity were expressed in art, theatre, and style, but most dramatically in music. By the end of the decade, millions of kids were singing along with a variety of lively, catchy songs that opposed the war and disdained the establishment. I felt we might have a better chance to transform society than the Old Left, even though they'd had much more developed organizations, because the 1960s rebellious cultural ferment involved a whole generation.

Rock 'n' roll started as a rip-off of Black music. In the 1950s Rhythm and Blues was the form that had the most energy, creativity, and appeal to youth, but back then most white audiences weren't open to Black groups. Colonel Tom Parker, the man who later found and promoted Elvis Presley, reportedly said, "Give me a white man who can sing like a Black, and we'll make millions." Elvis's breakout hit was "Hound Dog." Big Mama Thornton, who did the original, much spunkier version, received a $500 royalty and remained in obscurity as far as white America was concerned. But the vitality and energy of Black music couldn't be contained. White emulators began to evince increasing soul, and Black groups and singers quickly "crossed over" to success with white audiences. To me, the excitement of Rhythm and Blues and rock wasn't only in the beat, the youth themes, and sexual innuendoes; even more I responded to the deep expression of emotion. My favorite song early on was Marvin Gaye's "I Heard It Through the Grapevine," where he sang, "A man ain't supposed to cry/ But these tears I can't hold inside." What a thrill to hear that, contrary to the ubiquitous images that a strong man never gave in to emotion, it was only human to cry over a lost love! Later examples included Aretha Franklin's "Respect" and Smokey Robinson's "Ooh Baby."

While the Beatles were the rage, the number one rock group for me was the Rolling Stones—with their beat and themes bursting directly out of Blues and of Rhythm and Blues. The Stones were a lot better than most rock stars in acknowledging the Black artists who had inspired them, such as Tina Turner and B.B. King, and introducing some of them to white audiences. They also expressed a strong sense of rebellion against dominant society. In the 1960s, I enthusiastically identified with the Stones' macho posturing about sex, celebrated in songs like "Under My Thumb."

Drugs, too, were very much part of the mix. Here the rank hypocrisy of the keepers of society's morals played a big role. The same establishment that advertised and promoted alcohol and tobacco made other drugs illegal—which gave them the allure of being subversive. We had been raised on the crass anti-marijuana propaganda of films like *Reefer Madness*. When young people found that a joint didn't instantly turn them into hopeless addicts and fiendish murderers, they became suspicious of all the warnings and discounted claims that other drugs, like cocaine, were addictive. The practice of millions showed that marijuana was not an automatic conveyor belt to harder drugs, but some became susceptible. Most radicals I knew smoked marijuana in moderation—a few joints a week with an occasional foray into hashish. But sadly, a few bright and promising young people I knew became lost in it, totally "zonked out" every day, and dropped out of political activism and most other purposeful work.

Pot had some positive effects: it helped many young people "expand consciousness" in the sense of breaking from the repressed way they'd been trained, to get in touch with their sensuality and to move away from the dominant culture that was trying to mold us into compliant cogs in the corporate and military machines. It also involved millions in breaking and defying the law, which became a major source of legitimacy and support for political revolutionaries who fought the government. But our romanticization of drugs also had heavy costs. First there was the tacit but serious racism in our not looking at the devastating effects the heavy importation of a raft of drugs was having on the ghettoes and barrios—what the Panthers labeled "chemical genocide." Secondly, our blasé attitude left many in the youth rebellion vulnerable to the harm drugs can do.

An even worse harm, with staggering costs, has resulted from the government's war on drugs—making them illegal and therefore highly lucrative, guaranteed that drugs would become a fountainhead for crime and violence. It's not like the government didn't know this—they had gone through the experience of Prohibition, and many studies showed that a public health approach is a much more effective way to lessen drug use. Instead, the war on drugs was launched as a cover for attacking the Black community, which was the spearhead of social rebellion, and mobilizing broader public support for police power and repression. (For more of an analysis on this point, see "Capitalism and Crisis: Creating a Jailhouse Nation," in *No Surrender*). The results today are that police forces across the U.S. have created a total of thirty thousand paramilitary "SWAT" teams, the Fourth Amendment protections against unreasonable search and seizure have been shredded, and ghettos and barrios have been ripped apart by both drug violence and wholesale incarceration. In a way, we abetted the government's bad faith and destructive policies by being so facile in celebrating "soft drugs" without understanding the dangers.

The much-caricatured cultural rebellion of the 1960s had real problems: celebrating sex in a way that reinforced male supremacy and an irresponsible romanticizing of drugs. But at the same time, there was an exciting, mass breakout from the confines of the straightjacket thinking and cultural conformity of corporate society. Millions of kids got involved at some level in breaking the law, and many more in completely disbelieving government pronouncements. And the dominant values of competition to achieve commercial success and the unfettered right of the United States to run the world were being replaced by some mix of hedonism, peace, and community. What I most loved about this mix was the emerging sense that we were all brothers and sisters and that a better world was possible, indeed was actually in the making.

Political Theory

"The philosophers have only interpreted the world, in various ways; the point, however, is to change it."
— *Karl Marx, "Theses on Feuerbach"*

In high school my trajectory had been toward a profession that helped individuals directly, such as psychiatry. By the time I reached Columbia, my passion was broad social change, so I majored in political science. But, damn, poli-sci at Columbia was boring! It was severed from the real-life concerns that moved me.

One poli-sci course was especially promising and especially disappointing in its focus on the basis and legitimacy for having a government. We read and discussed the classics without commenting on the obvious problem—that their scenarios, based on men coming together to form a social contract, were all clearly mythological—so what good did it do?

For my term paper, I tried to reconstruct what life must have been like for the earliest humans and how that would have led to creating political formations. But all I had to go on was my crude understanding of "human nature" from reading Freud. My essay was atrocious, though I suspect my low grade resulted from its originality rather than its weaknesses. (Later I formulated "Gilbert's Inverse Law of Grading": the more time I put into a paper, the lower the grade because professors found unconventional ideas threatening. The papers that I just hacked out the night before, where basically all I could do is regurgitate what the professor had said, got the A's.)

There were only two graduate students I knew of who were radical and open to talking with undergrads, Shinya Ono and Victor Wallis. One of them (I forget which) suggested I read Marx's *German Ideology*, particularly the essay on Feuerbach. It was like a door opening. Marx didn't start with a myth but rather with the real world: the need to produce for survival under primitive conditions, the divisions of labor and reproduction (men and women) that arose, and how that led to different roles in society and political structures. It certainly didn't solve all the issues, but it was a *real* beginning. I also loved the sense of "species being" in his *Economic and Philosophical Manuscripts of 1844*: central to who I am is that I am part of a *species*; therefore anything that oppresses or degrades other human beings also hurts me, undermines my sense of myself.

Excited about these insights, I went to tell my academic counselor that I had found something by Marx that spoke to the questions about the origins of society. He smiled and said, "I know that, but you can't *say* that in the university." Only a single survey course studied *The Communist Manifesto*—and only to trash it. When the eminent professor completely distorted a point, and I raised my hand and politely disagreed, his response was to give me an icy stare and say, "Thank you, *comrade*." No discussion of the issue, just the threat of being labeled a dirty commie. Despite my distaste for the repressive Eastern European regimes, Marxism now seemed like a worthwhile source of political analysis.

National SDS meetings brashly flew both the red (socialism) and black (anarchism) flags. They weren't displayed in opposition, but rather because both represented the spirit of rebellion. The emphasis in SDS was on activism, and there was very little discussion of political theory. Our guiding ideal was "participatory democracy"—something that went beyond elections every four years, but instead was based on people being directly and actively involved in the decisions that affected their lives. This mandated group discussions and decisions in everyday life, including in the economic sphere. Participatory democracy sounded great to me, and still does, although there are many questions about how to achieve it. In practice, in SDS, it could be both liberating and frustrating. My first national council meeting was right after the anti-war march on Washington on April 17, 1965, and I came in bursting with excitement about bringing the protest back to the campuses. Then, once in the relevant workshop, we spent most of the allotted three hours debating whether or not to have a chairperson for the discussion. In a plenary, the chair, Todd Gitlin, who claimed to be calling on people in an unstructured, nonhierarchical way, kept going by me, only recognizing, sometimes repeatedly, people he already knew. My first national SDS meeting was quite a lesson in what feminist author Jo Freeman later (in 1970 and now available online) cogently critiqued in *The Tyranny of Structurelessness*.

Anarchism had the appeal of a freewheeling cultural spirit and the critique of hierarchy, but Marxism seemed to have a more coherent and useful analysis of society. That first national council meeting convinced me that there had to be some level of organizational structure, with care to make it democratically accountable. But what totally tipped the balance for me, and for thousands more, was what was happening in the larger world: revolutions were sweeping the planet, and almost all of them, especially the ones involving the most oppressed and pushing for fundamental economic changes, were led by Marxist-Leninist parties. Just in our lifetimes, at a pace unprecedented in human history, there had been revolutions in China, Cuba, North Korea, Ghana, and Algeria. The world was on fire with people's war in Vietnam and all of Indochina, the Philippines, Palestine, Eritrea, South Africa, Zimbabwe, the three Portuguese colonies in Africa (Angola, Mozambique, and Guinea-Bissau), and guerrillas were operating throughout Latin America. It was breathtaking, and it underlay the tremendous hope for dramatic social change that infused the youth rebellion of the 1960s. Each of these Third World struggles relied on its own history and culture, each applied and developed existing theory for the particular conditions of its colonized or exploited nation. But almost all that were revolutionary drew their theory from the Marxist-Leninist tradition, or at least its broader philosophical method, historical materialism. This method centered on the social relations of (i.e., who owned and controlled) production; the conflicts thus engendered; and how all of that developed over time.

For me, this overwhelming real-world sweep coincided with the central question that drove me to get into theory: why did the U.S. so systematically work against democracy, overthrow popular governments and install dictators, throughout the Third World? The answer, of course, was "imperialism": the fabulous wealth of the capitalist economy was based on the systematic plunder of the Third World. The human costs of policies to keep labor and raw materials cheap meant that ruthless repression was required to keep those who suffered down.

I didn't start with reading Marx and Lenin. Instead, I was devouring business magazines like *Fortune* and *Business Week*, with their emphasis on the need to open up new markets in the Third World. Others in the new wave of SDS activists were examining the same issues. David Loud of Harvard's chapter was writing a history of how the U.S. emerged as an imperial power. We combined that work in 1967 to write the first national SDS pamphlet that named the system "U.S. imperialism." I'm proud of that contribution, but it certainly had its shortcomings theoretically. When I was working on it, a friend in the Columbia's Student Afro-American Society tactfully cautioned me, "That's fine, but there are already some high-powered thinkers who've written on it, like Lenin, who you should check out." While I did read Lenin, I followed the business magazines in zeroing in on new markets. In reality, profitable investment outlets and cheap raw materials are even more important factors. What was best about the pamphlet was the opening I did, with eight key examples, from Guatemala to Iran to Indonesia, of destructive and anti-democratic U.S. interventions. Despite its weaknesses theoretically, the pamphlet was a crucial advance. While the old SDS leadership defined the system with the contentless phrase "corporate liberalism," we were now thinking in terms of *imperialism*, which both captured the international scope of the capitalist economy and helped explain the centrality of the national liberation movements.

Along with the inspiration from abroad, our movement faced a crisis within the U.S., one that SNCC had understood and articulated in 1966 when they called for "Black Power." Our idealism had failed to turn America around. In fact, power was becoming more entrenched and repressive; Black activists in particular were being imprisoned and killed. Even for those of us sheltered on campus, our disruptions of the war machine were met with the possibility of expulsion, which would subject the males to the wartime draft. Moral protest was not enough, we needed a clearer analysis of society; ardent students didn't have the power to overthrow the government, we needed to find a bigger "agency for social change." Broad sectors of SDS turned to Marxism for a way to solve the crisis. Those of us interested in women's liberation began to read an emerging set of theorists using Marxism to develop feminist analysis, such as Eleanor Leacock, Juliet Mitchell, and Sheila Rowbotham.

One well-organized Marxist-Leninist party was already a strong force within SDS, Progressive Labor. Back in 1965 they had combined the flair of cultural rebellion with militancy against the war. By 1967 they'd become a conservative force, condemning youth culture as decadent and pushing for a turn from militancy to organizing the working class. PL even opposed the 1968 Columbia strike. They didn't acknowledge how conservative the majority of white workers were when it came to the war and the Black struggle; or to the degree that they saw it as a problem, it was one that could be solved with their correct organizing line. In fact, these 1967 "Leninists" were behind where Lenin himself was in 1917, even before the rise of national liberation, in recognizing that the working class of an imperial power enjoyed significant material privileges from the plunder of the Third World.

Still, the student-based SDS had real weaknesses in terms of class perspective. Also, as students felt more powerless, this image of millions of workers had a certain appeal. For those of us who considered ourselves New Left, who craved a more coherent approach to the struggle but without abandoning the emphasis on support for national liberation around the world and within the U.S., there was twofold crisis: how to move forward against awesome government power, and how to stop a takeover of SDS by PL or the like. As Marxism-Leninism increasingly became the source of ideological legitimacy, many debates degenerated into competing recitations from their works—a real farce for a method that's supposed to be based on "the concrete analysis of concrete reality." Also, many in SDS mimicked the highly competitive, polemical style of debate designed to totally discredit opponents. It was bad enough when Marx or Lenin did it, they at least made some trenchant points, but a travesty and a real impediment to fruitful dialogue to have SDS filled with all these little Marxes and Lenins, invariably male.

Soon after arriving at the New School in the fall of 1966, I met two like-minded SDSers—Bob Gottlieb and Gerry Tenney. We liked to call ourselves "neo-Marxists" to emphasize the need for fresh analysis that grappled with the ways the world had changed. Bob, who had a lot of both drive and creativity, organized us to write a major new theoretical work for SDS, which we labeled the "Port Authority Statement" (PAS) after New York City's central bus station, as a satirical takeoff on SDS's founding document, the "Port Huron Statement."

My role was rooted in the research I was already doing with business magazines; in fact it was the section on imperialism that I did for the PAS that became the basis for the more developed *U.S. Imperialism* pamphlet later in 1967. But we were also highly motivated to find a way to counteract PL, and specifically to establish Marxist legitimacy for the student rebellion, which PL dismissed as petit bourgeois but which we felt was by far the most progressive sector within white America. The trends I found on job categories showed an increasing importance for highly educated workers, especially in science and technology. That data meshed with Bob's theoretical overview about a "new working class." We took that concept from French theorists he'd studied, especially Andre Gorz, and tried to apply it to our situation in the U.S. What was exciting to me was the way it legitimated student rebellions: according to Gorz, college was a crucible for developing workers for the most dynamic and strategic sectors of the workforce. While we talked a lot about racism, we didn't integrate it into the analysis. In a way there were two different papers slapped together: one on imperialism and racism, the other on class within the U.S. While the second part had elements of truth, the failure to integrate the whole, to put race at the foundation of class analysis, was a fatal flaw.

Most people in SDS didn't like the Marxist rhetoric and abstract theorizing, whether old-line PL or our "neo-Marxist" approach. But many were looking for a way to move forward and especially to counter PL's influence, so they supported "the new working class" as the alternative. For the first time, SDS's organizational journal, *New Left Notes*, added a theoretical supplement, "Praxis," which stands for the unity of theory and action—developing theory by reflecting on activism and then trying to apply the theory to develop the activism. Gottlieb, Tenney, and I—jokingly labeled "the praxis axis"—were the editors, and we focused much more on articles about changes in the working class than on, say, Ted Allen's (as it turned out, far more relevant) essay on the formation of white supremacy in U.S. history. While the interest in theory felt exciting, most SDSers found what we published too abstract and off-track. But an important sector of Left intellectuals loved "the new working class" theory. Requests to reprint these writings far outstripped those for my imperialism pamphlet or anything else I ever wrote.

Theory was perhaps the most male-dominated area of movement work. Women weren't expected to do it and generally weren't listened to when they did—which both discouraged them from entering the field and denied then the dialogue so vital to development. Naomi, with her keen intelligence and interest in theory, tried to swim against the tide. Study, brainstorming, and analysis were important parts of our relationship and benefited me greatly. She developed new working class theory in relationship to the role of women in advanced capitalist society, and we had a lot of discussion, although I ended up receiving more recognition and credit, on analyzing the prodigious drive to boost consumption within the domestic economy—both the economic role and cultural impact. Naomi went on to relate this to the changing sexist stereotypes and the pressures placed on women.

I wrote a pamphlet, *Consumption*, with the unfortunate subtitle *Domestic Imperialism*, chosen to stress the drive for new markets and the analogy of colonizing people's psyches. But that subtitle missed how the core of domestic imperialism is the oppression and colonization of U.S. people of color within the U.S. The *Consumption* pamphlet became the first release of a new organization, "Movement for a Democratic Society," launched by Gottlieb, Susan Sutheim, Marge Piercy, and others. MDS was a sincere effort to implement new working class theory by starting organizations in those job categories in a way that maintained ties to the student rebellion. The most successful was "Teachers for a Democratic Society," where Ted Gold and others later broke into schools to teach freedom classes in opposition to the teachers' union's racist strike against community control of schools. But Naomi and I, increasingly influenced by the more radical trends in SDS, felt uncomfortable with the elitist implications of MDS. At first my participation was half-hearted, and later (after Weather emerged), I withdrew from MDS. Overall, "new working class" is a good example of how theory can send us off on fascinating but mainly unproductive or even misleading tangents—usually creative ways to downplay racism and put whites at the center of "revolutionary" activity.

The Weapon of Theory

Despite these pitfalls, theoretical work can be invaluable. The analysis of imperialism was totally central to understanding what we were up against and to moving forward in a coherent fashion. *Monthly Review* magazine and publishing house was a particularly useful source. For example, they helped us to see through and refute the unilateral chorus among mainstream economists that Third World countries would develop over time if they opened themselves to Western investment and trade.

(About every ten years there is a new version of the "open yourself to the West" theory of development, without any analysis of why the preceding models failed so miserably.) The September 1966 *Monthly Review* ran Andre Gunder Frank's essay (which built on Che Guevara's critique), "The Development of Underdevelopment," which showed that it was precisely the way Western investments distorted those economies and extracted their wealth that kept the Third World poor and in bondage. This analysis was developed and explored in many subsequent *Monthly Review* books, detailing the way the process played out in specific countries.

Theory helped us debunk other sacred cows of the day, like the truism that the fixed value of thirty-two dollars for an ounce of gold, set up at the end of World War II, would never change. A few of us steeped in *Monthly Review* analysis of how foreign wars and bases were draining U.S. reserves, knew that Nixon would have to devalue the dollar relative to gold. So in 1968 I tried to get some SDS donors to buy $2,000 worth of gold, but since we were always living on the brink of financial disaster, there was no way that amount could be set aside. It was just as well: by 1971, when that $2,000 gold purchase would have been worth over $20,000, we were already underground and wouldn't have been able to cash in.

We often grappled with the role of campaigns to win reforms. Now that we understood the nature of the system, we knew that what was needed was a total change in the structure and nature of power. We were wary of reforms that co-opted (bought off) or deflected the struggle for qualitative change. But the oppressed have immediate, survival needs and people just don't rise up instantaneously for revolution. Intermediary forms of struggle are needed. One idea we played with was "structural reform," where the results strengthened the ability of the oppressed to keep fighting. For example, forming a union as an intermediary forms of workers' power was more important than specific wage concessions. Another concept was "insurgent institutions," where a facility to meet people's needs, say a community health clinic, also served as a base for building struggles against the state. In practice these ideas, while relevant, provided no guarantee against co-optation.

A most essential role of theory is to give young activists a sense of history. We were rightfully eager to change everything, overnight. But expecting quick, easy victories is a setup for disillusionment and burnout. Those of us who studied history had a sense of how long it took—and how many defeats were suffered—before feudalism or slavery was overturned. That sense of the complexity of the forces involved, and the many ups and downs, helped us to do much better at maintaining a long-term perspective and continuing our activism. On the other hand, many people who had delved heavily into theory pulled away from the militancy that was pushing the struggle forward. For example, at Columbia a few months before the strike, I was walking through the campus and ran into one of the grad students who identified with praxis. He was upset. "You know what those crazy kids are doing? They're sitting in to block an office that facilitates war research; such disruptions will discredit us." My response was to ask where this travesty was occurring—so I could head there to join the sit-in.

In opposition to the armchair tendencies of the "praxis axis," the emerging wave of campus SDS leaders, like Mark Rudd at Columbia, dubbed themselves the "action faction." While there were real and serious limitations in spurning theory, the "action faction" had a much better sense of how to move things forward at that key juncture, with the Columbia strike a powerful example of refocusing SDS on the centrality of militancy in solidarity with Vietnam and the Black struggle. Nonetheless, such mass militant action would not have been possible without the preceding years of dedicated and consistent organizing. In turn, the strike made the issues of war and racism central to the entire Columbia University community.

In the wake of the strike's tremendous impact and success, there was a growing distrust for "praxis" people and for theory in general. I got partial dispensation due to my founding role in the ICV and campus SDS, as did Teddy Gold for his highly dedicated activism. But in general it was a rough time among our peers to be identified with theory, and that tarnished my prestige and sense of self-importance within the movement.

Political developments and changes were so rapid in the 1960s that each year felt like a new generation, not only with a new leadership on campuses but also on the national level. Activities quickly escalated from marches to disrupting military recruiters, to draft resistance, to affinity groups ready to break window and avoid arrests. Politically we moved from awakening the moral conscience to resistance and then to revolution, and theoretically from democracy to socialism to Marxism-Leninism. Within all of these various changes, there were key strategies for the particular moment. Individuals who had brilliant ideas to move things forward one year often got stuck in the concept that had made them leaders, and had difficulty getting behind new strategies. I believe this is one of the many ways that ego plays such a major role in weakening the movement. People got all wrapped up in what had made them leaders, made them important, and resisted new advances.

I was already moving away from the "new working class" by the end of the Columbia strike. Still, it was that theory and my role in praxis that had brought me to prominence in national SDS. Now, with a new wave of militant leadership expressing disdain for the role of theory, I felt alienated. I didn't leave SDS but I pulled back considerably. In a way that time of limited activism was precious, as I dug much deeper into study. I read and thought about and worked with all three volumes of Marx's *Capital* (using Paul Sweezy's *Theory of Capitalist Development* as a kind of study guide) as well as related contemporary works. At the time, I was living in a rent-controlled little apartment in the West Village—a fifth-floor walkup, with no bath, for fifty dollars a month—which had a beautifully sunlit little study. What a pleasure it was to read slowly, stop and pace to think about it, and then read some more—often for ten to thirteen hours a day. While the study was valuable and enriching, my limited activism didn't feel good.

Revolutionary Youth Movement

The morning mail brings my copy of New Left Notes, *which includes the new strategy paper adopted at the Boulder NC. I open it thinking "Let's see what foolishness these young whippersnappers who know nothing about Marxism-Leninism have come up with now." But as I read the Revolutionary Youth Movement (RYM) paper my competitive bile evaporates. This analysis validating the student rebellion is qualitatively better than "new working class," and much more promising for organizing. RYM holds that students are more open to rebellion because among whites young people are the least integrated into the structures of white supremacy and imperialism, such as reformist unions. RYM recognizes the problem of students' limited class base, but instead of looking to the most elite sectors of the workforce, advocates building off the new cultural links with working-class youth.*

Some of the young staff members at the New York regional SDS office generously and thoughtfully stopped by my apartment regularly to keep me in touch with what was going on and to invite me to help out. So I was involved with SDS, but certainly not full-time, and I didn't bother going to the national council meeting in Boulder, Colorado, in December 1968. But despite my distance from national SDS, I became excited about the emerging RYM strategy.

More and more white working-class youth were identifying with the youth rebellion through music, pot, anti-authoritarianism, the sentiments of universal brotherhood and peace. Some of these youth were paying the heaviest costs, as cannon fodder in Vietnam, but getting the least benefits for maintaining imperialism. According to RYM, the way to extend the movement and to have more of a working-class base was to go to young people already identifying with the counterculture, and to reach them in places like community colleges and the military. Unfortunately, the RYM paper failed to make the other potentially revolutionary connection with the emerging feminist movement.

Soon after reading the RYM paper, I signed up as a community college organizer for regional SDS. I ended up working with some great young students, as anti-war protest was already burgeoning on those campuses. On regional staff, I was also in touch with the work to set up coffee shops near military bases such as Fort Dix, where we connected with the growing GI disenchantment that played such a key role in ending the war. Once again, it felt like a heady and exciting time to organize.

But even as an activist, I didn't give up my love for theory and continued to do such work, sometimes on my own, often in various collaborations or dialogues with other people. Naomi and I were at times called up to lead study sessions to help counteract the power PL tapped into by citing Marx and Lenin. Even beyond the defensive role, some of the work seemed useful.

In looking at repeated failures to build a successful U.S. working-class movement, most communist groups attributed the setbacks to the "opportunist" (unprincipled) leadership at the time. Implicitly, this simple solution says, "Now that *we* are leading things, everything will be fine." By this failing to grapple with deep material and historical realities, such as white supremacy, these sects were bound to repeat the same failures.

The most common oversimplification by those claiming the ML mantle was "economism," the tendency to reduce the problems in society to a simple economic explanation. The rich Marxian concept of "mode of production" got restricted to workers at factories; the many different conflicts that can lead to revolution were all narrowed down to the coming depression.

Similarly Marxian economics got reduced to one simple law, inexorably leading to a great depression. For some it was the falling rate of profit; for others it was "realization crisis" (the inability to sell what is produced at full value). In reality, both these tendencies exist, and capitalism's effort to solve one can make the other worse. Together, and with other factors, they produce deep tensions in the economy. But there is nothing mechanical or automatic about a collapse. These contradictions generate huge political battles such as imperialist expansion, wars, anti-labor offensives, and mechanisms for boosting consumption.

In my reading of Marx, the mode of production was the sum total of all the relations of production, of all the key ways production was organized. So national liberation struggles weren't some peripheral theater, always secondary to workers in the U.S. and Europe. Rather, because imperialism subjected the economies of whole nations, those struggles were crucial to how capitalism was organized, on a global scale. Also, the oppression of women had everything to do with the way the work force was reproduced (the unwaged labor to raise children who will become workers) as well as with maintaining patriarchal inheritance and property rights under capitalism. In a way these theoretical positions affirmed what was already at the heart of our politics: racism and sexism are far more than bad ideas; white and male supremacy are deep, fundamental structures which, along with class, are central to defining the system.

One area of particular interest for me was the way that "waste expenditures" (such as advertising, military, etc., that don't directly lead to new production for the market) had burgeoned and the role they played in the modern capitalist economy subsequent to *Capital*. Waste helped keep the system going by boosting sales, but it also was a drag on output and profits because the expenditures were unproductive. The mixed role of giant waste expenditures was sustained in part by imperialism's highly profitable and productive investments in the Third World—when political conditions permitted.

Most Western Marxists dismissed the great majority in the Third World—peasants—as nonstrategic and backward, since they were not industrial workers. But the products they grew were often exchanged on the world market at great profit for the transnational corporations, so the exploitation of the peasants and their role in national liberation struggles were key factors under imperialism. Our understanding of the U.S. as an international economy mandated analyzing class structure in global, as well as the usual national, terms.

But events in the world were moving much faster than the speed of my thought. All this theoretical work was soon to be put on the shelf when we formed Weathermen collectives—a life of full-time militancy—in the summer of 1969.

COINTELPRO

"Just my roomie and me / And our mimeo makes three / In our red haven…"

Meanwhile, in the mid-1960s, things were cranking right along, as my jolly rewrite of "My Blue Heaven" attests. The mimeograph was the primitive tool we used to make leaflets back then. You typed out the text on a stencil, which went over an ink drum, and then you cranked out copies. Someone donated one to our Vietnam committee, the ICV, and since of course we didn't have an office at Columbia, the machine went into an alcove of the little West 106th Street apartment I shared with Jimmy, the ICV treasurer. While the sound of the mimeo could grate, we came to enjoy it as expressing the way the anti-war work was progressing in 1965–66. Then a (figurative) grenade was thrown into our lap with a confidential and apparently documented charge that five members of the ICV were police informants.

The ICV wasn't doing, or even remotely considering, anything illegal. I recently had participated in the first East Coast demonstration where four young men had apparently burned draft cards, but it wasn't an ICV event, and exactly what was burned wasn't visible, and in any case the government did not want to call attention to such defiance by prosecuting it. But coming off the McCarthy era, people were wary that the government would collect names and information for subsequent persecution. (Freedom of Information Act (FOIA) documents later revealed that the FBI started keeping track of the ICV, its activities and members, right from the beginning—solely on the basis of our opposition to the war.) In addition to informing, police agents could influence and distort strategic and tactical decisions. The charges had to be taken very seriously, but expelling people could turn ugly.

The names were brought to me by Jimmy's girlfriend, K. She was somewhat older than us, with a sophisticated but jaded air and a style that had more in common with '50s beatniks than '60s youth. She was working her way through school with a part-time cleaning job, and explained that she had seen the names on a document while cleaning up in police headquarters. The list presented quite a dilemma: no one would want to work in an organization riddled with infiltrators, so we had a responsibility to expose and expel them. But these five were hardworking and popular; accusing them would lead to bitter acrimony and possibly even a fatal split.

Despite my inexperience I was lucky on this one because a good and trusted friend of mine had known one of the five since childhood. She knew everything about how and when he became radical, and that had happened way too early for it to be subterfuge. Confident that the list was wrong, I never raised it in the ICV. A year later, when Jimmy and K's affair was over, she was busted for heroin, and evidently had a history of problems. We inferred that the NYPD had held a pending heroin charge over her head to get her to plant that false and divisive story in the ICV.

Understanding how and when a person becomes radical became a primary technique for weeding out infiltrators later, when we prepared to go underground. Of course the method isn't foolproof, but infiltrators could fake anger and militancy much better than a real process of radicalization. When people did move to armed struggle, the greatest vulnerability to police agents came when seeking out people with access to military skills and materials. Also, learning individuals' histories was less successful for the Black movement, where the government had gone to greater lengths to develop long-term informants. Gene Roberts, famously seen in his role of the bodyguard giving mouth-to-mouth respiration to the assassinated Malcolm X, was recruited by the NYPD out of high school and had an impressive movement history. He wasn't exposed until 1970 when he was the key government witness in the notorious frame-up of the Panther 21.

This 1965 police-planted phony "snitch jacket" was not yet the official and later notorious COINTELPRO (CounterIntelligence Program), the illegal campaign to destroy the Black liberation movement and other struggles by people of color, and to turn back the New Left. The program's launching document was dated August 25, 1967, although the antecedents went back to the campaigns against the Communist Party and the Socialist Workers Party in the preceding decades. All serious activists today need to study and draw lessons from that history. The best single book I know is *Agents of Repression*, by Ward Churchill and Jim Vander Wall. But even these 510 pages describe only two of the many campaigns—the blood-soaked offensives against the Black Panther Party and the American Indian Movement. Not only was COINTELPRO much more extensive than that, but it was only one of several illegal government counterinsurgency programs. The CIA, Army Intelligence, local police forces, and later a special presidential task force all had their own versions.

One major target of the government was the "underground press"— small, radical, alternative newspapers. At their height this range of publications had about six million readers." The establishment couldn't stand exposure of realities such as Vietnamese children with napalm burns or the Panthers' side of the story in a confrontation with the police. In addition to the standard techniques of sowing distrust and divisions among people, they used multiple busts, on any pretext, to bankrupt these shoestring operations with legal costs. At the same time, the FBI systematically worked to scare off advertisers. (For a fuller account, see *UnAmerican Activities*, by Geoffrey Rips).

The classic example of how the government used fabricated legal charges against dissidents was the "Panther 21" case. In 1969, twenty-one leading members of the New York Black Panthers were charged with conspiracy to bomb Macy's and other department stores. A few took off, but most were rounded up and held on high bail. I made mobilizing support for them my top priority. While I could imagine revolutionaries building for armed struggle, I knew these charges were bogus, designed to turn the public against them. The Panthers would never bomb stores where people of color and working-class folks were shopping. After a drawn-out prosecution based on Gene Roberts's perjured testimony, it took a jury just ninety minutes to declare all defendants not guilty on all charges. But the two years of jail time, bail money, trials and legal costs left what had been a very effective Panther chapter completely decimated.

Another front was the concerted effort to split off white solidarity with the Black movement. The FBI, even as defenders of white supremacy, could see and exploit our internal racism. One tension was that while the Black movement was under much heavier attack, white leftists (poor as we were) had more resources. So a question arose as to how often the SDS printing press in Chicago would be devoted to urgently needed Panther defense material. On one hand, political priorities and solidarity meant putting the press at their service; on the other hand, we also had other responsibilities—to support other Third World groups under attack and to continue organizing work among white youth. A real dilemma of scarcity was made worse because we undoubtedly had a certain level of unconscious racist arrogance about "our" resources. In 1969, the groups almost came to blows, which would have been a colossal setback for the movement. Fortunately, the political understanding of several key people averted violence. Later, when COINTELPRO was exposed, we learned that phony phone calls, claiming to be from the SDS national office, had been placed to the Panthers saying that we were reneging on our agreements to print their material because we had too much of our own work to do. And the two people who had been pushing the confrontation toward violence turned out to be police agents.

By the late 1960s, we were feeling that something more systematic than local harassment was going on. A friend of mine in SDS was told by a young intern with access to the House Judiciary Committee that there was some secret program of attack. When I told various liberal and moderate Left friends what I thought was happening, the response I got wasn't in the form of a different political analysis; they simply and emphatically called me "paranoid." It's hard to argue against a psychological characterization, a charge that your very perception of reality is off. Yet when COINTELPRO was exposed in 1971 by a group of pacifists who broke into an isolated FBI office in Media, Pennsylvania, the documents showed that our late-'60s perceptions were a gross *under*statement compared to the scope and viciousness of the government crimes in progress.

Being accurate about persecution didn't exempt us from the dangers of political paranoia. When under pressure, it's easy to panic about phantoms while also missing very real dangers. In fact, sowing panic and distrust is a main goal of the attacks. For this reason, the FBI rated the false snitch-jacket as its most effective tactic. (Like the CIA, they don't admit on paper to assassinations.)

It is always upsetting to find, many years later, how far we are from systematically learning and passing along the lessons. The scenario is all too common even today. When there is circumstantial evidence that a trusted comrade might be an informant, some folks close to the situation don't want to deal with it because it is so unpleasant and disruptive; others try to prove they are "leaders" by denouncing the person publicly—even without proof and despite all the examples of how damaging false snitch charges can be. The sensible alternative to both sides of this bad coin is careful, sober, closed-lipped investigation. Often one can trace back and talk with principals in the incident that led to the rumors, or learn more about the individual's history of development, or even find other situations where he or she was privy to information the government wanted. Such methods are far from a guarantee but are preferable to either burying one's head in the sand or broadcasting unproven charges.

Similarly, much-needed political discussions are often cut off based on "security" ("Who knows who's listening?"), while damaging gossip is freely bandied about. A key success of COINTELPRO was to turn comrades against one another based on sexual jealousy or personal competition. Gossip can be a valuable weapon for the agents of repression, so it's important to minimize such backbiting and instead deal with tensions through open discussion based on mutual respect. At the same time, if we cut off needed political discussion, we hand the government a victory. We can't derive our concept of security from James Bond movies, with a strict "need to know" principle, where strength lies in the individual hero. Open political discussion is essential for a movement for the oppressed, and people can't be counted on to take high levels of responsibility and risk if they aren't fully involved in developing the political and strategic direction. So, we often are stronger, even with the vulnerability of openness, with full political discussion, while certain tactical issues that can be used against the movement should be handled in a more restricted way—but based on the overall politics and with democratic accountability.

In my experience, the best defense against the divisive tactics of COINTELPRO is to work hard to be true to our principles. We have to honestly look at and grapple with the ways that racism, sexism, homophobia, elitism, and competitiveness affect all of us who grew up in this society. We have to learn to handle differences among us in an open and loving way. We have to commit ourselves to full, participatory discussion of politics, while at the same time protecting specifics that can be used by the state. (For an excellent account of the experiences of the Panthers and helpful guidelines for dealing with internal conflicts, see Safiyah Bukhari, *The War Before*.)

Of course there was a qualitative difference in how COINTELPRO played out for the New Left and for Third World groups within the United States. Dozens of Panthers were killed between 1968 and 1971, and sixty-nine AIM members and supporters were killed on the Pine Ridge Reservation from 1973 to 1976. For the Panthers, 1969 opened with "Organization Us" gunmen publicly murdering stellar young activists Bunchy Carter and John Huggins in Los Angeles, and ended with Mark Clark and the most promising young Panther leader, Fred Hampton, shot to death by police while sleeping in their Chicago apartment. Later documents showed that the FBI directly egged on Us (and the triggermen may well have been police infiltrators) to attack the Panthers. In Chicago, subsequent investigations revealed that the police pretext for the raid was bogus, that all but one of the more than ninety shots fired were incoming, and that Fred Hampton had been drugged with a powerful sleeping pill. (For a more detailed and gripping account see Jeff Haas, *The Assassination of Fred Hampton*.)

It's hard to give an exact number for Panthers killed as a result of COINTELPRO. Figures I've seen vary from twenty-eight to forty; many more were wounded. While many Panthers were killed directly by the police or their agents, some died in internal violence fomented by the government. As with most aspects of COINTELPRO, the movement's internal weaknesses played a big role. (For a thoughtful discussion of why the Panthers were susceptible to aspects of COINTELPRO, see *We Want Freedom* by Mumia Abu-Jamal.) Please remember the circumstances and pressures on a still-immature movement. It was FBI plant William O'Neal who gave the police the floor plan and then drugged the victims so that Fred Hampton had no chance to wake up and defend himself. Informants were also responsible for hundreds of Panthers being framed and sent to jail, including Mondo we Langa and Ed Poindexter, who are still in prison today. Agent Cotton Smith tried to set up a violent confrontation by feeding "information" to both Huey Newton and Geronimo Pratt that each was trying to kill the other. So the issue of weeding out infiltrators took on a life-and-death urgency, even while there was still much to learn about humane and effective methods to do so.

By 1971, the combination of this bone-crushing pressure and internal weaknesses led to the West-East split in the Panthers. The West Coast BPP, led by Huey Newton, pulled back from armed confrontation and focused on the Panther community programs like free breakfast for school children. Others, including many East Coast Panthers, went underground to fight the repression by building the Black Liberation Army (BLA), which included other revolutionary nationalists. In retrospect, many of those involved wish they could have avoided the split and developed both aspects of the struggle in tandem, but the pressures and acrimony of the moment were overwhelming.

The split of the Panthers and the setbacks to the Black liberation movement as a whole, as well as to other Third World militants, broke off what had been the main inspiration and example for all kinds of radical awakening and change throughout the U.S., and set different, more difficult terms for our entire movement. The blatant assassination of the charismatic Fred Hampton, and the failure of much of the broader white movement to make this a central rallying point, joined with the earlier napalming of children, were the events that pushed me, with others, toward a total determination, maybe even a frenzy, to fight this murderous government. And it was a time when revolutionary struggles around the world were having great success.

From Protest to Resistance

It's a nightmare of sorts but I'm wide awake, alone, well past midnight, on a dimly lit Greyhound bus crossing the Great Plains in the summer of 1965. It's not ghosts or ogres or other phantoms that are scaring me; rather hard cold reality in our all-too-brutal world. The results of a much longer process were crystallized into these traumatic thoughts: Now that I recognize that imperialism's violent suppression of all attempts at reform has made armed struggle necessary by and for the wretched of the earth, now that the sturdy dam of guaranteed personal moral purity I felt as a pacifist has broken, could I possibly turn into another Stalin, become drunk on the power and paranoia that can transform an ardent idealist into a cold-blooded murderer?

What a difference a decade can make. In 1960, I was a model citizen-in-the-making, carefully studying candidates' programs and itching to be able to vote. By 1970, I was headed underground to fight "the monster." Compared to many people in the '60s—when some leaped from Republican families to militant radicals in a matter of months—I was as slow and deliberate as a turtle, grappling with every step in the process: from liberal Democrat, to social democrat (hoping to bring about moderate socialism through elections), to nonviolent civil disobedience, to building resistance through street militancy and draft defiance, to supporting revolutionary armed struggle. With each step, I took my commitment to that approach seriously. But I also felt the responsibility to relate political theory to the real world—that any strategy had to be measured by its results in terms of people, by showing some real potential to stop hunger and provide education and opportunity for every child in the world. Given that constant check-in and verification, two factors impelled me up that staircase toward revolution. The more we tried to change things and the more we studied, the more we saw how systematically our government had crushed peaceful and democratic efforts to level the playing field for the poor. At the same time, revolutionary movements around the world were mobilizing the oppressed and achieving dramatic social change.

The center point of my transitions came in the spring and summer of 1965. While passionately opposed to the war in Vietnam, I didn't support the National Liberation Front (NLF). With the exception of the Cuban Revolution with Castro's vital relationship with the people, I felt that communist governments weren't democratic, and I was wary of regimes that resulted from military victories. My hope, what I saw as the alternative to the U.S.-imposed dictatorship, was the "third force," the Buddhists and various middle-class pacifist and democratic elements opposed to the repressive and reviled South Vietnamese regime. That spring I went to a major educational program on Vietnam, at some big auditorium. The speaker had worked in Vietnam for years, with the U.S. Agency for International Development (AID), so he certainly hadn't started out as a radical. He described how the U.S.-backed regime had systematically destroyed all opposition with prison, torture, and assassination. I was sitting there gasping: the reason there is a national liberation front, the reason people in Vietnam are waging an armed struggle, is that the U.S. doesn't allow anything else. The "third force" was decimated and doomed; the only way to achieve change was to be organized to fight for it.

That insight about Vietnam developed into a worldview during that super-charged summer bus trip. A grad student in the ICV had come to me with a suggestion from a woman of the Old Left: it would be valuable for the different campus Vietnam committees that had sprung up across the nation to share experiences and begin to consolidate strategy. She offered to pay for airfare out to the West Coast, and then a bus ticket back through many campus stops for an organizer to make the connections. It sounded like a good idea to me. Before leaving, I assembled some reading for the long hours of travel. Among the books was one recommended by a PL friend: *The Great Fear in Latin America*, by John Gerassi.

Schools were crackling with anti-war energy and the exchange of ideas felt dynamic as I visited Berkeley, the University of Wisconsin, and several more. I was also able to connect people to the national anti-war coordinating office (the precursor to the "Mobe") that Dave Dellinger and others of us had started after the SDS march on Washington. In between these rushes of activities and ideas and people, were the long hours on buses, during which *The Great Fear* blew me away.

When Gerassi went to Latin America, he was pretty mainstream, a reporter for *Newsweek*, but what he saw changed him. His book provided a thumbnail sketch of each country in the region, and showed that every time there was a serious move toward economic nationalism—every time there was an attempt to use some of the wealth of the country to better the conditions of the poor, rather than fatten up U.S. transnational corporations—the CIA engineered an overthrow, usually violent, and set up a pro-U.S. dictatorship. The excuse would be to "stop Communism," but the coups were often against elected governments and sometimes even against right-wing nationalists, such as Vargas in Brazil. Then Gerassi took each of those countries and broke down the figures: the illiteracy rate (often it was two-thirds), the vast numbers without potable water, the absence of health care in the countryside, and so on. He described the bone-chilling brutality of U.S.-installed dictators such as Somoza in Nicaragua and Trujillo in the Dominican Republic.

One example (which later opened my *U.S. Imperialism* essay) was Guatemala. A democratically elected president, Jacobo Árbenz Guzmán, dared to take some fallow United Fruit Company land (giving them compensation at tax-assessed values) to redistribute to poor peasants to grow food. The CIA organized a military coup led by Colonel Castillo Armas, with air cover flown by CIA pilots. The Castillo regime returned the land to United Fruit, allowed plantation owners to cut wages by 30 percent, closed down opposition newspapers, and reinstated policies that kept 70 percent of the people illiterate and almost all the best land in the country in the hands of a few families. The vicious repression to enforce such conditions engendered a guerrilla opposition and a bloody civil war that was still raging as I read.

A quick summary with one brief example can't capture the impact of reading that series of sketches and seeing the figures for each country—and feeling how each person living with squalor and disease was a real human being. Part of what brought the statistics alive was my summer of study in Mexico two years earlier. The sight of children picking through garbage heaps for food—moving aside the dead dog covered with flies—was burned into my consciousness. The one clear exception to this pattern was Cuba, where a revolution overthrew the pro-U.S. dictator, Batista, and then made free education and health care for all the top priority. On all the key indicators of health and welfare, Cuba stood head and shoulders above the U.S.-sponsored governments of the region.

The lesson that screamed out to me was that the greatest violence of all was the social violence of hunger and disease and wasted potential that characterized the conditions of more than two billion human beings in the Third World. At the same time, history showed that the ruthless use of military, economic, and political power made peaceful change impossible. Caring about people, wanting to stop the massive, excruciating social violence, mandated a willingness to fight. I now understood where the guerrillas in Guatemala came from and I supported them. But then another troubling thought entered my mind: Now that I know it is necessary and right for Guatemalans to fight and die because of what *my* government is doing, what is *my* responsibility? Can I continue to be a pacifist while they are paying such a price for what the U.S. does?

The only ethical answer I could come up with is that I had a responsibility to fight too, but alone on the bus that night, I also had to confront the possibility that force and violence could corrupt even the most sincere idealist. I had felt a great comfort in being a pacifist. I was on the side of the oppressed and I knew that I personally would never harm anyone. There was almost a guarantee of a certain level of moral purity. But *The Great Fear* put me in touch with the need to also look at results in the real world: stopping intolerable social violence was more important than my personal purity—true morality is based in caring about other people and (as opposed to the false ends vs. means debate) requires both good intentions and intelligent strategies to achieve qualitative change.

I would have loved to have been able to talk with other friends that night. But I came to a rudimentary understanding on my own that got developed in later discussion and studies of Third World movements: there had to be clear standards that defined revolutionary armed struggle as the opposite of imperialist violence. Revolutionary action must be clearly in the interests of the vast majority, the oppressed, and action must be geared to build their participation and power rather than to consolidate the organization as a power over them; any such action must be rigorously tailored toward mobilizing the people and weakening the power structure; the greatest care must be taken to avoid hurting civilians.

But a rational set of standards didn't dissolve my terror at setting off from my secure home ground of pacifism into the uncharted wilderness of armed struggle. My main comfort was that these troubling challenges had no immediate practical application. In 1965 it was still hard to imagine a role for or participation in revolutionary armed struggle. In fact at that point (and for a couple of years to follow) I hadn't even thrown a brick.

Morality was central for me. After political science proved so disappointing my freshman year, I switched my major to philosophy, for one basic reason: now that I knew my life would be dedicated to political activism, I wanted to have clear moral guidelines for what I did. But the philosophy department was as unreal as poli-sci, and even more pretentious. The main schools of ethics we studied derived moral principles from some absolute, such as God's will or the Platonic ideal. But of course those absolutes were articulated by men and—not coincidentally—mainly served to reinforce the dominant ideas and forces in society. The alternatives presented were forms of relativism, the most extreme version being logical positivism, which held that all ethical statements are subjective, similar to saying which flavor of ice cream you like or which baseball team you root for. The philosophical flavor of the day was existentialism, and some Marxist students liked it because it seemed "dialectical." But to me it was another jazzed-up version of relativism, with each person just making an individual, inherently "absurd" choice about morality. Even while taken with Albert Camus's affecting novel, I felt that *The Stranger*'s failure to grapple with colonial violence revealed the pitfalls of his existential approach to ethics.

I was an odd duck among the radical philosophy students in feeling closer to utilitarianism. While I recognized its deep problems of being rooted in a middle-class perspective and in its potential misuse to shortchange minority rights, I felt that "the greatest good for the greatest number" at least got at the basic terms. Morality was neither an absolute dropped on us from the sky nor a purely relative choice like ice cream flavors. While there are no verifiably perfect judgments, there are qualitatively better and worse choices. The basis for a real morality is humanity, what works for people. Naturally there will be many different interpretations, but all human beings strive to have the basics of survival secured, and then beyond that some opportunity to develop their potential. Various social policies and actions can be measured against that standard. To me, morality in the real world entailed various imperfect but qualitatively different choices, based in a sense that every human life is equally valuable. Of course, the middle-class bias of utilitarianism was not the way to develop that. But I'd already learned from Malcolm X of the key division in the world between oppressors and oppressed and of the need to see choices in terms of the interests of the vast majority. Similarly, Marxist analysis was teaching me that the human condition had to be grappled with in terms of class and power in society.

The campuses were seething with both growing energy and mounting frustration in the mid-1960s. We felt tremendous frustration that the war continued to escalate despite our polite protests; and we felt greater strength and energy as more and more students became active. What would you do if you were close by as a machine-gunner was mowing down rows of people, and he wouldn't respond when you implored him to stop? We wanted, we felt impelled, to find a way to take the machine gun out of his hand, to make it inoperative. In the urgency and promise of the day, we would excitedly recount and discuss each and every successful example of heightened opposition to the war, anywhere in the country, and immediately look for ways to apply it on our campus. I remember the rush I felt when I heard about 1965 effort in Berkeley to block trains carrying troops to bases for subsequent deployment to Vietnam. It was time to confront and disrupt the merchants of death.

Columbia University was part and parcel of the war machine in many ways, from sophisticated weapons research to inviting recruiters for the Selective Service System (the draft), the CIA, Dow Chemical (makers of napalm), and the like. When the Vietnam Committee at Columbia stagnated, the SDS chapter, led by John Fuerst, took the initiative. Students, tired of the same old picket lines that the government disregarded, felt the affront when these agencies and corporations worked right on our campus to continue to perpetrate mass murder.

The actions usually weren't sit-ins. Instead SDS would bring scores of demonstrators to crowd and question the recruiters, who, under those circumstances, could get nothing else done. These new actions were controversial. University officials and leading academics, who had never said a word when it was *verboten* to criticize U.S. foreign policy or when teaching Marx could ruin an academic career, now discovered and defended the absolute value of free speech—when it was exercised by the establishment, anyway. Their hypocrisy notwithstanding, free speech is a fundamental principle, and when eroded, the restrictions are overwhelmingly used against the Left. So the charge that we were suppressing free speech had to be taken seriously and could turn students, even many who opposed the war, against us.

Equal Rights and Unequal Power

SDS had a pivotal confrontation with University President Grayson Kirk in Low Library. When he said such protests couldn't be tolerated because they violated free speech, people looked to me to answer him, with my reputation for being articulate in debates—on campus and on citywide radio programs—against young conservatives or government representatives about the war. But this time I blew it, and all because I wasn't radical enough in challenging the myths of liberal democracy. Understanding that the issue was the difference between *speech*—which should be equally open to everyone—and *power* to act in ways that affected others, I told Kirk that the problem was inviting recruiters for the war machine when the opposition (e.g., SDS) was not given such university support. But of course SDS was allowed to function on campus, even if our budget was only pennies compared to the megabucks of the corporations and Department of Defense. The real contrast was that the university did vital scientific research and provided graduates for a war industry that was developing ever more "advanced," more gruesome weapons to use on the Vietnamese; but there certainly was no way Columbia would provide resources or personnel to help the Vietnamese fight back, no way the National Liberation Front or other resistance movements would be able to get the results of weapons research or recruit fighters. The central confrontation wasn't between the government and SDS but rather between imperialism and the people of the Third World. That would have been the clearest way to demarcate the power divide, to show that when it came to research, resources, and recruiting, the university certainly did not allow free access for the oppressed.

The claim of "equal rights" can be an very effective cover for enforcing unequal power. I should have been able to state it clearly, because I had read it in Marx's "Critique of the Gotha Program," or as the witty Anatole France put it early in the twentieth century, "The law, in its majestic equality, forbids the rich as well as the poor to sleep under the bridges, to beg in the street, and to steal bread."

The "equal rights" cover for grossly unequal power continues to be a major bludgeon today. If, in the face of giant advantages for white males with wealth and resources accumulated via centuries of outrageous discrimination, people of color demand "affirmative action," they are accused of bias. (In 2004 I heard President Bush speak with great indignation about a college admission program that didn't select purely by SAT scores and grades. This is the same George W. who got into one of the top colleges in the country despite woefully inadequate SATs and grades, because his daddy was an alumnus and big contributor.) Feminists who try to set up women-only meetings or other safe spaces are accused of "sexism in reverse," but they are responding to a reality where, by and large, it is men who harass, stalk, beat, and rape women and not the other way around. Republicans institute policies that weaken trade unions, give gigantic tax cuts to the rich, and gut programs for the poor; but it's only the rare Democratic critique of those actions that gets accused of promoting "class warfare." There are, of course, literally a million examples of how the rules are made and applied to favor those with power. One of the greatest shams precludes limits on political campaign spending because *money* is defined as "free speech." Similarly, the big media in the U.S. are "free" for any billionaires who can buy in. In contrast, our goal was to make speech freer—making it possible for a much wider range of people to be heard more fully—by opening up and equalizing resources. We wanted to implement the political principle of "one person, one vote" instead of the prevailing "one million dollars, one vote."

On campus, anti-war as well as prowar voices could be heard, and our ability to provide information and express our viewpoint helped us get to the point where two-thirds of Columbia students opposed the war by 1968. Free speech is an invaluable and central principle, and our goal was to defend it and extend it to the voiceless and powerless. But speaking out is one thing, and the power to implement policy is another. However inarticulate I was that day, SDS activists understood that war research and recruiting—which were available to only one side in the conflict—were aiding and abetting crimes, indeed crimes against humanity, in progress. Those supporting the war were welcome to speak and debate as much as they wished; but we would not stand aside and allow murder incorporated to operate on campus.

This way of challenging power felt like a big step beyond the periodic marches, walled in by the police. Here was something happening in the community where we lived, on a regular basis, where we could least hamper the machinery of death. There was a tremendous sense of energy and excitement in the air, accompanied by greater creativity on the cultural front. One fun form of that was "guerrilla theater," graphic skits in the middle of the campus, to expose the "work, study, get ahead, kill" logic of the status quo. These developments at Columbia were part of broader changes across the country, summarized by the new slogan, "From Protest to Resistance."

First Bust

"They're framing me for 'assault on a peace officer' when I didn't even raise my hands! They jumped me! So, take that!" I throw a quick punch to the breadbasket and the cop doubles over... That's my fantasy as I enter the courtroom and see the policeman who arrested me. It's odd and disconcerting for me to have any violent impulse toward any person, even the cop who busted me. It's a fantasy that I don't have the least desire to implement. What's odder still is that the "revolutionary" who analyzes the system as imperialism is so shocked at being framed.

It was April 1968. An emergency demonstration had been called because the charismatic European student leader, Rudi Dutschke, had been shot down and almost killed by a right-winger in Germany. The site was the New York office of the German Springer Press, which had been whipping up hysteria against the European student movement. We felt a lot of affinity with the German students; their organization also went by the initials "SDS" (Sozialistischer Deutscher Studentenbund or German Students Socialist Organization). When they were attacked, we wanted to show solidarity. The demonstration, called on short notice, was simply to be a peaceful picket on the sidewalk.

As much as I wanted to be there, I already had a commitment to meet my dad, who was in New York City on a business trip. I put a copy of my recently printed *U.S. Imperialism* in my pocket to give him (I knew he wouldn't agree with the politics, but *maybe* he would be pleased that I'd been "published") and decided to stop off at the Springer protest on the way to our midtown lunch. A couple of blocks away from the picket, I heard sirens. "That can't be us, can it?" But I broke into a trot. When I got there, there was no demonstration—just debris on the sidewalk and one kid, I didn't know him, being beaten by about four cops. Then another six police came charging out of the alleyway, but there was nothing to attack but this one helpless kid. I was stunned. I had no idea what to do. I couldn't imagine fighting the cops, but it went against the grain to step out of the way while they vamped on this lone demonstrator. So I stood in the way, and they all piled on me.

Surprisingly, I didn't fall down. At 155 pounds, I wasn't all that solid, but with so many of them on me, they got in one another's way, neutralizing the impact. This infuriated the cops, and one pulled my legs out from under me. As I fell, I saw a club swinging for my head and instinctively rolled as I hit the ground. The club missed and (I later found out) the cop scraped his hand on the sidewalk. As they started to kick, a flash bulb went off. Someone (a sergeant?) yelled, "Cool it, the press." And that was it. No beating, but I was cuffed behind my back and hauled down to the police station. Some of our people had regrouped and saw the swing of the club, heard the crack, thinking it hit my head. So I tried to give them a look to let them know I was OK; I also knew they'd be calling a lawyer and working on bail. I was charged with misdemeanor "assault" on two officers. The one with the scraped hand went to the hospital for "treatment"—a band-aid. I missed lunch with my dad, and the cops found my *Imperialism* pamphlet to be of great interest. In jail, I saw some of the other demonstrators, who had been busted before I arrived. J.J. tried to yell to me from another tank. I answered but didn't keep the exchange going. I don't like to shout and didn't see what it would accomplish. Later I realized that, once again, I'd been too stodgy; there's definitely a value to being boisterous to keep group spirits up.

Naturally, I wanted to fight the case all the way. I hadn't assaulted anyone; all I'd done was exercise my constitutional right to a peaceful picket; it was the cops who illegally broke up the demonstration and then assaulted me. After several court appearances, the DA offered my movement lawyer a plea bargain: I would plead guilty to a misdemeanor "disorderly conduct" charge and pay a fifty-dollar fine.

"No way, I'm not guilty of disorderly conduct!" I protested.

"I know," the lawyer replied, "but if it goes to trial it's going to be your word against six police officers. You'll be found guilty and you could get a year in jail."

"I don't care, let's fight it."

"Look, I'm swamped with pro bono work for the Panthers, many of them are facing *life* in prison. I'm not going to spend all the time it would take to go to trial for a misdemeanor, when it can be resolved for fifty dollars."

He had a point: he was doing far more important work for the Panthers. But on the way up the courthouse stairs to plead guilty that day, I couldn't help that fantasy of getting a little satisfaction for my fifty dollars.

The day in court went worse than I had imagined because the lawyer, knowing my reluctance, hadn't prepared me. It wasn't enough just to enter the plea; adding insult to injury, the judge forced me to recite for the record just how I'd been guilty of the offense. While my righteous innocence is amusing, the experience in court was an eye-opener. The buildings are colossal and intimidating, the language incomprehensible to a layperson, the procedures unfamiliar. As a defendant you sit there and watch these exchanges among lawyers and judges, feeling you have no say in your fate. I found out that, contrary to all the hype about "trial by jury," over 90 percent of the cases in New York City were resolved by plea bargain—standard for anyone without the money to hire a lawyer. It is common for the police to inflate the initial charges, so the compromise, the "bargain," is to plead to what should have been the maximum in the first place. I also was shocked by the explicit racism. I remember one judge taunting a lawyerless, uneducated Black man who got tongue-tied. "What's the matter? What drug are you on now, Mr. Johnson?" It finally dawned on me, this student of radical theory, that the criminal justice system is an integral, central part of the repressive apparatus of the state.

Affinity Groups

It's November 1969. We're running hard; it's a misty night; no streams of light from street lamps, just luminous fuzz balls; there are sounds of sirens, breaking glass, and the pop of tear gas guns. Don't know what our original "objective" was; right now it's simply to get away from police sweeping down the street, busting heads and making busts. Then as we turn a corner, it hits me full blast—a direct cloud of tear gas. Eyes burning, choking, I'm still standing, but disoriented, have no idea which way to run; I'll be busted for sure. Lost in that cloud, I feel a hand firmly grabbing my arm, guiding me as we run off in the right direction and get safely away. At first all I can see, looking down, are the long, sturdy legs in blue jeans. When I can look up, I recognize the wet bandana covering the mouth and the light freckles high on the cheeks, see the motorcycle helmet, and can picture the sandy-colored ponytail now tucked away. It's Noelle, a college student a couple of years younger than me, who is planning to go to medical school.

Noelle's aid at that point is no accident; we're part of the same affinity group of six people. That's the way we go to demonstrations these days. Affinity groups form beforehand, often on the basis of friendship and trust. These small units allow for greater mobility and initiative if/when the demonstration gets raucous, and can be a way to carry out different tasks if it's a situation where people are going to move around police barricades or break windows at government or corporate buildings. And most practically, and most often in my experience, the affinity group is a way for people to look out for one another, to try to make sure no one is left behind to be trampled or busted.

In 1969–70, I was in six situations where we got gassed. Sometimes it bothered me, sometimes it didn't. I don't know what made the difference, whether it was the type of gas or just the way the wind was blowing at the time. But half the time I pulled others through it, and half the time I got rescued. In each of those demonstrations, my affinity group accomplished little offensively, but all of us made it through intact.

My first experience with that new form was on November 11, 1967, at the citywide demonstration against the Foreign Policy Association (FPA). This was a conclave of the establishment behind the war in Vietnam and other interventions into the Third World, and Secretary of State Dean Rusk himself would be attending. As with the earlier move toward disrupting recruiters on campus, we didn't want to merely "protest"; we wanted to stop this ruling class body from carrying out their dirty work.

The inspiration came from the demonstrations against the draft board in Oakland, California, a month earlier. After two days of massive peaceful protests did nothing to stop the induction of draftees for the war, people switched to mobile tactics—with shields and helmets, breaking windows and running to avoid arrest—and managed to shut the induction center down that day. As always happened back then, we immediately wanted to emulate their success.

Bob Gottlieb, Susan Sutheim, and Marge Piercy of MDS called together a citywide coalition to plan the demonstration. Still close with them, I was on the steering committee, but I have to admit to not playing a very active role in this terrific success. They had the idea of the focus on the FPA, to illustrate who's who in the power structure. While there would be thousands doing a traditional-style protest, hundreds would be in affinity groups with missions such as blocking the side streets where the FPA elite tried to enter; throwing bags of cows' blood on their limos, to represent the blood they had on their hands; and then moving on, before the police could respond, to block another side street. Knowing the police penchant for busting demonstration organizers, Gottlieb created a fictional character, Ernest Chaison (for Ernesto "Che" Guevara) to be discussed on all tapped phones as the coordinator.

Personally, I was in the traditional part of the demonstration, where several thousand protesters gathered on the sidewalk. My main memory is of the police riding horses into the crowd, and how intimidating that was. Columbia SDS was a major source for the more active affinity groups. The police were caught by surprise, and those responsible for so much blood-shed also got some on their limos. The demonstration was a tremendous boost to morale and a watershed for more active and militant protests—so much so that ten years later I saw a film produced by a Marxist sect that hadn't even been on the steering committee, which claimed that they were the ones who organized the November 1967 FPA demonstration.

"Ernest Chaison" as the pseudonym for the phantom coordinator of the FPA protest, while completely in jest, wasn't accidental. Our daring and creativity in that period sprang from adopting a guerrilla mentality, and the personification of the heroic guerrilla was Che Guevara. What's hard to recapture now is the hope and excitement we felt as guerrilla warfare raged in dozens of countries throughout the world, and how it worked as a method for villagers, firing old rifles at B-52 bombers flying far overhead. Soon, however, a simplified version of the guerrilla experience became the rage in much of the world, at great costs to revolutionary movements.

Foco

We also felt Che's urgency about making the revolution, as opposed to the passivity of many in old-line Communist parties in Latin America. In late 1967, Regis Debray, a French intellectual who had close ties to Che and Cuba, published *Revolution in the Revolution*. A polemic against those who felt that the time was never right to launch armed struggle, Debray's lesson from the Cuban experience was that the people know they're oppressed and need only the confidence that they can win. The small group (or *foco*) success-fully employing guerrilla tactics can therefore become the basis for rallying the people. Debray's theory was called *focoism*, and his book sent a major buzz among those chafing to propel things forward throughout the world.

I read *Revolution in the Revolution* in my period of self-imposed isola-tion following the Columbia strike. I liked Debray's emphasis on action, and his (oversimplified) version of the Cuban Revolution was attractive.

At the same time, I was well aware that the successful revolutions in China and Vietnam, and the ongoing struggles in other Asian countries, such as the Philippines, followed a different model: people's war. They also used guerrilla military tactics, but the strategy was painstaking and massive organizing among peasants and workers to enable them to fight a long, drawn-out war to drain imperialism's superior technological and economic strength. I started to write a review of *Revolution in the Revolution* that said essentially that the push to action was positive and healthy, but that the model of people's war should not be so readily dismissed. I shelved my review when another SDSer wrote one with a similar analysis, but a big factor in my reluctance to publish was political cowardice. Some of the leaders of the Columbia strike were very taken with Debray, and I was reluctant to risk further disapproval as "anti-action" by criticizing *Revolution in the Revolution*. In conversations I raised my concerns about the negation of people's war, but only cautiously, as a sort of addendum to my support for the push to action.

In any case, an intellectual understanding of some of the problems didn't stop me from being part of a subsequent focoist error; nor, despite learning from that experience, from repeating it a good decade later. In a world of excruciating oppression of millions that was seething with rebellion, there was tremendous allure in a position that said "Just do it; it will work!" Of course that theory also appealed to our egos—our privileged sense of self-importance and destiny as individuals—as well as our lack of patience, or rather perseverance, for the much longer struggle that was needed.

Even my initial reading was too sanguine in accepting foco as a model for Latin America. Tragically, the results there were disastrous as a generation of the most idealistic and courageous youth launched guerrilla warfare in places like Guatemala, Bolivia, Argentina, and Uruguay, only to get isolated, trapped, and murdered. In part they had underestimated the ruthlessness of the enemy, who proved quite willing and able to carry out wholesale massacres to wipe out popular bases of support and to commit widespread torture to get information that would lead to the guerrillas. But we 1960s SDSers had no idea of those dire consequences yet to come.

Revolution in Our Lifetime?

"I agree, man, these are exciting times—but you don't really believe there could be a revolution here, in the United States, in our lifetime, do you?"

"It feels like there could be. Look, Hal, rationally I'd rate the odds at about ten to one against us. But by historical standards— in most periods it's a million to one—those are fantastically good odds. Who knows when there'll ever be a chance like this again?

"I worry about you, Dave, the way you're throwing yourself completely in, like there's no tomorrow. Che says, 'In revolution, one wins or dies.'"

"Yeah, I know, but not for us, at least not yet. And there's so much at stake for humanity! I, all of us who see what's going on, have to give it our all."

As we tried to feel more connected to world revolutionary trends and to be more effective within the belly of the beast, we definitely weren't ready for the "warfare" part; but we consciously tried to apply "guerrilla" methods—an approach that could challenge a vastly superior physical force by employing hit-and-run mobility and popular support. That was the inspiration behind shifting from the old civil disobedience, where protesters just got carted off to jail, to the mobile affinity groups, causing disruptions and moving on quickly. The Oakland draft board and the NYC FPA protests were early, successful examples of applying this guerrilla mentality to the slogan "From Protest to Resistance."

More than just a spirit of the times, guerrilla warfare pointed to a strategy to win, a way that the most extensive and powerful empire in world history could be defeated. Che had summed it up in an essay that came out in April 1967 by saying, "Create two, three, many Vietnams." We understood this to mean that the imperial monster, for all its overwhelming firepower, could be overextended and worn down. While scores of Third World nations chafed under the stark conditions resulting from imperial exploitation, the U.S. could not afford to wage three or four Vietnam wars simultaneously. Che was calling on people throughout the Third World to seize this opportunity to push revolutionary struggle forward. Che himself had left Cuba in 1965 to lead a small guerrilla group in Bolivia. They got isolated and trapped by CIA-led commandos, who then executed Guevara on October 8, 1967, a date later honored as the Day of the Heroic Guerrilla. Even with Che dead, his example and strategy seemed to point the way forward.

For some of us there was a key internal dimension to this worldwide uprising: our becoming revolutionaries within the U.S. In our analysis, the majority of white people in this country had been deflected from the class struggle against capitalism by the benefits, the privileges relative to Third World people, from the spoils of empire and from white supremacy at home. The strength of U.S. capitalism, its global reach and plunder, would now become its weakness, as it was drained by a series of costly wars and as successful national liberation limited the plunder of the Third World. The arms of the octopus would be cut off, leaving the head weak from the loss of blood. And national liberation was tearing the U.S. apart internally too with the surge of the Black, Native, Puerto Rican, and Chicano/a struggles.

Under those conditions, the great possibility—and our job—was to win large numbers of white people to solidarity with people of the world, to see that the alternative to bloody wars and a declining economy here was some form of socialism, combined with a less wasteful, more cooperative lifestyle. While many in the white Left characterized us as "Third Worldist," we also saw anti-imperialism as the only possible route to socialism within predominantly white America.

What most distinguished the 1960s from previous (and subsequent) decades was the tremendous *hope* we felt, a hope expressed in the youth culture's sense of universal brotherhood and a vision of peace. That hope arose from the reality of dramatic contemporary developments: the most oppressed people in the world were rising and had a real chance to win by overextending the imperial monster—and we would be part of that. We avidly studied struggles around the world, not just for strategy but also for inspiration. For example, China. The nature of the regime today means that we have to look back critically, but at the time the Chinese Revolution was one of the most impressive achievements in human history. Hundreds of millions of people, most of them poor and illiterate, were mobilized to fight and win against overwhelming economic and military odds in a war that lasted for decades. Then they rolled up their sleeves to work on the prevailing backwardness and poverty, to stop mass starvation, bring health care to the countryside, begin industrialization, and support women's rising against feudal restrictions. This experience came home to me in an engrossing read of William Hinton's *Fanshen*. The book detailed the process of change in one Chinese village: how people organized to grow enough food, how women collectively put wife-beaters in check, how the whole village discussed key political issues.

The 1960s were animated by that great sense of hope. The oppressed seemingly had a way to win in the strategy of "two, three, many Vietnams." And at home, there was an emerging youth culture infused with a sense of universal brotherhood. Looking back forty years later, those hopes obviously haven't been realized. Many guerrilla movements were defeated while most of the national liberation struggles that seized power have not achieved (due to a combination of external pressures and internal weaknesses) major economic improvements for the people. Within the United States militarism and reaction are surging again. But our hope was not completely unfounded. Every empire, no matter how strong it looks, eventually falls. People living in ancient Egypt believed the Pharaohs were gods on earth; the Han Dynasty in China seemed eternal; the Roman Empire invincible. Today's imperial rule will also fall, even if over a broader historical span than we envisioned then; it oppresses too many people. What worries me more are the human costs and environmental destruction that will result from its decline, and whether we will have the ability to create a more humane alternative. It seems to me that the central problem/tension is still between imperialism and the conditions of life throughout the Third World, even if it won't necessarily be fought out in the form of national liberation struggles. Even without a clear, immediate winning strategy, there's a compelling need to keep humane visions and possibilities alive.

Making Choices

Some opponents of our "Third Worldist" tendency charged us with the white arrogance of picking the leadership of other peoples' struggles. Even if the critics' motive was to discredit us, they'd seized on a real issue: How could SDS decide to ally with the BPP instead of the NAACP? Or, in Angola, support the MPLA (Popular Movement for the Liberation of Angola) but not the FNLA (the National Liberation Front of Angola)?

I hadn't made my choices sitting in an ivory tower, passing down judgments on others. Quite the contrary, my politics developed in response to the advances of national liberation struggles throughout the world, and the criteria I applied about who to support came from the political leadership they had provided me. I studied them to see which ones achieved dramatic changes in their peoples' conditions of life and sense of participation.

While each nation has its own particular characteristics, those struggles that were about more than just changing the flag, that made a qualitative difference for the people, generally had these features in common: 1) The revolution was based in the majority, the most oppressed, which in Third World countries meant peasants, workers, women, and minorities. 2) Their political program went beyond changing regimes to a fundamental restructuring of the economy in the interests of the oppressed. 3) Because such economic changes brought fierce attacks from imperialism, such movements almost always needed to build a popularly based armed struggle capability. 4) Real revolutions had a strong and visible practice on women's liberation. 5) Such national liberation movements were also *inter*nationalist in allying with other peoples fighting imperialism. (These basics were later articulated much more directly and clearly by the BPP in the distinction they drew between "cultural" and "revolutionary" nationalisms.) The organizations that had the above

politics usually were Marxist-Leninist or at least used historical materialism as their method of analysis.

Having good criteria didn't magically eliminate white arrogance or
automatically resolve every dilemma in the messy real world. In the fight
against South African Apartheid, should we ally with the PAC (Pan
Africanist Congress), which seemed to have the more revolutionary line,
or with the ANC (African National Congress), which had a much larger
mass base? I felt we should build support for both, but that was almost
impossible in practice, given their bitter disputes. Or, I believe SDS was
right in 1969 to prioritize solidarity with the BPP, given its revolutionary
politics, popular support, and level of confrontation with the state, but we
erred in doing very little to build, even if secondarily, support for other
revolutionary Black and other radical Third World groups within the U.S.

So there are no pat answers. But there is a valid approach in drawing
our criteria from studying the revolutionary struggles of the oppressed
and doing our best to develop dialogue with and accountability to their
organizations. Within these parameters, we still have to make, and be
responsible for, conscious political choices about alliances.

Sectarianism

*We're at opposite ends of a chest of drawers, carrying it up four
flights of stairs, but somehow we have enough wind to argue
heatedly the whole way—and during the next few carries too.
Ned had been a stalwart in the ICV, and we've been friends
since 1965—so much so that when I decided, in the summer of
1969, to move out of my fifty-dollars-a-month rent-controlled
apartment in the West Village, I promised it to him. But Ned
can't believe that I'm leaving to join a Weather collective and
he's vehemently attacking the politics, which he characterizes as
irresponsible posturing about revolution and adolescent breaking
of windows and throwing of bottles at riot police. I'm taken aback
by the intensity of the bitter anger from this old friend. Yet, I'm*

only feeling the initial sprinkles on the edge of the thunderstorm that's blowing in…

Some of the New Left's passion and urgency got turned inward. Fighting to stop horrible destruction and to release incredible potential, we felt a tremendous amount riding on our decisions. As both the costs of repression and the possibilities for revolutionary change intensified, it felt like the world itself was at stake in every debate about ideology and strategy. In some situations, the differences were of fundamental importance; but more often we were floundering in a swamp of sectarianism: narrow, internal disputes that deflected us from concentrating our efforts on the state and that served as a big turn-off to new people considering getting involved in the movement.

Inspired by revolutionary movements around the world, we mimicked them in many ways—sometimes to the point of farce. We had read about historic splits that had been turning points on the path to revolution: Lenin's repudiation of the reformism of the Mensheviks; Mao's breakthrough in seeing that the peasants would be the main base for the Chinese Revolution; Castro's resolve to go to the mountains to initiate the armed struggle. Each time, everything was at stake.

Any complex endeavor—and there's nothing more complex than making a revolution—requires thorough debate, constant point and counterpoint, as part of a continual process of testing and reevaluating ideas. None of us is smart enough to figure it all out in one fell swoop. It's not just a question of intellectual capacity; even more limiting is the fact that each of us grew up in this society, dominated by the prevailing ideas and inundated by the culture of competitiveness. So we need to pay close attention to and grapple with the ways the rulers' perspective has influenced ours. For us to build a movement worthy of any claim to be revolutionary, we have to consciously struggle with the oppressors' values and culture within us. We way overemphasized the role of individual genius when we most needed a qualitatively better collective process, and we forgot the core value of revolutionary humility.

"Two-line struggle" became the rage, our pet formulation adopted from the Chinese. This format posited that in any political struggle there were two main opposing positions. The underlying basis for different points of view in society is class: so in these arguments one side represented the bourgeoisie and the other the proletariat. A major problem with this model within the Left was that, naturally, each side saw itself as representing the proletariat while the other side stood for the bourgeoisie. Once the opponent was seen as the class enemy, then all kinds of antagonistic methods—moving from pure argument to power maneuvers and manipulations—became legitimate.

Before long my standard joke was, "There's a two-line struggle here, and in class terms it's between more and less radical sectors of the petit-bourgeoisie." My quip was unfortunately accurate because of the very limited class base of the student movement; and because, while our differences may have been significant (hence, "more and less radical"), neither side was close to an adequate overall theory and strategy.

"Two-line struggle" was supposed to be a dialectical method of political argument. In reality, for us, it played out as a simplistic division into mutually exclusive spheres of pure good and pure evil. This approach was a natural for a generation raised on TV shows about "good guys" (cowboys or cops) vs. "bad guys" (Indians or criminals). In philosophy this pure dualism between good and evil is called Manichaeism, and it characterizes much religious thinking (God vs. the devil). Ironically, and sadly, the Left's sectarianism mirrored that of religion: complete disdain for opponents' views, lack of introspection into one's own sins, and a penchant for debating by citing authority. Just as religious denominations quoted the Bible, Left factions would trot out quotes from Marx, Lenin, or Mao (often plucked out of context). We called ourselves "scientific" socialists, but do physicists with differing hypotheses validate them by citing competing quotes from Newton or Einstein?

Unlike religion, our doctrinal disputes were about matters very much in this world, often freighted with life-and-death implications for the oppressed and their movements. Did we support independence for various peoples of color within the U.S., or should we strive to forge a multinational working class? Did an independent women's caucus give needed power to the oppressed or create divisions diverting us from the overall struggle? Should our limited resources be devoted more to big national demonstrations or to community organizing? Were election campaigns a good arena for organizing or a diversion from building a movement in the streets? Should you organize people based on immediate bread and butter concerns or was it essential to emphasize the major issues for society as a whole? Do we respond to growing repression with increased militancy or by restricting the movement to nonconfrontational tactics? Some positions had to be discredited; they weren't "Left" at all because they ran completely counter to the interests and aspirations of the oppressed. But on most questions there were sincere differences of opinion about a complex and changing reality. And often neither side had the whole answer. The situation called for open, healthy debate, but more often we responded with posturing, quote-plucking, and name-calling.

Our model of struggle became a competitive, winner-take-all approach as each group sought to triumph as the true, correct revolutionaries, the leadership. This mentality reflected the power and privileges of growing up within an imperial nation, especially as white, male, or college-educated. But people of color and women weren't automatically exempt, as egoism can infect anyone. Too often each group's focus, energy and maneuvers were mobilized around proving their position correct as opposed to how to best move things forward for the oppressed. There are three giant costs to sectarianism: it's a big turn-off to new people; it leads to unnecessary splits, undermining unity against the state; and in demonizing opponents, it leads us to exempt ourselves from similar problems and overlook our own internal weaknesses.

Today we still don't have that foolproof method for distinguishing crucial debates from competitive bickering; we don't have a Geiger counter to ring a warning when the toxic radiation of sectarianism pollutes the air. But clearly some approaches and methods are better than others. The highly polemical style of Marx and Lenin may have its place, but it can't be the main model for internal struggle. We have a lot to learn from feminism and from the Christian Base Communities in Latin America. While I am still wary of the manipulation that can come with the more informal means of decision-making, I'm definitely interested in learning more about the consensus methods activists are working on today.

In challenging, heady, scary periods, we need ways to keep our grounding, to try to always base decisions on the interests of the oppressed, to always stay in touch with the humanist basis for our activism. Looking back I'm amazed at how many times I thought everything I was doing was about making revolution, but my actions were self-aggrandizing; at how, with my consciousness and ideals, I could still maneuver so strategically for self-interest. And I definitely wasn't unique in this regard. I now believe it is healthier to be conscious and explicit about self-interest (whether for an individual or a group) in a given situation—such as the impetus to minimize physical risk, the drive to be "the leader," the desire to appear attractive. It's not inherently evil to have self-interest, and in any case it's not completely avoidable. What messed me up was when I couldn't admit it to myself and then unconsciously maneuvered in dishonest ways. My method now is to try to be open and explicit about my personal concerns and then to rigorously evaluate them relative to collective principles and goals. Sometimes my personal needs are a legitimate consideration; at other times I'll want to subordinate them to what's needed by everyone.

In any case, we need ways—even in the heat of battle, facing unexpected challenges, forging new breakthroughs, or scared out of our wits—to always look at what we're doing in terms of the needs and interests of the majority of humankind. Is this particular battle mainly about building power for the people? Is it consistent with our humanitarian values? Does it advance the interests and aspirations of the vast majority of humankind, the oppressed?

A Seismic Fault Line

In 1968, the towering heights of SDS's successes felt breathtaking, but we didn't know that the earthquake fault, deep in the ground we stood on, soon would bring most of what we had built tumbling down. The combination of the dramatic advances for revolutionary movements along with the intensified state repression created an overpowering crisis. We became starkly aware that students did not have the strength to seriously challenge the most powerful government in world history. Excited about revolutionary possibilities but unnerved by the dangers, many activists became frantic about finding any immediate base powerful enough to confront capitalism. Traditional Marxist theory offered a ready-made answer: the industrial proletariat. Proponents stressed that workers constituted the majority of the U.S. population, were tough, and could bring production to a crashing halt.

This approach was comforting in the abstract but, whether or not the varied versions recognized that people of color were generally the most exploited and militant workers, it had a fatal flaw in reality: It evaded the fundamental problem of the impact of white supremacy on U.S. workers. Even when invoking the attractive terms "the multinational working class," these politics led to pandering to the white majority and to wiping out the independent and leading role of national liberation movements. In contrast, some of us passionately embraced the understanding that the cutting edge, the defining aspect of any revolutionary movement worthy of that name, was to fight on the side of Black and other Third World struggles, the forces challenging the very foundation of the system. But in our urgency of the moment we tended to give up on the difficult but important task of organizing significant numbers of whites in an anti-racist way, which would also strengthen the solidarity we could provide.

SDS experienced the tensions in the forms of heated debates and antagonistic personalities, with charges and counter-charges about who was "opportunist" (selling out). But the problem wasn't just on the level of our consciousness; it was based squarely on material reality, going deep down to the giant and perilous seismic fault line in the bedrock on which this country had been built: white supremacy. The material benefits of white supremacy even to those oppressed in other ways are substantial: from who gets the better jobs to all the historical reasons that result in an average accumulated wealth for white families that is ten times that of Black families; from who does and who doesn't die in childbirth to the myriad consumer goods that are affordable because people producing the raw materials in the Third World are living on a dollar a day. Of course the consumer society is very destructive and the separation of whites from everyone else in the world is corrosive of our humanity. But the promise of a revolutionary change usually seems distant and unachievable, while these benefits from white supremacy are immediate and tangible.

Historically, radical movements either tried to appeal to the majority whites or prioritized fighting racism, but rarely, if ever, managed to do both in any kind of sustained way. White workers, women, poor farmers had an ultimate interest in a revolutionary transformation of society, but as the overall history of the trade union, suffrage, and populist movements showed, in any given situation they opted to settle for the immediate benefits the system provided from the more intense exploitation of people of color globally and within the U.S. So, while there had been periods of fierce struggles by whites for immediate reforms, there had been precious little in the way of revolutionary challenges to the system itself. (For a more in-depth discussion of this dilemma, see my essay, "Looking at the White Working Class Historically," reprinted in *No Surrender*.)

Revolutionary class consciousness cannot peacefully coexist with white supremacy, which was overwhelmingly the main basis for the failures of radical movements in the U.S. For those of us who, at our best, understood that, the most inspiring historic example was abolitionism, but they hadn't organized widely among working-class whites. The divide we experienced pushed us toward a sense of isolation and self-righteousness. RYM had been a breakthrough in providing at least part of a strategy, given the upheavals of the day, of working with a growing sector of militant whites on an anti-racist basis. But given the revolutionary advances, the frightening repression, the palpable sense of urgency, and our own inexperience, would we be able to build a movement that was principled and solid enough to stand on that seismic fault line?

The Split of SDS

Check it out: the photo in the National Guardian *of the crowd standing and cheering Bernardine Dohrn's speech expelling PL from SDS at the June 1969 National Convention. That's me in the middle of the picture, waving a clenched fist and looking a bit dazed.*

My stunned look comes from being simultaneously staggered and inspired. For several years now, I have thought of myself as "an SDS organizer," and that has been the most satisfying identity of my life. It expresses me and more than me. "SDS organizer" stands for something out there in the world, a visible set of humane, radical values that I have tried to put into practice. Now I'm staggered because with this catastrophic split, does "SDS" mean anything at all?

Yet the other side of this disaster is a new opportunity to move past the posturing and the rhetoric to a revolutionary direction for real. Bernardine's is the most inspiring speech I've heard since Malcolm X, as she clearly and fully articulates the core principles we've stood for and how those principles are the only basis for us to move forward today.

While I never imagined a total split, I certainly went to the convention prepared for a battle. The PL vs. RYM maneuvers had been in high gear for over a year. A key skirmish had taken place at the April 1969 National Council meeting in Austin, Texas, where we passed a resolution mandating support for the Panthers. We considered this the key dividing line because the Panthers were the most dynamic and leading political force in the U.S., under vicious, murderous attack by the government. Solidarity with the Panthers was a top priority, although our resolution should also have acknowledged other Black nationalist groups as well as revolutionary Native American, Puerto Rican, and Chicano/a organizations. Given PL's bitter opposition, we saw the passage of the resolution as a decisive defeat for them. We underestimated their willingness and ability to pack the upcoming convention.

As we prepared for June, different tendencies emerged within RYM. One conflict occurred during discussions about open admissions, an exciting demand that emerged out of student struggles to make free college education available to everyone. Chicago regional staff drafted a resolution demanding open admissions for all people of color, or as we said back then, Third World people within the U.S. When New York City regional staff discussed it, we felt it should also include poorer, working-class whites. New York City staff sent the two people who'd been clearest in the discussion, mainly Dionne but secondarily me, to Chicago to work out a unified position.

We saw the meeting as completely fraternal, a few adjustments to arrive at a unified resolution, so Dionne and I had no discussion of tactics, as we would have if we'd expected hostility. Because she had been the most articulate in our staff discussions, she made the presentation, with me there to supplement her in the discussions.

As soon as Dionne finished her presentation of our position, the immediate and intense reaction of the Chicago leadership was to attack me. No one even referred to what Dionne had said. It was simply, "Gilbert was responsible for the reactionary 'new working class position'; this criticism of our draft is just 'new working class' in different clothes." I was literally dumbfounded. Dionne leapt to my defense: "That attack is totally unfair. 'New working class' is one mistake, in the past, that doesn't at all define David's overall politics. Reaching out to the poorest sectors of white working-class youth to align with Third World people around open admissions is very much what RYM is all about."

Somehow we did eventually come together around one proposal, although I don't remember the exact wording. But we were less than pleased. The surprise attack had revealed a deeply flawed politics. Those male SDS leaders were so anxious to discredit me as, in their view, a competing theorist that they totally disregarded Dionne, treating her as simply a front-woman for me, and didn't address a word she said. It never even occurred to them that this woman was speaking precisely because she had led in developing the political position.

A clear tendency within RYM crystallized with the "Weatherman" paper, published in the June 1969 convention issue of *New Left Notes*. The full title was a line from Bob Dylan's "Subterranean Homesick Blues": "You don't need a weatherman to know which way the wind blows." I was sure that the title was a creative way to say, "You don't need elaborate Marxist-Leninist theory to see that the revolutionary upsurge of our era is coming out of the Third World." When I gave my translation to one of the authors, he said, "Nope. The line doesn't mean anything in particular: that just happened to be the song on the stereo when it was time to pick a title."

Regardless, the line resonated with me. Most Western Marxists insisted that the working class in the industrialized countries was, by definition, the most revolutionary force. That dogma flew in the face of reality, and the strategy based on that view repeated the errors through U.S. history that led to building unions that turned out to be racist, sexist, and proimperialist. Since the end of World War II, every single struggle that overturned or even seriously threatened the old state power, with the partial exception of France in 1968, had come from the Third World. Within the U.S., the Black, and the Native, Puerto Rican, and Chicano/a liberation movements, as well as the Asian-American anti-racist struggles, had done far more than the mostly white union movement to inspire and lead the movement for social change.

Even back then, parts of the Weather paper seemed a bit forced or excessive to me. The long argument that Black people could make the revolution in the U.S. by themselves alone seemed a bit convoluted. But I understood the context: many elements in the white Left were cautioning the much more militant Black movement to slow down because the majority population wasn't ready to support them. The Weather paper's position was absolutely clear: The Black struggle wasn't beholden to the white population. Racism was totally central to what America was about. Black liberation had an independent initiative and fundamental power in dismantling the system. Our job wasn't to tell them to wait but to minimize casualties and speed victory by mobilizing support. I especially liked the emphasis on building a "white fighting force" in solidarity and for revolution. The Weather paper also correctly saw sexism as stemming from a structure of male supremacy, but it lacked any kind of women's program beyond promoting women as fighters.

Working relationships with some of the authors made me predisposed to welcome the Weather paper. Even if a few arguments seemed awkward or exaggerated, overall the paper was the best statement I'd seen from our movement on the leading role of national liberation worldwide, the centrality of the Black struggle within the U.S., and the urgent need and potential for building a militant anti-imperialist movement. After reading the paper, I was happy to call myself a "Weatherman." Many in RYM didn't agree with Weather and distinguished themselves as RYM II, which included groupings that went on to form the Sojourner Truth Organization, the Revolutionary Union, and the October League.

Heading out to the convention in Chicago, my car, as usual, was packed. In addition to some veteran SDSers, Patty and Frank were coming to their first national meeting, representing the new Queensboro Community College chapter, which had led a successful campaign against the firing of a radical professor. I had worked closely with the chapter during that campaign and encouraged them to relate to national SDS. Because the professor at issue was a PLer, I feared they might be biased in that direction. But on the drive out, I learned that they felt he'd been condescending and manipulative; they didn't regret the struggle to prevent his firing, but they deeply distrusted PL.

That didn't automatically put them in the RYM camp. They liked RYM's emphasis on community colleges and my work with them, but wisely weren't ready to commit to a number of ideological issues. National SDS was a new scene for them both, and remembering how unwelcome

I'd felt at my first national meeting, I did my best to prepare them for what the gathering would be like and provide some initial introductions. But I myself wasn't prepared for the lions' den we entered, and I fear that once I got absorbed in the sectarian battles, I wasn't very attentive to Patty and Frank. In a way, they represented many in SDS—distrustful of PL but not necessarily agreeing with RYM—who may have constituted a plurality but didn't have a strong, well-organized voice at this crucial turning point.

The factional fighting was ferocious. Every single detail, even the order of the agenda, was cause for battle. As so often happens in these situations, positions were rationalized in objective terms, to appeal to swing voters, when the real reasons were factional advantage. While it occurred to me that it would be better to state honestly: "We propose this order for agenda items because it does more to emphasize anti-imperialism," such niceties felt quite secondary to breaking PL's stranglehold on the organization.

Political struggle got reduced to name-calling. I took a turn at the mike and talked about how PL's position was, in effect, racist. The PL speaker who followed retorted that I was clearly anti-working class. To be more accurate, they had a position on "fighting racism," but only as a source of divisions within the working class. We wanted to organize working-class youth—but not the traditional way, in the factories. Our problem with PL was that even though they verbally opposed racism, they refused to support the leading struggles of the day. Their position that "all nationalism is reactionary" denied the very independence and self-determination that oppressed people had been fighting for; the stance served as a "Left" cover for abandoning the groups under the fiercest attacks by our government. When PLers, who had hardly thrown a brick and had even opposed the Columbia strike, denounced the Vietnamese for "selling out" in agreeing to peace negotiations, Clayton Van Lydegraf, a longtime communist who had left PL for this very reason, thundered back, "PL is very courageous: they're willing to fight U.S. imperialism to the very last drop of Vietnamese blood."

While PL had done a much better job of bringing people to the convention, a RYM strong point was our alliance with the Panthers, still revered by much of the Left. When the Panther speaker addressing the convention made a sexist remark, PL, themselves deeply male chauvinist, jumped on it with glee. Then, as I described earlier, Naomi Jaffe intervened not, as I had expected, to score points against PL but rather to boldly assert that women's liberation was too important to be used as a political football.

On and on the battle raged. At a certain point it became clear that, while definitely not representing a majority of members nationwide, PL had brought enough delegates to win crucial votes, perhaps enough to be able to turn SDS into its opposite, something we would not allow. Bernardine Dohrn led a walkout of almost half the delegates, which entailed a certain contradiction to formal democracy—who were we to expel them?

The answer was articulated in Bernardine's historic speech. Democracy wasn't defined by the vote at one packed meeting. Bernardine went back to the inception, growth, and history of SDS. We were born in response to the courageous breakthroughs of the civil rights movement. We had been nurtured and mentored by a special, fraternal relationship with SNCC. We had blossomed and grown to be the national organization spearheading opposition to the war and educating white youth about imperialism. We had been inspired by and learned much of what we knew from the national liberation movements in the Third World and the determined struggles of people of color within the U.S. Solidarity with the Black struggle and with national liberation worldwide had both created who we were and defined our bedrock principles. People who turned on the Panthers and the Vietnamese when they were under fire were a total contradiction to what SDS was all about. We would now carry forward our principles in a clearer and more determined way.

{ THE MOST SANE/INSANE OF TIMES }

*T*he police car screeches to a stop in the Chicago night, and six officers leap out, firing into the air. The reports are loud and rapid, the muzzles flash a garish orange against the black sky. I turn to take off but Sam shouts, "Don't run—they're only firing blanks, trying to scare us away." He's a Vietnam vet and knows a lot more about guns than I do, so I pick up a rock and throw it at the cluster of cops. They're just beyond my range, but the rock catches an officer's attention. As he glares at me and raises his gun, my feet overrule my belief in Sam's technical knowledge. The next morning I learn that two of our people got shot at that corner, one with a serious neck wound.

It was the most insane of times; it was the most sane of times. Those nine months, from the split of SDS (June 8, 1969) to the tragic townhouse explosion where three bright and idealistic but badly off-course activists were killed (March 6, 1970), were the most frenetic, transforming and out-of-kilter months imaginable. We, who had lived sheltered lives, were pushing ourselves to undertake the violent forms of struggle that our solidarity with Black and other Third World people, combined with the government's murderous repression, seemed to mandate. So we psyched ourselves up with what was, at times, a disgusting romanticization of violence; a sectarian arrogance toward leftists who wouldn't join us; and an organizing style based on showing our willingness to fight. All the mainstream and most of the Left histories center on this period that serves so well to discredit us, with barely a mention of our preceding years as activists who led in building the anti-war movement and in forging alliances with the Black struggle, and with little discussion of the six ensuing years of the WUO's carrying out focused armed propaganda against imperialism while taking great care not to hurt anyone. But if reducing a decade of history to these nine months is unfair, we are responsible for providing the ammunition—for discrediting ourselves with a manic politics and practice. Inevitably my own account will also linger on these nine months: a most intense and controversial period but one to be seen, I hope, in the context of all the years of solid organizing that preceded it, and the six years of focused and competent underground action that followed.

How can I say it was also the most sane of times? The sad reality is that the status quo, the day-to-day comfort, the conventional wisdom of empire is insanely anti-human. True human sanity does not consist of remaining calm, cool, collected—going on with life as usual—while the government murders Black activists, carpet-bombs Vietnam, trains torturers to "disappear" trade-union organizers in Latin America, and enforces the global economics of hunger on Africa. In particular, we felt that the passivity of most of the white Left toward the violent attacks on the Black movement gave the government the green light, let them know there wouldn't be a serious political cost among the "majority" population for their campaign of annihilation. Our sins of commission were more visible, but sins of omission can be just as deadly. So our identification with the majority of humankind and our urgency to act were the height of sanity. But our unadmitted fear, our inexperience, our loss of our humanist moorings led to a crazed period with many setbacks.

After expelling PL, the "real SDS" held elections for national officers. I was pleased that the candidates from the Weather tendency won all three positions. Now we had a clear revolutionary direction and would soon rebuild SDS to be stronger and bigger, or so I thought. Soon plans were brewing for the next major national action: a large, militant demonstration to "bring the war home" in Chicago that October.

At the same time, Weather was going through a radical self-transformation. We'd talked about organizing white working-class youth; it was time to move into their neighborhoods and get down to it, and also time for us to learn to live and work collectively. We were moving from radical activity to living in and for the revolution.

My affinity for Weather politics and for the new level of commitment did not make joining a collective (or as we said, posturing as street toughs, "gang") easy. I was wary of the chaotic culture. And more to the point, many of the militants still distrusted me as a stodgy pre-Weather "theorist." In fact there's not a chance I would have become a member if not for Ted Gold, who both actively recruited me and lobbied for my acceptance.

Ted Gold, two years behind me at Columbia, had always been a sincere and dedicated activist. In his senior year he was one of the outgoing SDS leaders Mark Rudd and others had surged past to set off the strike. But Teddy, putting his ego aside, had no problem becoming a committed and hardworking member of the new team. Less than a year later, he was one of the recognized leaders of the Weather collective in New York City. The other leader, Dionne, had been an outstanding regional SDS organizer.

Ted told me that he had admired and learned from my work in building the Vietnam committee and SDS chapter at Columbia, and that he wanted me to help him and Dionne build Weather in NYC. What was unusual for that time of incredible self-consciousness about status was his willingness to risk disapproval and go to bat for me. It probably also helped that Dionne and I had enjoyed a good working relationship on regional staff. Soon I was part of the "gang" as we looked for housing in Park Slope, Brooklyn. Although it has gone through gentrification since, in 1969 "the Slope" was a predominantly white working-class neighborhood with a sizable Puerto Rican community. Without any reliable source of income or even a conscious budget, we made the initial plunge by cashing in our middle-class chips. I had over $2,000 (over $12,000 in 2011 dollars!) in Israel Bonds that I had received as Bar Mitzvah gifts twelve years earlier. I redeemed all of them, giving half the cash to the Panther bail fund, with the other half going to our collective's living expenses.

Criticism/Self-Criticism

Walking out of the meeting in the grey predawn feels like being in the middle of an acid trip without having ingested any drugs. I never could have envisioned such a experience, and two contradictory thoughts blare inside my head: A twenty-four-hour criticism/self-criticism session has to be the height of insanity; and, the revolutionary process means that Teddy can finally come to fully love women!

We may have moved to Brooklyn to organize the youth, but our first order of business was to transform ourselves. Living collectively, putting our entire lives into the revolution, and learning to fight were all new and intimidating challenges. Our main tool was criticism/self-criticism. We all had to go through it, but since Dionne and Teddy were leaders, we started with them. Somehow the session with Teddy became a super-marathon. He wasn't any more male chauvinist than the rest of us, but as a leader he was the first one challenged to change—fully and immediately! The main sticking points all involved his resistance to accepting woman as equals. The session was intense and grueling. I could hear the clucking in Teddy's dry throat as he tried to speak, but he didn't bolt; he stuck with this excruciating process because he wanted to be a revolutionary and he knew that a full-hearted embracing of women's equality was an essential component. Thus to me, the session was simultaneously mad and hopeful.

The theory of criticism/self-criticism is great. In bourgeois society, the norm is to bad-mouth people behind their backs but never make constructive criticisms to their faces; at the same time each individual fiercely resists admitting mistakes. The communist ideal is to admit and learn from errors, to benefit from the perspective of others in order to grow and move forward. There were some guidelines we had picked up from reading about the Chinese and Vietnamese, designed to keep the process open and constructive: a cadre should listen carefully to the full criticism before scrambling to defend himself; those making criticism should use the person's strengths to defeat her weaknesses—i.e., not just criticize but help the person see how she can grow.

That was the theory. In practice, almost all our criticism/self-criticism sessions were horrendous. Whatever the collective ideal, our practice was still permeated by the dominant culture of competitive individualism. So instead of being a loving, constructive process, most of our sessions were marred by efforts to pull people down in order to gain a higher rung in the hierarchy. (The very constructive and helpful criticism of me by six women, described earlier, was an extremely rare exception.)

A companion mania of the time was "smash monogamy." One reason for this was the political analysis of the traditional nuclear family as a key institution of male supremacy. The other reason was that a couple would have more loyalty to each other than to the collective. So there was tremendous pressure on couples—although a few managed to resist—to break up, and move toward sexual promiscuity. But without yet having a strong feminist culture, the "new forms" meant less caring, commitment, and respect in relationships. Actually, even promiscuity suffered a temporary setback. With the push for women's political leadership, there was an epidemic of male sexual impotence. Men withdrew politically and emotionally as well as sexually. Then women had to struggle again to teach that passivity was not a form of accepting leadership but rather a way to undercut it, because everyone needs engagement and dialogue to grow.

But the early collectives were not entirely defined by these grim trends. A formative experience was the trip, involving some Weather leaders and other radicals, to Cuba—both to experience the revolution there and to meet with Vietnamese representatives about the course of the war and the efforts to end it. Teddy came back from that trip brimming with energy and optimism; I'd never before seen anyone so inspired. He felt that both the Cubans and Vietnamese exuded an incredible humanism and embodied how revolution was winning worldwide. He felt a strong personal bond with the people he met, and the discussions of strategy gave him a sense of grounding, depth, and possibility. One way he expressed this energy was to take a form of humor I'd started at Columbia—writing revolutionary lyrics for popular Motown songs—to new heights.

Later, when Teddy and two other comrades were killed in the tragic townhouse explosion, J. Kirkpatrick Sale immediately published a piece in *The Nation* defining Teddy as the epitome of "guilt politics." I don't think Sale ever met Teddy; he certainly didn't know him. Sale's rush to judgment probably came from his urgency to discredit any political push toward armed struggle. The "guilt politics" mantra just didn't fit the deep level of identification we felt with Third World people; and far from feeling guilt, with its condescending sense that we are so much better off than they, we were responding to their leadership. The national liberation movements were providing the tangible hope that a better world was possible. Those who caricatured him never saw Teddy on his return from Cuba—the very picture of inspiration, energy, and hope. The word that captures Teddy's psyche as he built the NY collective was not guilt but exuberance.

Despite our identification with the humanism of those struggles, our internal process ran roughshod over people, and our collective became a crucible that an outsider wouldn't want to touch lest she get burned. But 1969 was a year of widespread radical upheaval, and despite our crazed style we found political allies in Park Slope. We even organized a little local demonstration against police harassment and also helped someone evade the draft.

Personally, I got close to two of the young men in the neighborhood, with lots of discussions long into the night. They initially hadn't taken the student movement seriously, seeing it as rich kids on a lark, like the college "panty raids" of the day. It was only with the Columbia strike and then the confrontation with the Chicago police at the August 1968 Democratic Party convention that Mario and Peter saw us as serious about risking privilege and fighting the state.

I latched onto their approval as a validation of our overall skewed organizing strategy: the key is to demonstrate that we are willing to fight. Borrowing from foco theory, we felt that people already knew that the system was oppressive; what they needed were examples that showed it could be overturned (you *can* fight city hall). Also, echoing the BPP minister of information, Eldridge Cleaver, we confronted people with the dichotomy: "You're either part of the solution or part of the problem; either on the side of the people of the world or of imperialism." Obviously (in retrospect), there's a lot lacking in this simplistic approach to organizing—and it contravened our many years as organizers when we combined lively demonstrations with painstaking educational efforts, working through doubts and questions, challenging the government's versions of reality that people had been raised on, and, as any good organizer must, listening to people's concerns and perspectives rather than just preaching the new gospel to them.

We enthusiastically borrowed Panther rhetoric—some of it quite creative in challenging the dominant culture. A prime example, quickly adopted by white street kids, was to rename the police "the pigs." While today one might balk at language that dehumanizes anyone, this term played a provocative role in breaking the mental shackles of the day. The media always portrayed the police as fair, restrained and just (and therefore always justified), a pervasive image completely contrary to their role as the occupying army of the ghettos and barrios and as frequent attackers of anti-war demonstrations. The shocking label "pigs" was meant to pierce this false facade and convey both their brute violence and their role as enforcers for the forces of greed.

One reason we didn't listen to criticisms of our language was that the same charge, "rhetoric," had been used against our naming of the system as "imperialism." But that had been essential to showing why the war wasn't just an isolated "mistake" but rather part of a deep and ongoing pattern of interventions that was linked to racism and class rule at home. But the invaluable role of fighting for a radical analysis, especially when well explained, is not the same as posturing with rhetoric that gets in the way of dialogue and organizing.

Breaking and Brawling

Nationally, the two main Weather tactics of the day were beach sorties and "jailbreaks" at schools. The first involved a group of us running down a white working-class beach carrying the flag of the National Liberation Front of Vietnam, the so-called "Vietcong" flag. The rationale was that this was a good way to polarize things, and indeed it was. This tactic usually resulted in brawls. The one time our "gang" did it, I got isolated and surrounded by about eight guys. One blow caught me on the chin and knocked me down, but I quickly regained my feet, otherwise I would have been kicked senseless. Then the police arrived. If they'd known who we were or what led to the brawl, they wouldn't have broken it up. What an embarrassment for a revolutionary to be saved from the working class by the pigs!

The jailbreaks involved charging into high schools or community colleges and taking over a classroom or auditorium. We would make a speech about siding with the people of the world and invite the students to "break out." The first one we did was carefully planned, but I never made it. My affinity group was headed out to the high school in Brad's Chevrolet (for some reason he wasn't there that day) when a tire blew out. The trunk required a separate key, which we didn't have, and the jailbreak was over before we managed to change the tire. Months later, someone chanced upon Brad's wallet and saw a business card and contact phone number for a detective in the "Red Squad"—the unit of the NYPD that infiltrated and harassed radicals. Brad was immediately told to leave the collective.

I did make it, in a support role, when a group of women in our collective took over a class at a Brooklyn community college. Their assertion that there are more important things happening in the world than what the professor was teaching really resonated with me—and did with a few of the students. But I also saw the discomfort many students felt with the disruption, and it was difficult to get past that to any content. Emotionally, given my upbringing, I realized how hard it was for me, and for many of us, to be so "impolite." For me it had been easier to be beaten and jailed as pacifist than now to barge into a classroom and interrupt.

The national women's "jailbreak" at a Pittsburgh high school became the most infamous Weather action of the period, because a local paper reported that the women ran through the high school bare-breasted. The fact that this was totally false didn't stop the mainstream media and the white Left from trumpeting this "news" to discredit and dismiss us. Even in a website dialogue about the WUO over three decades later, a noted and generally excellent Left columnist said it wasn't worth even discussing the politics of a group whose women would run through a high school topless. Two even more grotesque apocryphal stories circulated about the Weather gangs: in one, a collective killed, skinned, and ate an alley cat to prove their toughness. In another, a woman had her arm broken because she wouldn't sleep with someone.

Given all we were genuinely doing to discredit ourselves, why did such false stories arise and circulate? To me these slanders were a way to avoid discussing our politics at all and thereby evade the challenge of what we were doing right. Up until 1969, being a campus radical was a fairly comfortable position. One had the moral prestige of siding with the oppressed without any threat to one's safety and comfort. As national liberation struggles advanced and government repression escalated, we insisted on breaking out of that cocoon and into real-life battle. For all our mistakes, our staunch identification with Third World people and our zeal in dedicating our lives to the revolution represented a formidable and unsettling challenge. No wonder people were pissed! Nonetheless we were doing a whole lot that was terribly wrong, as would become painfully apparent in the organizing for the October national action in Chicago.

The plan was to protest the opening of the Chicago 8 conspiracy trial, the government's most visible move to repress and intimidate the anti-war movement. Eight men were charged with "interstate conspiracy to riot" for having organized the protests at the 1968 Chicago Democratic National Convention. (The official commission which later investigated what happened summed up the extensive violence as a "police riot.") The selection of these "ringleaders" was somewhat arbitrary, and the one Black man in the indictment, BPP Chairman Bobby Seale, hadn't played any role at all in planning the demonstrations; he was simply an invited speaker. But the Federal and local governments had a policy at the time of bringing multiple legal charges, no matter how farfetched, against Panthers to bankrupt them with legal costs and to tie up valuable cadres in court battles.

The slogan for the Weather actions, "Bring the War Home," was in large part created as a satirical critique of the dominant slogan of the "respectable" anti-war movement, "Bring the Boys Home," which, while a just demand, pandered to a white-centered worldview that the tragedy of the war lay in the U.S. soldiers killed—when the number of Indochinese deaths, mainly civilians, was fifty times greater. We also felt it important to emphasize that the Vietnamese weren't our enemy, the U.S. government was—and we would fight it here. These points were essential to building a movement that could stop future interventions into Third World countries. And, in a period when a couple of million youths considered themselves revolutionary, there was a rising potential to reach people with our anti-racist and anti-imperialist politics.

I was amused by how many who claimed the mantle of Marx and Lenin blasted "Bring the War Home" as outlandish and irresponsible. It was Lenin, during World War I, who vowed to "turn imperialist war into class war" and urged the proletariat of each country to fight its own ruling class. He saw the lower strata of the working class, who got the least benefits from imperialism, as the most promising. We were appealing to youth as the sector of the white working class least integrated into imperialism. (The more "respectable" socialist parties of Lenin's day succumbed to an orgy of patriotism and supported their respective governments' war efforts.) More practically and urgently for us, with our strong identification with the Black struggle, the war had already come home. Between 1964 and 1969 hundreds of cities were rocked by urban uprisings, with thousands of people in the streets smashing windows, setting fires, throwing stones, and occasionally even sniping at police. We wanted to make sure that these communities, with the full force of state violence raining down on them, didn't fight alone.

The militant sections of the youth movement, while not at the level of struggle of the urban rebellions, began to emulate their tactics with what became known as "trashing": breaking windows, setting fires in corner trash cans, throwing rocks at charging police. We were far from the first or only ones pushing the envelope. Just in 1970 alone, there were hundreds of actual and attempted bombings, usually fire bombings, against symbols of militarism and corporate greed. There was a palpable sense that even among white youth, revolution was in the air. Of course "war" was hyperbole for what we were doing, but there was a healthy recognition of the reality of the broader world: our government was waging a bloody war against Vietnam and against Black people in the U.S. We were determined to be on the side of the oppressed and of the rebels.

Whatever was right about our anti-imperialist politics got swamped by our making a fetish out of violence. Fighting itself became the main organizing tool, almost the political point in and of itself, as we tried to "psych" ourselves up to break into this new territory. We identified, but still persisted in, our own internal excess, the "gut-check"—daring our cadres to be brave enough to fight. The gut-check turned out to be a terrible motivational method. When someone takes risks mainly to prove his manhood or her womanhood to peers—when one doesn't feel a deep political and humanitarian basis for facing new challenges—he or she often makes dumb mistakes and has trouble maintaining commitment over the long haul. Macho is not only a male-chauvinist style; it doesn't work, at least not for us, going up against such a powerful enemy and needing to build a long-term struggle.

I was shocked to hear that some organizers talked of many of us getting killed in Chicago. To me, they had lost sight of our own political analysis of white supremacy: the system was not ready to massacre white kids, mainly middle-class, who didn't have firearms. My analysis, while mainly right, underestimated the police's willingness to shoot. Still, the talk of death had more to do with our own drive to push ourselves to take on risks than with any reasonable political analysis.

The high school "jailbreaks" and beach brawls didn't work to organize new people. The New York collective managed to turn out only about thirty or forty people for Chicago, and as our bus loaded the NYPD Red Squad showed up to taunt us for being so few.

The national action had been conceived in June with the high hopes of bringing a fighting force of ten thousand to Chicago. When we actually gathered there in October, we numbered about six hundred. Under the circumstances it might have made sense to call off some of the more confrontational tactics. If our leadership ever considered that, not a whiff of such doubt reached me. The strategy was still to fight the police to set an example for white youth, although the unstated mission was even more of a priority: to prove ourselves.

Fighting in the Streets

Having escaped gunfire but unsure what to do next, I make my way to one of the predesignated movement centers. I'm looking forward to the respite from the action and the camaraderie of sharing stories of the night. But the front room is the first aid station, and there's Marsha, her lip swollen to the size of a banana, a gash sealed with stitches, and two teeth gone. "What happened?"

"A cop got me with his billy club, a direct swing to my mouth." While there are no tears, she looks a bit dazed. But even more determined: "We'll have to face and overcome physical assault if we're serious about tearing down imperialism."

As we gathered in Lincoln Park, I had a surprising déjà vu: Boy Scout camp! Comrades around bonfires, nervously anticipating action and telling scary tales. I was neither seriously scared nor highly confident because I had no idea what to expect. It was October 8, 1969, the international Day of the Heroic Guerrilla, named in honor of Che Guevara who had been killed by the CIA and the Bolivian military exactly two years before.

One of the speakers called for people to head out for the rich "Gold Coast" neighborhood and the Drake Hotel residence of Julius Hoffman, the repressive judge presiding over the Chicago 8 trial. As we marched out, a line of the notorious Chicago police—intimidating in their leather jackets, billy clubs in hand—moved in to stop us. Then I saw something I'd never ever imagined: our front line, wielding the staves used to hold signs, knocked a few cops to the ground and the rest of them broke and ran. I must admit that after all those times our urgency to stop mass murder had been turned back by police force, it was a rush to see our people rout their line. From that point on, the night was chaos. With little sense of either the objectives or Chicago geography, I was mainly just running around. At one point I joined a few of our people in turning over a car and felt a kind of collective physical power in doing so. Later I ended up on the corner where two of our people were shot. My most vivid memory of that night is Marsha at the first aid station: Marsha with her missing teeth and swollen lip.

The next morning's event was the women's march on the draft board. With the police completely prepared, and the women outnumbered, many felt disappointed that they did not prove to be more of a "fighting force." But to me, that was a realistic result of the balance of forces. Simply having an all-women's action at all was a major advance. When Illinois called out the National Guard, some of the other actions planned for what the press had now dubbed the "Days of Rage" had to be canceled.

The last action, on October 11, took place downtown in The Loop, and was in some ways the most intense. I remember our marching down a street completely lined with police when fighting broke out. I headed for the end of the block, where we were supposed to break out to trash the business section, but a cluster of three or four cops moved in to tackle me. I threw a bottle—as close as we were, I must have unconsciously not wanted to hit them—which shattered at their feet. With that distraction, I dove, spun, rolled back onto my feet still running—and shot past them. That moment was fairly emblematic of my brief "streetfighting days." My offensive reflexes were close to nil, but my defensive reflexes were spectacular.

While I was personally lucky, close to half our people were arrested during the Days of Rage. Still, for many of our people Cook County Jail was a place to build revolutionary spirit and unity as well as to have direct personal contact with people of color and the poor, so badly abused by the criminal justice system.

In evaluating the action, I was aware that the Chicago BBP leader Fred Hampton had denounced our tactics as "Custeristic" (suicidal). As much as we respected him, his critique did not prevail because other BPP leaders, most vociferously Eldridge Cleaver, praised our push toward greater militancy. The BPP itself would soon go through a split, in the face of withering repression, between a push for armed struggle and a step back to a purely legal, nonconfrontational approach. While Cleaver was the best known figure on the militant side, the forces we admired and aligned with were better represented by people from the Panther 21 and other groupings who went on to build the Black Liberation Army.

Rocky Mountain High

Whatever reevaluation the New York collective did of its organizing work, I missed it, as I was soon off to Denver. The Weather Bureau (as the leadership collective was then called) called New York to say I was to immediately join our Denver collective, where we had only about eight people, most of them with little political experience. I inferred that I was a good choice to strengthen Denver because the Bureau thought it would be healthy to move me out of NYC, where I had a long history and many contacts, some of whom represented a more antiaction tradition.

The way things worked in those days, if the Bureau (and to us that represented the revolution) said I was needed someplace else, that was it. I was expected to pick up and be there within two days, although of course we had no money for plane tickets.

Both my sisters lived in New York, and I combined quick farewell visits with requests for money to help with the airfare. While Brenda and I weren't super close, our relationship was still warm. Ruth and I had had a falling out about the 1967 Arab-Israeli war, but we'd stayed in touch, and I assumed she was still sympathetic to civil rights and anti-war work. Whatever her politics, she articulated a criticism that I should have taken more to heart, expressing anger that I had paid so little attention to family in the past months but now came asking for money. I heard her and felt embarrassed but nevertheless thought my family should know I loved them even as I devoted all my attention to the cause. I didn't come up with enough to make it all the way to Denver, so I bought a ticket to Chicago hoping I could scrounge more money there. As the plane entered the Midwest the pilot announced we'd run into a major storm system and that we had to go all they way to Denver to land. The airline would arrange a next-day connecting flight back to Chicago, a courtesy I didn't need.

That flight commenced an almost magical relationship to Denver. I called our collective's house—I'd never met any of them before, but they knew I was slated to join them—and they picked me up at the airport. As I remember it, that same night (or maybe the next) we were off and running, literally, to create a vocal political presence at a rock concert. It was my first time running in mile-high thin air and I felt it. I don't think we had any plans beyond banners and leaflets but many of the kids were frustrated about being denied access to the concert. Our agitation added to their anger, which threatened to generate a riot. One of our members, Bill, seemed frantic as he made a major effort to get us to chill out and withdraw.

Two weeks later, three of our members stopped in at a bar when someone walked in and immediately blurted out: "Why, Bill, I haven't seen you since we were at the Police Academy together." That was the last time we saw Bill…out of uniform. Both Brad, in the Brooklyn collective, and Bill are examples of a broader point. In the movement people only talked about "agents provocateurs"—infiltrators who promote violence in order to bust or discredit an organization—and there are many grim examples of such. Some of the worst provocations were set up because the police, frustrated by their inability to stop political bombings, wanted to create a stark deterrence. At least twice in the 1970s, once in Seattle and once in Puerto Rico, naïve radicals were enticed by infiltrators to place bombs, only to be shot down by police who had staked out the target.

But the state also fielded a stable of *agents suppressants* who tried to put a damper on evolving movement militancy. Provocateurs are more dramatic and damaging, but much of the Left has an anti-militant bias in not discussing the problem of *suppressants* at all. There is no simple litmus test to differentiate sincere militancy from provocation or honest caution from suppression; there is no substitute for having a sound analysis of specific conditions and a deep feel for people, their histories, and their values.

Denver proved to be an incredibly valuable and transforming experience because it brought me into contact with the Chicano/a struggle. On the northern edge of the half of Mexico's territory that the U.S. conquered in 1848, Denver didn't have nearly the brown population density of many cities in Texas, California, and New Mexico. But it did have the Crusade for Justice (CFJ), founded by the charismatic and brilliant Rodolfo "Corky" Gonzalez. He had been a successful professional boxer who then went into Democratic Party politics, but bolted when he saw them repeatedly sell out his people. He later wrote an epic poem, "Soy Joaquin/I am Joaquin" that grappled deeply with the dual identity of a people descended from both the conquistadors and the colonized Indians.

Corky and the CFJ became a center for the "Plan of Aztlan" which entailed looking at the U.S. Southwest (or "El Norte" of Mexico) as a spiritual and ancestral homeland for the Chicano/a people, rooted in the history and continuity of the Indians on that land. While some criticized "Aztlan" for being too mystical a concept, it did play an important historical role in forging a sense of Chicano/a identity and struggle. The CFJ was also very conscious about building links with other Chicano/a organizations around the country and helped develop the concept of "La Raza" which, as explained to me, represented both the "brown race" of all Latino/as but also the way their multiple racial heritage—Native American, Spanish, Black, Asian—could be a bridge for and unifier of the whole human race.

When I arrived in Denver most of the local white Left disdained the Crusade as too nationalistic and too violent. I didn't know what to expect, hearing how "anti-white" they were, but they seemed worth checking out. Just going to their office was an experience in itself because it was in a large building they owned that served as a vibrant community and cultural center. As we walked through, we saw workshops for local artisans and classes on Chicano/a history. We also saw top leaders, like Corky, helping sweep up and clean out the auditorium. Before making it to the office, we got to talk with some of the community members, who carried themselves with great dignity and also struck me as politically conscious and astute. I remember a middle-aged gentleman who lauded our political activism but cautioned that we seriously underestimated how deep and pervasive racism was among white people. He wasn't saying it was biological; he was encouraging us to organize, but he cautioned that historically it went even deeper than we accounted for—and he was right.

The political dialogue was instructive on the value of nationalism. With the CFJ fully confident that they set their own political terms and ran their own organization, they were completely at ease and even warm with us; I didn't feel any of the difficult dynamics that I'd heard about in SNCC when it was still a mixed organization. Contrary to the conventional Left wisdom, oppressed people's nationalism does not equal being anti-white. The Crusade had no problem working in principled coalitions. In fact, when a local church reneged on serving as a meeting center for the anti-war movement, the CFJ offered its auditorium. I found them to be a stunning example of radical politics with a deep community base. Several months later their developing community consciousness got expressed in a high school walkout to protest a curriculum that negated their culture and history. We quickly mobilized to organize support among white students. Our high school organizing subcommittee—three or four out of our overall collective of eight—rushed out a leaflet and ran over to the high school to pass it out. When they came back that night to describe their work, they brought the leaflet, which hit me like a punch to the solar plexus.

The content, though crude, expressed our line of the time, that you're either on the side of the oppressed or of "the Man." Here's why I was terribly upset: the leaflet hadn't been signed—didn't say who issued it. We were speaking as white allies, but an unsigned leaflet would be taken as written by the Chicano/a students and sound as though they were calling for a race war. It was too late to retrieve the leaflets that had been handed out, but we cut a stencil that put "SDS-Weatherman" at the bottom of each leaflet in the batch for the next day. A night later I went to the CFJ building to apologize for this terribly wrong intrusion into their struggle. In another good sign about how the Crusade functioned, the high school leader, Ernesto, met with me without any adult higher-up supervising.

When I explained to Ernesto what had happened, he laughed out loud—and then told me why. Earlier that day there had been a meeting between the students and the administration with some of the teachers who represented a potential swing force. The administration then produced this "race war" leaflet to show how dangerous and irresponsible the students were. Ernesto knew it wasn't theirs, so he sent one of the kids out to the street to track down the leaflet and its source. He came back with the same exact leaflet but with "SDS-Weatherman" at the bottom. It was then the administration who had egg on its face since it looked like they had doctored the leaflet—deleted the "SDS-Weatherman" in order to slander the Chicano/a students.

Denver was a breath of fresh air for me in many ways. Even during this period of monomania for revolution, I couldn't help marveling at the Rocky Mountains. We often drove out to the mountains to visit rural supporters and do some rudimentary target practice. We sometimes could hear right-wing Minutemen nearby doing serious training with heavy-caliber weapons. We even took time for occasional trips to sightsee. The mountains were gorgeous. Ironically, Denver's air wasn't so fresh. The combination of overreliance on automobiles and the way city air was held in by the mountains created a serious pollution problem.

My first time living in the West, I liked the open spaces and the sense of an open culture, less self-conscious and less driven than the East. Denver was also where I got in touch—as assimilated as I'd always felt—with the role the legacy of the Holocaust had played in my own anti-racist sensibilities. I became conscious kind of in reverse, acknowledging the relief I felt in meeting so many blond and blue-eyed radicals. Denver had its own militant history. I arrived just after Cam Bishop had fled the police; he was legendary among radical youth for allegedly blowing up the power lines to the main defense industry in the area.

Whether due to our small size or because nationally Weather had learned from our October failures, we were no longer doing "jailbreaks" or provoking riots. Our focus in Denver was on street kids, students at high schools and community colleges, and rock concert fans. While our line was still pretty much "you're either part of the solution or you're part of the problem," we did make much more of an effort to organize—to leaflet, to talk with people (and even listen a little!), and to speak at colleges. Two of the street kids even joined our small collective. They later came under tremendous police pressure, given their vulnerability to drug charges and their lack of family resources. We discussed the situation and agreed on their friendly withdrawal from our collective. They had been strong in never acceding to the pressure to become informants.

With my political experience and commitment, I soon became the leader of our collective. Back then we had no formal positions below the Bureau—local leadership was neither elected nor appointed, it just sort of emerged. The positive side of this was that it created was a sort of consensus. But the negative side was more telling, because this was a time when we were frantic to push ourselves and others forward, when our culture was extremely competitive, when the "gut-check" was still common.

In discussing those days with old comrades, I've noticed that most remember vividly the times when they were badgered by others, rather than vice-versa. To try to work around the vanity of memory, I've invited a member of that collective, who saw problems with the dynamics and didn't later go underground, to write his view of me. Given our friendship today, and the distance from the events, his account undoubtedly errs on the generous side, but it will give an idea:

> I remember you as forceful, driven, good-humored, prone to machismo. A great deal of the thrust was to push ourselves to take more risk and dare to take actions that involved danger. You embodied perfectly the powerful psychological need to shuck all white skin privilege, which could only be done by casting oneself into the fray. Unfortunately this need overcame the complicated mission to reach out and involve more and more people in the movement, to win by organizing rather than direct action.
>
> In a debate on the current world situation at the University of Denver, you were comfortable and civil and offered a sweeping characterization with just enough urgency to speak to and move the audience... In terms of the internal dynamics, I remember when you lit into a penetrating critique of me based, as your examination advanced, on my identification with my father's professorial

distance. You just relentlessly pursued my ego and rendered me defenseless and not particularly empowered to be a revolutionary. It was your ego trip at my expense, but not without some illumination…

I also vividly recall you receiving a phone call at dawn telling us that Fred Hampton and others had been killed in bed. This punctured our "life trip" phase… Your voice conveyed your utter disbelief.

On a Life Trip

Right after the Days of Rage, Weather had enthusiastically moved into what we later called our "life trip" ethos. Partly a reaction to the morbid talk of death in organizing for Chicago, the emphasis now was on living exuberantly, with freewheeling use of drugs and promiscuous sex. This new hedonism wasn't meant as withdrawal from struggle but rather as a way to energize ourselves for it. One night two of our members got picked up on a surprise harassment bust while they were high on LSD. We were worried that they'd succumb to paranoia, but fortunately they handled themselves with aplomb.

The push on sexuality was to defy society's norms and restrictions. The new line was that being liberated meant enjoying sex with both women and men and with multiple partners as well. I remember guiltily confessing to the Bureau member visiting Denver, and feeling my local leadership role was in question: "I don't know why, but I just can't get myself into having sex with a man." He responded with a laugh and said, "There's absolutely no requirement that you do." But even if our attempts to be "polysexual" were artificial and often crude, they did help people break through the prevailing sexual repression. It was in that context that two of the men in our collective came out as gay, and it was a pleasure to see their sense of themselves open up and blossom. As far as I know there was no put-down or loss of status in our collective—quite an advance for a Left organization in 1969. On the other hand, we still had no understanding of the need to struggle against internal homophobia or of the role of gay and lesbian liberation as a political issue and force.

The energy of the "life trip" swept us across the country for the November 1969 mobilization. Two carloads from Denver joined half a million people massed in Washington to protest the war. Within that, there was an explicit "revolutionary contingent" determined to make the connections to racism at home, and to raise the level of militancy to the "trashing" that was becoming increasingly popular among radical youth. The first night, our contingent marched on the South Vietnamese Embassy in Dupont Circle. In Chicago, strictly as Weather, we had numbered in the hundreds. Here we were part of a fighting force of a few thousand. A night of street battles ensued, with demonstrators breaking windows and throwing stones, and cops firing tear gas and clubbing those they could catch. Overall, it was a powerful expression of anger against the war and brought at least a part of the U.S. Capitol to a standstill for the night.

In the spirit of the "life trip," about fifty Weather cadres celebrated the successful street-fighting with a preannounced "orgy" at a movement center with a lot of floor space. Although there had been lots of talk about orgies, this was my first, and it turned out to be my last. I tried to look for someone I felt attracted to, but I could feel no sexual spark in such a public setting. So I simply sat alone at the edge of the crowd. While shamelessly promiscuous, I still, deep down, felt sex to be extremely intimate. I saw a lot of writhing bodies, but I suspect that, while some may have found orgies new and exciting, most just went through the motions to maintain the image of being liberated.

The next day a revolutionary contingent of about ten thousand broke off from the main march on the Pentagon and headed for the Justice Department—the symbol and the actual operating center for the systematic attacks on the Black movement. When we started to throw rocks at the windows, anti-war security monitors, mainly from the SWP, tried to stop us, but we pushed them aside. There was a skirmish with police as demonstrators pulled down the American flag in front of the building and some shrubbery was set on fire. We considered this "trashing" of the Justice Department an important victory. Attorney General John Mitchell—himself a key figure in running COINTELPRO, and later in the "Watergate" scandal—was looking down from one of the top floors. He was later quoted as saying that the scene reminded him of Russia in 1917 (the year of the revolution). His statement was quite an exaggeration—but one we happily embraced. We were finally directly confronting "the Man."

Weather was part of but didn't directly lead the revolutionary contingent. Still, we felt that our example of fighting in October had done a lot to spark this new and broader militancy. Later, we similarly felt that the ten thousand who participated and then returned to various cities did a lot to lead the range of "TDA riots"—the outrage expressed in February 1970, the day after the Chicago 8 were convicted. These riots in turn were precursors to the millions in the streets after the U.S. invasion of Cambodia and the killing of four anti-war demonstrators at Kent State on May 4, 1970—the biggest outpouring of anti-government outrage in U.S. history. Of course, by the time of this dramatic high point for the revolutionary youth movement, Weather had gone underground and was not directly part of it.

The Panthers in Denver

"We have to do something to expose this racist judge!" Frustrated, we sit in a Denver courtroom as supporters for two Panthers, Rory Hithe and Landon Williams, facing an extradition to a bogus trial in New Haven, Connecticut. Despite brilliant arguments by their lawyer, every ruling goes against the Panthers. But what can we do in a courthouse loaded with cops? I get an idea. We need just two props—one from a slaughterhouse, the other a standard toy store item. The next day, in the middle of the hearing, the courtroom door swings open and a pig's head rolls in, straight toward the judge's bench. A dropped bag of marbles trip up any pursuers. No busts and no injuries; the only riotous aspect is our laughter.

The Black Panthers had a small chapter in Denver. They didn't have a long history there or a strong base, but the cadres were intelligent and dedicated, and many charismatic Panthers passed through Denver when traveling between coasts. We met with them often and were inspired by them. A couple of the Panthers were fascinated by the Holocaust and often asked the Jewish members of our group why there hadn't been more widespread resistance. They understood the U.S. treatment of Black People as genocide and were determined, even at the cost of their own lives if necessary, to stop it.

Their talk of sacrifice wasn't fantasy. In 1969 alone, more than twenty Panthers were murdered and over seven hundred were arrested. We in Weather felt that the lack of white solidarity had given the government a signal that they could proceed with their campaign of extermination without heavy political cost among the "majority" population. One moment in particular crystallized this failure. During the Chicago 8 trial— the most visible confrontation between the anti-war movement and the government—the one Black defendant, BPP Chair Bobby Seale, was singled out for abuse. Seale, having been denied a postponement so his lawyer of choice could represent him, insisted on speaking out to defend himself. The judge called in the sheriffs, who chained and gagged Seale right in the middle of the courtroom. The other white defendants objected verbally, but only the pacifist, Dave Dellinger, the oldest of them all, put his body between the sheriffs and Seale. The seven white defendants then proceeded with the trial, making some good political points along the way about the war and the police riot at the Democratic Convention. But we felt it was wrong for them to proceed with Bobby chained and gagged—that once that happened, the white radicals should have refused to participate and disrupted the trial.

On December 4, 1969, Panthers Fred Hampton and Mark Clark were executed in their apartment. The Chicago police claimed the Panthers had fired on them, but later examination of the apartment showed ninety to ninety-nine incoming bullets, and only one wild outgoing shot. A later autopsy revealed that Hampton had been drugged with secobarbital—evidently by FBI infiltrator William O'Neal. Four days later the LAPD laid siege to the Los Angeles Panther office. But Vietnam vet Geronimo Pratt had organized a defense, and the Panthers held off hundreds of police until morning, when the presence of the media allowed the Panthers to surrender without being gunned down.

Two of us were visiting the Denver BPP office one afternoon when a gunshot was heard outside. We saw the Panthers immediately pull out sandbags and go into defensive positions, after moving the two of us to a more sheltered spot. Thankfully it was a false alarm. Whatever the gunshot was about, it wasn't the beginning of a police siege. But the incident in the context of all that was happening nationwide impressed on me that, all the rhetoric about revolution aside, it was indeed a life-and-death struggle for the Panthers.

County Jail

The main consideration for planning our Denver actions was solidarity with the Panthers. We even had a discussion about whether, in the event of an assault on the Panthers, we could fire on the police to divert a least a few of them—but we soon realized that we weren't capable of that level of confrontation. Still, most of our actions of the period were to point to the police as the front line of racist assault and to encourage white youth to side with people of color. In January 1970, a month after Hampton and Clark were killed, our actions resulted in my two Denver busts.

The first bust came during a women's action. The plan was that Weather women would disrupt a police science class at a local college with a smoke "bomb" (no explosion, but a thick cloud of smoke) while the Weather men supported their action by passing out leaflets outside, explaining why people shouldn't join the police force. Worried that the women could get cut off inside the building, I insisted on having two of us, posing as students, in the hall. When the women set off the smoke and ran, a burly police-officer-to-be in the hall grabbed one around the neck. I convinced him (verbally) to let her go. The women later (rightly) criticized my paternalism. It was their action, my presence made them more passive, and if I hadn't been there they would have fought harder to get away.

My paternalism had another cost. After the women got away, I went out to leaflet with the other guys. When the student I'd encountered in the hall came out, he identified me to the police, who arrested me and charged we with arson. Unlike my first NYC bust, I can't claim complete innocence, but "arson" felt outlandish: the smoke device caused no fire (we made sure of that before using it), and I'd never touched it and never entered the classroom.

My second bust, amid our growing frenzy about the Panthers, was more serious. We planned to leaflet cars and pedestrians in a main hangout area for white street kids—but this time when the police came to stop us, we were going to stop them with rocks. When the cops got out of their car, they got a surprise, but most of our people froze and didn't let loose. One cop got knocked down, and I saw the other, enraged, start to draw his gun. I instinctively plowed into him and knocked him to the pavement. At that point, good tactics dictated kicking him hard enough to keep him down so that I could retreat with the rest of our group. But I couldn't bring myself to do it, and instead just rolled off and ran—right into three off-duty GIs. After a bit of tussling, I was on my back with the GIs holding my arms and head and with my legs sprawled apart. I saw another cop charging me. Just as he raised one leg to give me a running kick in the balls, I did a quick scissors motion on his other leg and he was down. But so was I. Busted—and with an incriminating rock in my pocket.

The pleasant surprise at the station was that, except for a couple of well-telegraphed punches, I didn't get worked over. They weren't quite ready to whomp on white, college-educated kids. Their approach was more psychological as they told me what a nice guy this cop was, about his family and all he did for the community. (Fortunately, he had no injuries beyond a couple of scrapes and bruises.) The unpleasant surprise was what they had already done to the guy in the holding cell with me. A young Chicano arrested for drunk and disorderly, he was in intense pain because the cops had systematically pounded his ribs.

This more serious bust meant a week or two in jail before I got bailed out. My parents, who were on a trip out West, came to visit. Talking with me through the screen separating prisoners and visitors, they were highly upset and couldn't understand how the courteous and responsible young man they had raised could be arrested on such charges, ruining his prospects for a respectable profession. But with incredible dignity they didn't resort to the guilt tactic of "you are killing us." And I guess they decided that now that I was twenty-five years old, even though I needed them to bail me out, they could no longer give me orders. (Sly and the Family Stone's hit song that month, "Thank You for Letting Me Be Myself," kept running through my head, in appreciation of my mom and dad.) They urged me to stop what I was doing and return to academics. I regretted the pain I was causing them, but there was no changing the trajectory I was on. Our government was carrying out mass murder on a daily basis. All the values of community service my parents had instilled in me meant—given my understanding of the world we lived in—fighting the monster.

One of my first social encounters in jail was with a white biker with a ponytail and lots of tattoos. Cautious, I told him my charges but not my political affiliations. He came back with, "As soon as I get out I'm going to contact the Weathermen to get guns so I can go after the pigs with some real weapons." It's not that this guy represented the working class or that he had embraced our anti-racism, but to a sector of white youth their identification with our fighting the government was a possible bridge to engaging with them on the fundamentals of racism and the war.

Jail also provided some time for reading, which had fallen by the wayside in this mad-dash, nine-month period. Rereading *Hamlet* in these circumstances, I just couldn't understand his hesitancy to take action. But I discovered a gem of a short story, Herman Melville's "Benito Cereno," a textured and subtle account of slaves taking over the boat transporting them.

War Council

My two January 1970 busts had followed on the heels of the quarterly SDS national council in December. With Weather people the elected leaders of what now was only a fraction of the old SDS, and with discussion of moving to armed struggle in the air, the Flint, Michigan, meeting was renamed "The War Council." My number one impression and what hit me the most emotionally was the bank of posters of Fred Hampton, who had just been assassinated by the police and FBI. I also remember the two sick comments, in the efforts to "psych" ourselves to violence, that became notorious. One speaker discussed the recent grisly killings by the "Manson family." She may have meant to ridicule the American fascination with violence, but in the context of all our war talk it sounded like she was extolling these cruel murders. The other, a tortured discussion of the necessity of armed struggle even if a white baby was accidentally killed (this from someone who wasn't a leader), seemed gratuitous, since nothing that would kill babies was on any agenda I could imagine. My discomfort with these two remarks at the time didn't lead me to criticize them or even explicitly demur. I saw them as rhetorical excesses accompanying a correct direction, and I didn't want to be left out of the cadre who would be chosen to pursue armed struggle—to be, in the status consciousness of the day, revolutionaries "on the highest level."

A few months later in Denver, our collective did two armed actions, one firebombing and one small explosion, against the war and police repression of the Panthers. Both were small and directed at buildings, symbols only. Along with our precautions, we were lucky because in our haste to move into armed struggle we took action before having a thorough grounding in all the factors that go into ensuring safety. We didn't see these actions as an alternative to organizing; we still were out talking to youth and doing various stunts like the pig's head in the courtroom. As open exponents of militancy, we were under heavy police surveillance. One kid we worked with, whose father was with the Denver police, told us that there were over twenty plainclothes cops assigned to our collective of eight. Spotting and then losing tails became a day-to-day part of our work, almost a sport. There was also a political lesson to be learned: it is not viable over time to have the same group be both the main public exponents of revolution and the ones carrying out armed actions. As we would later see in the example of the Irish Republican Army (IRA) and Sinn Fein in Northern Ireland, a more mature model is to have political unity but clear organizational separation between public mass work and underground struggle.

There was another attempt to infiltrate the collective. We regularly went out to a local park to talk with the kids who hung out there. One night one of our female members came back with a potential new recruit, who quickly homed in on me. I don't know whether she was guided to or just zeroed in on me. In our long discussion about politics and life, she said she was part Native American and that had made her acutely aware of racism and injustice. Her manner seemed temptingly seductive, as though it was assumed we would sleep together that night, and she had a definite sensual appeal. But something didn't compute: her political understanding just didn't correlate with the level of commitment she was contemplating. So my questions became more thorough and pointed, and her responses didn't hold together well. Finally she admitted to some "incidental" past work for the police department. At that point we mutually agreed that it didn't make sense for her to work with us.

At first I congratulated myself on being so principled in resisting the James Bond mystique (powerful in the mass culture of the day) of having sex with an alluring counterspy. But later, when I thought about it more soberly, I realized that it was probably her apparent belief that sleeping with me (the enemy) was required that had led her to so quickly blow her cover.

The Townhouse

The phone rings in the middle of the night. "Three of our people, including Teddy, were killed in an explosion yesterday. I can't go into details on the phone, but we think the police did it. We'll get back to you when we know more. In the meantime, watch your back."

Soon our small world in Denver got blown apart by a blast 1,800 miles away. A couple of our people heard a news item with poor, crackling radio reception while driving in the mountains, about an explosion in New York City and a Gold, sounded like Theodore, being killed. I couldn't and wouldn't believe my best friend was dead. It must have been the writer Herbert Gold, a big enough name to make national news. While I knew Teddy was in New York City, I had no idea who was in his collective or what they were doing. The last I'd heard, Teddy was going to be one of the key people to lead SDS, to be the public, mass anti-imperialist organization after most of Weather went underground.

That night I got the phone call. I was shaken to my core. Three of our people, including my best friend, suddenly dead. My grief was compounded by real fears. A death is even more unnerving when you feel it could have been you. In the context of what was being done to the Panthers, the "police attack" version was entirely credible—and in Denver we were under intense surveillance. Were we being set up for the kill?

When a Weather Bureau member made it to Denver a couple of weeks later, we got the real story: our own people had accidentally caused the explosion as they frantically rushed to build bombs. The two others killed in this tragedy were later identified as Diana Oughton and Terry Robbins. Two women who had been on another floor of the collapsing townhouse had managed to escape both death and arrest.

My earlier caller understandably hadn't wanted to give incriminating details over the phone. But the "police did it" cover story was a serious disservice as it pushed us into an immediate fear for our lives and made it hard to function intelligently. It was an early lesson that "security" in communications doesn't always trump political discussion or emotional impact. The caller, without spelling out incriminating details, could have given us a more realistic sense of the situation.

Denver, with our small group and geographic distance from Weather strongholds, was the only one of our collectives without a Bureau member nearby, which left us isolated from many internal political debates. This Bureau visit was to bring us into the debate that was raging after the townhouse: between militarism and building a revolutionary youth movement. Militarism was defined as determining effectiveness by the size of the armed blows against imperialism. (I didn't learn until much later that the politics that led to the townhouse went beyond militarism. The planned action, directed at a military ball, would have killed some officers and their dates, thus sinking into a cavalier attitude toward human life and "collateral damage" all too reminiscent of the U.S. government.) The alternative to militarism had a role for armed struggle, but only as an integral component of the overriding goal of building a bigger and more militant revolutionary movement. Organizing was key, and actions were to be evaluated not based on the size of their bang but rather for their impact on consciousness.

The Bureau members who led the struggle against militarism, Bernardine Dohrn, Jeff Jones, and Bill Ayers, thought that Denver would be a strong ally. In contrast to the New York collective, we had never stopped working with and trying to organize white youth. We used a range of tactics, and even our two armed actions did only minimal damage to buildings as our purpose was to highlight the institutions of oppression.

But by the time they got to Denver I had flipped and brought most of the collective with me. Out of my mind with grief for Teddy, my response was to feel compelled to carry out his mission—again, with no idea that the New York targets had included people. I was focused on what we could do to stop the war machine and the police repression of the Panthers. For example, the U.S. military was straining its air capacity to carry out continuous saturation bombings, killing many civilians in Vietnam. Wouldn't it be great if we could somehow incapacitate a major aircraft carrier? The police had done a number of raids on Panther offices. Couldn't we do something to draw police attention, impairing their ability to concentrate forces on the Panthers?

The Bureau's counterarguments were patient and clear: We will never be a match for the government's military might. Our strength, in fighting for the oppressed, is in potential numbers. The intensity of struggle and repression around the world and within the U.S., along with the growing militancy of white youth, does mandate a new level of struggle. But the model for us, as for the Vietnamese in the earliest phase of their fight against Japanese colonialism, is "armed propaganda": actions designed to educate about the oppressor and to show that there are ways to fight back without being crushed. Indeed, for revolutionaries it is almost never a question of military victories. Our prime focus is on the consciousness and mobilization of the people.

While I heard these sound arguments, they weren't yet enough to overturn my newfound militarism. I was supposed to represent Denver at the national get-together to thrash out these issues, but in the chaos of the period, the Bureau person who dealt with us lost touch. I never got the instructions on how to get to this clandestine meeting. Later, I wondered if he "lost touch" intentionally. Regardless of why I didn't get there, my presence and position at the meeting wouldn't have made much difference. The militarist direction was wrong, morally and strategically, and would have been disastrous. The revolutionary youth movement tendency won decisively. That left us in Denver with the choice of either working with a national organization that we saw as in at least partial retreat, or trying to escalate military damage as a tiny collective. However out of touch with reality I'd been for that six weeks, I realized we couldn't possibly handle the latter. We decided to work with national Weather, which was already largely underground. By late April the Denver collective was disbanded. A few went underground, dispersed among different cities; a few returned to more normal life and movement activity.

Later I was profoundly grateful to Bernardine Dohrn, Jeff Jones, and Bill Ayers for leading us out of the volcano, for knowing what to do in a crisis that had way overwhelmed my own political understanding, and for leading the successful construction of an underground. That appreciation, while definitely merited, also had a downside in that it became difficult for me to credit my own views in any differences I might have with them. But what mattered most was the new potential for building and sustaining a humane and coherent anti-imperialist underground. We were about to embark on a form of struggle that conventional wisdom deemed impossible and that was unprecedented in the U.S. since the 1850s and the abolitionist underground railroad.

Columbia, 1968. The strike was about war and racism, not grades, tuition, or student democracy.
Courtesy Columbia University Archives

Auburn Prison, early 1980s. David with codefendant and comrade Kuwasi Balagoon.

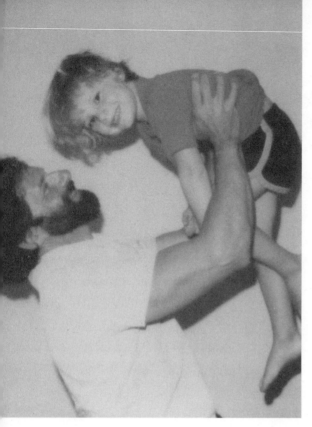

David with his son Chesa, 1980s. Parenting from behind prison walls is a challenge.

Inmate #83-A-6158, Auburn Prison, NY. David is a mentor to many young activists today.

{UNDERGROUND}

Tin soldiers and Nixon coming
We're finally on our own
This summer I hear the drumming
Four dead in Ohio
—Crosby, Stills, Nash & Young, "Ohio," 1970

We're well across the Continental Divide, headed for Utah. Traffic is sparse late into the morning of a weekday in the mountains of western Colorado. The conditions of my bail on "arson" and "assault on a peace officer" charges prohibit me from leaving the state, so we definitely notice the white Ford with the unusual antenna that's been behind us for a while. To check it out we stop at the next roadside diner. The Ford drives on by, but our relief turns into concern a couple of miles down the road when the Ford falls in behind us again.

An hour later, we pull into another diner, just past the turn-off for a small regional airport. Again, the Ford drives by, but this time we don't stop to sip our coffee. We get back into our car, double back to the turnoff that was always in our plan, and head for the airport where I have a reservation, under another name, on a small commuter plane making the short hop to Salt Lake City. My comrade, who is not under any legal charges, will drive her car back to Denver. If the Ford was following us, I'm in the air and out of the state before he realizes we doubled back.

Landing in Salt Lake City, I smile at the thought that this notoriously conservative town is serving as my jumping off point for underground resistance. But I don't linger to savor the irony. I move briskly to the gate for my flight out, reserved under yet another name. Once we take off I know I've made it. Now that I'm in the air, I'm securely "underground"...But where am I headed? What is the unknown life that awaits me?

The Crosby, Stills, Nash & Young song about the four anti-war students shot down at Kent State came out months after we went underground, but it became my anthem for the experience. As "independent" as I'd considered myself as a radical student, and as close as my budget was to the poverty line, I'd always had my parents and community to fall back on. Now, "we're finally on our own." And we were fighting Nixon and his monstrous military might, as imperialism waged war on the impoverished throughout the Third World, napalmed Vietnamese children, assassinated militant Blacks and other people of color, and was even willing to kill white college students to intimidate the anti-war movement.

Just six weeks after the townhouse, I was still recovering, still somewhat shell-shocked, still uneasy about Weather's rejection of a strategy of military sabotage. Despite that disagreement, leadership was willing to work with me, but they weren't about to place me in a position of responsibility. When I arrived on the West Coast, I was taken to the safehouse of two comrades. I knew one of the women well and knew of the other, but she hadn't been in SDS, and we'd never met. They gave me their underground names and headed out for some unspecified errands.

An hour later a neighbor knocked on the door. I didn't want to answer, but he could see that the light was on and he had probably heard movement. Given the sense of community in the local hippie culture, it would have been weird not to answer the door, so I did. "Oh, where are the girls?" After explaining I was a friend visiting from out of town, I answered, "Anna went to see a friend and Carolyn to do some shopping; they should be back in about an hour. What should I tell them?" "Just say their neighbor Bobby dropped by to say hi."

From the expression on Bobby's face, I could tell that something was wrong, and I had a good idea what it might be. When the comrades returned, I asked them if they used "Anna" and "Carolyn" with their neighbors. "No, those are our organizational names. Here we go by the first names that correlate with the ID used to rent the apartment." The immediate problem was easy to smooth over, given the subculture. I managed to run into Bobby in the hall the next day. "Did you drop by yesterday when Joan and Lisa were out?" "Yeah, I did." "I wasn't sure because I was zonked on hashish at the time…I hope I wasn't incoherent." "No," Bobby grinned, "You were just fine."

So we were fine, but clearly we had made a rookie mistake—partly based on inexperience, partly based on their uncertainty about how much information to entrust to me, only a candidate and still not a member. As we learned over time, any combination of us always needed to have a "conspiratorial minute" to precede any potential encounter with outsiders. The minute was used to agree on a believable and consistent narrative on who we were and what we were doing in that particular setting. This technique served on three different occasions over the years to enable me and those I was with at the time to talk our way out of more or less random encounters with the police.

My first underground task was disguise, which also entailed some changes of residences until my appearance stabilized. Our reliance on hair dye led me to do a spoof on a popular Lady Clairol ad of the day: "Does he, or doesn't he? Only his section leader knows for sure!"

Before long I'd gone from clean-shaven to a bushy beard, from short dark hair to long and light, from horn rimmed to rimless glasses, from an informal version of collegiate dress to tie-dyed T-shirts and bell bottoms. One day I walked right past an old college friend, who didn't recognize me. On the other hand, I later heard from contacts that someone I didn't know personally but who had often seen me giving anti-war speeches recognized me from a distance. She, like so many we knew from those days, was sympathetic; there was no danger she would call the cops. But we learned to play close attention to gait, carriage, and style, which could be more revealing than glasses and hair, especially for women, who didn't have the advantage of beards.

The lesson became clear when I read an inspiring story about Harriet Tubman. She was taking a group of twenty escaped slaves through a Baltimore train station to head north on a forged pass from their master when she saw her former owner heading right toward her. She couldn't bolt and run, so she immediately huddled over and shuffled forward like an old lady with arthritis. Her ex-owner just brushed on by without ever looking her in the face.

The most essential tool for staying underground was ID. The 1970s were pretty informal and we could often rent apartments or hold short-term jobs without ID, but you needed it in case you were stopped in the street, or to buy a car, or to cash checks, etc. It was best to not put all those functions on the same ID, lest a breach in one area brought everything else down.

Three alternatives were available. First, you could use an ID that someone had agreed to "lose" and not report for a while, or that had been stolen. Back then, most driver's licenses didn't have pictures and would survive a routine call to the Department of Motor Vehicles, provided that credit cards or checks hadn't been stolen with it. Counterfeit IDs were also widely available, with a wide range in quality. There would be no problem of such an ID being reported stolen, but it would not survive a call to the DMV. Finally, there was the morbidly named "dead baby" method. The idea was to get a real birth certificate and use it to "build" an identity. The method entailed reading old obituaries, or even gravestones, to find a child who had died too early to have applied for a social security number. If the child had been born in one county and died in another, the chances (back then) of cross-referencing were nil. Using the data in the obituary, one could request the birth certificate and then use it to get a social security card and other ID, and then use all that to get one's own driver's license, even in a state with a picture on it. There was no problem applying for a social security card in your twenties, especially for women who, in those days, often didn't enter the workforce until divorced or widowed. This last method produced the best quality and was what was we usually ran on, trying also to always keep at least one back-up set.

Our approach may sound quaint relative to today's much more complicated ID requirements, but at the time, when the conventional wisdom was that no underground could survive, these methods were creative and effective.

Money was another crucial need, with three main ways to obtain it: jobs, crime, and donations. Initially we were reluctant to get jobs both because of ID concerns and because we saw ourselves as full-time revolutionaries. Crime was risky. It didn't seem worth the risk of getting busted for the petty crimes—such as stealing and quickly cashing checks—that we may have chanced while aboveground. Armed robberies were highly dangerous and way beyond our abilities. Overwhelmingly, our funds came from political donations. Opposition to the war gave us a big base we could call on safely, whose middle-class backgrounds meant they had some money to spare. While my personal budget was extremely frugal, I had food and rent. Most importantly, the organization had operational funds.

Though our vision was all about action, our main activity was meetings—internal meetings for political discussion and strategy sessions, and individual meetings with aboveground backers to build our support network. Such a network was crucial for everything from money to cars to addresses for receiving IDs to feedback on what was happening in the broader political movement, which helped us evaluate the impact of actions.

As with most of us, my meetings would not be with an old best friend or with a prominent ex-SDSer. Usually I was working with a friend of a friend; we may have never met before and would not be linked on any computer, but my friend had assured me this person was committed and trustworthy. A few of the people in my support network had never even been to a demonstration. For example, I met a couple while playing frisbee in the park. There was no way the FBI would be looking for me there, so I could trust the political views these two expressed, and once I met their families, I knew they were solid. The young couple, with no college background, had never participated in the organized Left. So as long as I could ensure that they didn't brag about our contact to anyone, I could consider them 100 percent secure.

Meetings with movement activists were far riskier, but important for political dialogue. Great care had to be taken to be sure they weren't followed to the meeting. We learned some standard but effective procedures. The above person would watch, without constantly looking over her shoulder, for a tail, and if she saw one would abort the meeting. The under person would observe her come in, along a planned route or "trajectory" with a long or wide enough view to spot any tail.

We'd gone underground to wage armed struggle and, in the wake of the townhouse, our first priority was to do so safely. The political errors of the townhouse got expressed in the recklessness of not bothering with safety switches or test lights. I was assigned to a small group to work on developing a safer circuit. The others, like me, were seasoned activists whose current status was uncertain after the recent upheavals. Maybe the assignment was make-work, to keep us occupied; but two of the people in our group turned out to have a flair for electronics, the process among us was good, and the result was a new and much safer circuit.

In the early '70s, as activists in a range of movements felt impelled to initiate armed struggle, several were killed. Two ex-SNCC workers died in an explosion in the East, and a carload of Chicano militants blew up in the Southwest. Mourning these losses, I had no way to assess, given the nature of the times, whether these activists had been assassinated by police agents or had died, like our townhouse comrades, in a flawed effort to begin armed resistance. There were definitely crucial lessons that had to be learned about storing and handling explosives—had infiltrators purposely supplied them with unstable dynamite? I also wondered whether the police had put out deliberate disinformation about building circuits. In those days, many anonymous tactical guides were in circulation. Could one have a short circuit built into it? *The Anarchist Cookbook*, the most widely distributed manual on tactics, was a possible candidate—but I didn't manage to get my hands on it to analyze their diagram for a short. Even with my limited ability to do anything about this grave problem, I was extremely remiss in not pursuing the issue in a more determined way.

An unprecedented prairie fire of youth rebellion unexpectedly swept the country in May 1970. Following the U.S. invasion of Cambodia and the Ohio National Guard's killing of four anti-war demonstrators at Kent State, 448 college campuses went on strike or were shut down, with four million students and youth taking part, and scores of ROTC and Bank of America buildings were burnt to the ground. On May 14, police killed two students at a Black college, Jackson State in Mississippi, but unfortunately this atrocity did not evoke the same outrage from white youth. What better moment could there be for an organization that had envisioned a Revolutionary Youth Movement and sought to give it anti-racist leadership? But all we could do was watch as the events unfolded on the mass media. I had only been underground for a month; collectively we were barely two months past the catastrophic townhouse; our concentration on the demanding task of going under meant that we had no capacity for playing a role in this massive rebellion. Our passivity at that moment felt excruciatingly frustrating.

Weather Declares War

By May 21, 1970, Weather issued its "Declaration of War" against imperialism, signed by Bernardine Dohrn. This brash and militant statement highlighted the Black revolutionaries who had inspired us, pledging, "Never again will they fight alone." The declaration promised an armed action within fourteen days. Naturally, we had an action all ready to go. We wanted to attack a symbol of the criminal justice system, a central institution oppressing people of color within the United States. But we had done a better job of mastering safety than effectiveness. A small bomb placed in the San Francisco courthouse, scheduled to go off when the building was empty, failed to detonate. The police didn't find it, leaving the possibility of a later accidental detonation when someone was there. So we had the awkward but necessary responsibility of telling the authorities exactly where the device was hidden so that the bomb squad could find and defuse it, thus giving police forensics an intact example of our circuit and components.

On June 9, the oranization announced that it was alive and functioning with a blast at the NYC Police Department headquarters. Newspaper accounts said that the device had been placed inside a locker room and that seven employees sustained minor injuries from shattered glass. After this, the WUO never injured any person. We in the West were relieved that the comrades back East had bailed us out and we laughed about our laid-back "hippie" sense of time that had stretched the fourteen-day limit to nineteen.

By summer, I was accepted as a responsible member. At the time, there were several small armed struggle groups totally unrelated to us. In August 1970, anti-imperialist activists blew up a major war research center, the Army Math Building, at the University of Wisconsin. Even though the blast occurred at 3:40 a.m., a graduate student who was unexpectedly in the building to do some late-night research was killed. We had extensive discussions on how to do our best to see that other groups didn't make such deadly mistakes, and on how to set a clear example on safety for the other armed struggle groups that were emerging.

We soon had our basic approach down. Every target had to be a clear symbol of the power structure that oppressed people. Every action was accompanied by a communiqué explaining it politically. Several copies were sent to radical papers, in the hope that they would print it in full. One was also left near the scene for the mass media, hoping they would cover at least the main reasons, which were also summarized in a slogan that went with the warning call. The blast was usually timed for the wee hours of the morning, but only after extensive surveillance to make sure there was no graveyard shift of janitors or secretaries. And every action was preceded, by about a half an hour, with a warning call to clear the building. We soon learned that calling the police wasn't enough. They often claimed they received no call, and they made no effort to check and clear buildings. Perhaps they didn't want the risk to themselves of going in, or maybe they hoped that someone would be killed, which would turn people against us. To make sure the warning call got acted on and to cover ourselves, we started calling the media too and telling them to notify the police.

There was a lot to learn about handling and storing dynamite, making safe circuits, and placing and hiding a device without being seen. But while those aspects are always, and rightly so, a little scary, I soon felt confident about our technical skills in those areas, along with our political focus. Two aspects of the work carried the highest risks of getting caught. First, the early-morning surveillance, to make sure nobody worked in the building at that hour, because it meant being out at times and in places that might look suspicious. And second, the warning call, because many police stations and media offices could trace calls within two minutes. We had to time our messages to keep them focused and brief, take care not to leave fingerprints or provide a usable voice print, and to pick a phone location with many possible exit routes into more crowded areas. Despite the risks, these methods for making the actions as safe as possible were always followed.

Surveillance gambits produced some amusing incidents. One time a woman comrade and I were parked in a car near some government buildings, just off a freeway, and except for us the street was deserted. All of a sudden, police lights shone behind us and a cop walked up to check us out. Being the male, I was in the driver's seat. Per our earlier "conspiratorial minute," I explained that we had been driving on the freeway when we had a lovers' quarrel; I had pulled off so that our spat wouldn't cause an accident. My plaintive, flustered look said, "You know how temperamental women can be." The cop laughed paternalistically and told us to be on our way, without asking for ID.

By October 1970, we were adept enough to launch a "fall offensive," with four actions in two weeks. Hitting several targets helped us express a fuller politics. Three of the actions, against the criminal justice system, expressed solidarity with a rising tide of prisoners' resistance. A fourth action was carried out by an all-woman team, "The Proud Eagle Tribe," who attacked a war research center at Harvard. This example highlighted women as fighters (but didn't articulate any fuller program on women) and argued that Vietnam was very much a women's issue.

I was in charge of the one aspect of the fall offensive that didn't work: an effort to foster a more diversified resistance. I was working with a couple of anti-imperialist fugitives who weren't members of the organization. The idea was for us to carry out an allied action, which would extend the reach of the offensive and also encourage other independent collectives.

The planning didn't go well, and I soon spotted a serious breach in their security and quickly helped them clear out of the region, a few days before the FBI showed up at what had been their door. (Regrettably, after that I didn't do a good job of maintaining a working relationship when they were far away and feeling isolated.) If I hadn't been so wrapped up in proving my personal piece of the offensive a success, I might have seen the security problem earlier. If I hadn't picked it up in time, the heat could have followed me back to the organization. This setback in an effort for outreach and diversification, while not a disaster, was one of many factors that pushed the WUO toward a more centralized model.

Overall the fall offensive was a big success, but our most impressive and notorious action had happened a month earlier: helping liberate Timothy Leary from prison. Leary, an early promoter of LSD and a celebrity of the drug culture, had been sentenced to ten years for a small amount of marijuana.

High on Youth Culture

"Some of your Left sectarian friends will criticize us, but we're going to break Tim Leary out of jail. The point is that we're going to learn how to do it here so that later we'll be able to break out BLA prisoners who are held under much tighter security." That's how a Central Committee member (as the smaller leadership body that had replaced the Weather Bureau was now called) had first presented the idea to me that summer. With any political objection to the action preemptively discredited as "Left sectarian," I bite my tongue. It's not that I object on principle to helping someone convicted on drugs—Leary didn't belong in prison—but I didn't feel like this action would be the most political use of our limited capabilities. But the argument that this experience with a medium security would help us learn how to free political prisoners in max prisons was compelling, although it's not something that ever came to fruition.

The real push for this action was our evolving politics around youth culture. In the frenzy that led to the townhouse, we had seen ourselves as "exceptional whites"—the rare handful of white people who were sincerely anti-racist. This sense of being so isolated had driven us toward spectacular and dangerous actions to try to have an impact. But there was a double error embedded in the "exceptional whites" perspective: First, it led us to abdicate our responsibility to organize other white people in an anti-racist way; and secondly, it expressed the conceit that we were now magically free of racism. So the "exceptional white" vanity had diverted us both from internal struggle with our own racism and from the challenge to do broader anti-racist organizing. In short, the position was more about promoting ourselves than about building the strongest possible solidarity with people of color.

After the townhouse, our reaction against this error was to rediscover a base in radical youth. When we went underground, hunted by the FBI, youth culture provided the sea for us fish to swim in. I felt a comfort in living in and moving through communities where the prevailing values were anti-war and anti-police, where the sentiment was "peace, love, and happiness" rather than "kill commies." Hippy culture also had incidental benefits. The flowering of a range of hair styles and modes of dress gave us greater flexibility for disguises. The variety of living arrangements and the lifestyles not tied to nine-to-five jobs allowed us a lot more maneuverability without being conspicuous. We were able to get around by hitchhiking, easier for men but still usually safe for women. We changed our diets to center on brown rice, tofu and vegetables, and fruit and yogurt. At times, and only half jokingly, we referred to ourselves as hippies.

Liberating Leary would have a strong appeal to the major component of youth culture—perhaps bigger than those who were consciously political—whose rebellion centered on drugs. This actual "jailbreak" was a lot more complex than our previous actions, but it went off without a hitch. Leary then issued a widely read public statement that encouraged those in the drug culture to oppose the war machine and to support political prisoners. Eventually he ended up at the Black Panther Party international headquarters in Algeria. I wasn't privy to how this sanctuary was arranged. Years later, a Panther comrade who was there said they were unhappy about accepting Leary because of his advocacy of drugs, but reluctantly did so out of solidarity with us. That unhappy marriage in Algeria didn't last long. After leaving there, Leary was caught on a plane as he was hopping from one country to another seeking asylum. He then made a deal to testify against Weather in return for avoiding major jail time. Whether by conscious ploy or as a result of his excessive use of LSD, his accounts were so incoherent—he reportedly gave seventeen different versions of the escape—that he couldn't be used in any court case. But the feds most likely learned something about our operations and personnel.

New Morning

The most explicit articulation of our youth culture politics came in December 1970, three months after Leary's escape. Lyrical in some ways, "New Morning" gave the first public accounting of the townhouse and revealed that Terry Robbins was the third activist who had died there (his body had been too shredded to identify). The statement, signed by Bernardine Dohrn, explained the military error and vowed not to repeat it. We publicly changed the name of the organization from "Weatherman" (the language usage of that time had the male stand for the whole species) to the more gender-neutral and inclusive "Weather Underground," which later became known as the Weather Underground Organization, or the WUO.

"New Morning" also referred to a "youth nation" as though the oppression and resistance of white youth was now on a par with the national liberation struggles of people of color within the U.S. The statement warned against "hard drugs," such as heroin, while extolling the role that "soft drugs," such as grass and LSD, could play in expanding consciousness. While I was surprised by the term "youth nation" after so many years of debate within the Left on the rigorous criteria that designated a people as an oppressed nation, I welcomed "New Morning" as life-affirming, as clearly putting us past the military error, and as placing us within a broader culture that was moving toward resistance.

The next month a radical weekly, the *Berkeley Barb*, printed an open letter to us from the members of the Panther 21 who were in jail. They opened with high praise for our initiative to build an underground. They also expressed criticism of two points in "New Morning." They warned against endorsing drugs, which were a form of chemical genocide in the ghettos and barrios. They also were concerned that our reaction to the military error entailed pulling back from the crucial role of armed struggle. Their open letter, lauding what we were doing right and clearly stating their concerns, was an unusual and positive example of how to conduct comradely political struggle.

Greatly admiring the Panther 21, I basked in their praise but wasn't sure what to make of their criticisms. The line in the WUO, which I received simultaneously with the copy of the letter, was that there was a misunderstanding: the 21 didn't realize that we would soon be doing new actions. I don't remember discussion of the drug issue, but I guess we saw the devastation caused in the ghettos and barrios as a problem solely with "hard drugs." We could have easily responded to this thoughtful effort at dialogue by sending an open letter back to the same radical newspaper, but we never did. I was never in any discussions that even considered doing so. We did go on to carry out other actions, but the Panther 21 had picked up whiffs of retreat that would later become a major wind.

The feel of that first year under was amazing for me, almost like living in a fairy tale. Contrary to the common misconception, I didn't feel paranoid, at least after the first month; I wasn't constantly looking over my shoulder. Naturally the situation required an attention to detail: ID, disguise, mail drops, safehouses, how and where one moved, and persona. But once those aspects were in place, I felt confident and relaxed, and it seemed that most of us did. My main feelings in the situation were our sense of great purpose, a certain satisfaction that we were fighting the monster that was raining down military and economic death on so many human beings. We enjoyed the power of invisibility and the surge from spearheading a larger subculture rebelling against the powers-that-be. We lived many of the pluses, as well as some aspects that turned out to be minuses, of hippie culture. At times, we had the rush of knowing what tomorrow's news would be—because we were planning the events that would make the headlines.

An organization was a tremendous advantage for being safe and productive underground. Beyond creating knowledge and resources for survival essentials, the organization provided a sense of collectivity. With each other, we didn't have to cover up who we really were. When a security worry arose, you had others to help you evaluate it. Most importantly, the organization had a program and a sense of purpose. As I later found out from taking in and assisting an anti-imperialist militant on the run, lone fugitives often had a much, much rougher time, both psychologically and functionally.

Once underground, we rediscovered what had always been a main activity until the frantic months of 1969: reading. Soon, and over the years, a slew of books (especially any one recommended by a Central Committee member) were circulating throughout the organization—from Toni Morrison novels to radical reinterpretations of U.S. history to studies of the Tupamaros (urban guerrillas in Uruguay); from Gerda Lerner's analysis of patriarchy to Felix Greene's highly readable and humanitarian breakdown of the workings of imperialism, *The Enemy*, to the gripping account of Berlin's underground resistance to Hitler in *The Red Orchestra*. And we eagerly read all we could find on the role of and advances by women in the national liberation struggles. Initially the main sources were articles, but by 1974 we had books such as Margaret Randall's *Cuban Women Now* and Arlene Eisen Bergman's *Women of Vietnam*.

One thinker had an especially profound influence on me, Amílcar Cabral, the leader of the struggle for independence from Portuguese colonialism in Guinea-Bissau and the Cape Verde Islands. Cabral combined an incredibly detailed knowledge of his country and people with a penetrating historical-materialist method that wasn't tethered to the European origins of Marxism-Leninism. And he looked frankly at problems that other revolutionaries tended to paper over, such as the petit-bourgeois background of many movement leaders. Instead of simply declaring the party "proletarian," Cabral sought to develop a process that would lead those with these leadership skills to merge more fully with the workers and peasants. He also admitted that, for all the progress their organization had made on the status of women, they still had a long way to go. A reprint of one of his speeches in front of a solidarity group in Italy impressed me. Cabral argued that as damaging as imperialism had been for Third World people, it had been even more tragic for the European working classes by deflecting them from revolution, from fighting for their own full emancipation, and thereby wounding their very souls. (A collection of Cabral's essays is still available from Monthly Review Press.)

The hardest part of being underground was the separation from family and old friends. Still, I was with friends in the organization and I could stay in touch with a few of the most conscious and careful who had remained above. The situation with my family was much tougher. My mom and dad were extremely naïve about the state and in any case could not in any way be expected to carry out the clandestine measures required for safe contact. In fact, soon after I went under, they took out ads in a range of radical papers urging me to get in touch with them, which served as a big neon arrow pointing to them as prime candidates for FBI surveillance. Soon two agents called on them, and my parents invited them in for coffee, hoping for their help in locating me. That year the FBI went on to visit every person whose number appeared on my parents' phone bill. Agents also paid a highly visible visit to my oldest sister where she worked. Ruth, fearing she might lose her job, was extremely upset and withdrew even further from the rest of the family. The one gnawing tension I felt being underground was knowing of my parents' anxiety but having no safe way to see them. I wrote from time to time when a comrade passing through could mail my letter from another city in another state. In those occasional letters, I reassured them that I was fine and that I loved them, that my rebellion wasn't against them but solely against the government. Later I ran into an old college friend who, although aboveground and not working with the organization, maintained some contact. He thoughtfully took the initiative to visit my folks and assure them that I was healthy, safe, and sane. His visits were a little better than my letters from random cities, but, as I later learned, none of these steps did much to comfort them.

The amount of time the FBI put into checking out all my parents' friends was just one indication of the mammoth and often illegal efforts to catch us. In 1980, two FBI agents were convicted for "black bag jobs"—illegally breaking into the homes of family and friends of WUO cadres—and a few months later were pardoned by President Reagan. No agents were ever prosecuted for the far more serious and lethal COINTELPRO felonies committed against the Black, Native, and Latino/a movements.

When we first went under, the conventional wisdom in the white Left was that we wouldn't last six months because "the FBI always got their man." Two years later, when we penetrated and bombed the Pentagon in May 1972, some of these same Left elements claimed we must be a CIA operation—how else could we have succeeded? Both misconceptions were based in the myth that the state is all-powerful and that clandestine resistance is futile. We knew, of course, that the FBI was making every effort to catch us. Our code name for them was "the shoes" because of Director J. Edgar Hoover's ridiculous edict requiring all agents to wear brown shoes, which made them easier to spot.

The shoes, who under Hoover never really went after organized crime, made us a top priority, with all of their vast resources. But as that first year rolled on, we felt increasingly secure in our clandestine practice, our new identities and personas, our ability to function. For me, I felt the most "at home" ever, now that my whole life was lived in fighting imperialism, and there was also the ego boost of believing we were doing so "on the highest level." One of our most visible and satisfying actions was the bombing of the U.S. Capitol Building on February 28, 1971, in response to the invasion of Laos and in order to highlight Congress's responsibility for the war. The next day President Nixon got on national TV and denounced this bombing (in which, as was standard with our actions, no one was hurt) as "the most dastardly act in U.S. history." I was bursting with pride: this premier war criminal and mega-mass murderer pointed to us as his worst enemy—what a tremendous compliment! Little did I know then about the government's practice of manipulating public attention to notorious criminals to make itself look good. Often when the FBI was hot on a fugitive's tail, they moved him up onto their high-profile "Ten Most Wanted List," thus ensuring themselves a much better success rate in the public eye. In short, the government liked to spotlight wanted outlaws when the FBI was about to catch them.

Encirclement

The phone wakes us up at two in the morning. The ring is omi-nous because only the handful of underground cadres in the city have the phone number. "This is Sonny; everyone has to clear out of the apartment," the familiar but now breathless voices urges. "Immediately! Don't stop to pack. The shoes just tried to run me down in the Chrysler. I managed to lose them in a mad-dash chase through a maze of side streets, and I ditched the car. But they have the license plate number. As you know, we used the same ID to register the car as for the utility bills on the apartment."

The four of us are out of the Pine Street apartment and into the night in minutes, with just the clothes on our backs. I'm not even sure we gathered up all our back-up IDs. We hear sirens in the distance but we don't see any surveillance on the street, so we carefully weave our way to another safehouse, in a completely dif-ferent neighborhood. There we wait until six o'clock and the start of commuter traffic to send our one nonfugitive and little-known cadre back to check out the area. He reports that the Pine Street apartment is swarming with police and FBI…

It had started a few days earlier.

The upper half of my body was under the car, so there was no point in my coming out to show my face when the two men in suits, who looked out of place on this dirt road in the woods of Marin County, approached us. Cal and I were there trying to repair one of the collective's cars: as I remember it, a Dodge Dart with the well-engineered slant-6 engine, which had broken down the day before. The car was registered in a woman's name, actually a well-known fugitive, but there was no picture with the ID she had used.

I knew nothing about cars but Cal, from a Western and working-class background, was a pretty good mechanic. We were running partners at the time, and the idea was for him to teach me as we worked. That's why I was under the car, and he was giving me instructions. Although a fugitive like me, Cal had not been a nationally known figure in SDS. Of course we were both well disguised, and the car we had arrived in was out of sight, so we looked like a couple of local "freaks" (slang for hippies) who had been commissioned to repair some woman's car.

The two suits said they were real estate agents and asked if we knew of any property for sale in the area. Cal said, no, he didn't know of any, and the suits departed. Cal, who had been cool in facing them, became agitated as he told me he was sure they were FBI, he could just smell it. Brown shoes were too common to be a definitive sign, though, and I thought he might be a bit paranoid or hyper-vigilant, which can easily happen underground. Why would the FBI be looking for us on a rural road where we hadn't lived or operated? But Cal was the one who had faced them, so there was no choice but to take his worries seriously. We left the Dart, returned to our car, and headed back to San Francisco to sound an alarm. With nothing more definite, Cal's warning would only mean leaving the Dart for a while, and heightened alertness.

I was overdue to check in and talk politics with two supporters, friends of friends, whose address I'd used to get ID, so I called them the next morning. "This is Bobby; I'd thought I'd stop by today."

"We're kind of busy right now. How about tomorrow for coffee and ice cream?"

"Sure, sounds good." But it didn't. "Ice cream" was our code word for heat, to let me know that I shouldn't come near them. Over the next couple of days, a couple of other comrades had similar incidents, indicating that the FBI was onto some of our IDs. Something was happening, and we had to figure out what it was.

In assessing the situation, we debated whether to ditch the Pine Street apartment. There was a link to one of the possibly hot IDs, but the connection was indirect, a couple of steps removed. Real-life security issues were never as simple as "always put safety first." We rarely had the time and money to do everything absolutely perfectly. Jettisoning precious resources unnecessarily can also endanger the organization. If you get rid of every ID, safehouse, and car at every whiff of danger, you might end up on the street, unable to withstand even a routine police stop, and certainly without the ability to do actions—our purpose for being underground. Most security decisions required hard choices, trying to balance immediate safety with securing and maintaining adequate infrastructure.

Given the value of the apartment, leadership argued for a policy of watchful waiting. The links to Pine Street were indirect and not along any paths the FBI had been known to pursue. I argued, in opposition, that while the FBI might not be sharp in terms of political or psychological assessments, they could be expected to be bureaucratically thorough. We had to assume they could and would follow the links in the chain that led to this safehouse. The "watchful waiting" position prevailed over my "links in the chain" analysis, and thus we were still in the apartment when we got Sonny's 2:00 a.m. call and evacuated just hours, perhaps minutes, before the FBI and police arrived in force.

Sonny's close encounter had been part of a bigger cat-and-mouse game that night. Earlier, two Central Committee (CC) members had pulled up at Western Union to collect some money wired by a supporter to an ID name. They spotted three men who looked like they were surveilling the area, so they hotfooted out of there, and lost the car tailing them by weaving through side streets. Then Sonny, a nonfugitive, was given the job of fetching a back-up car, and he found he had a tail. Obviously if the FBI had come into the scene ready to do a bust, they would have brought enough cars to block any getaway. Evidently they were still trying to figure out who belonged to the various IDs they were tracking, hoping to spring their trap only when they had the whole organization, or at least the key people, surrounded. After these chases, the FBI knew that we knew, and must have moved into full-court press mode, leading them to find and raid Pine Street early the next morning.

Now, clearly, they were on to us in a major way. Just a year after the townhouse and our surprising success at establishing an active underground, we were on the verge of having the whole West Coast operation and some top leadership busted. On one of those frantic couple of days after Pine Street, when I was out doing an errand trying to help shore things up, I saw a shocking newspaper headline: "Black Panthers Split!" Huey Newton in Oakland and Eldridge Cleaver in Algeria had publicly attacked each other in an acrimonious international phone call that had been broadcast live on a progressive radio station. Having no idea that internal differences had risen to that level of tension, I was stunned that such a rift could happen, and especially right then. What a terrible double blow it would be to broader movement morale if the BPP split apart and the WUO was busted all in the same month. I felt a profound sense of responsibility; we had to get on top of the offensive against us in time to avoid capture.

When we tried to chart everything involved, someone spotted the connections that explained most of the pattern: all the compromised IDs were based on a single batch of birth certificates. In the early 1970 rush to go underground, a cluster, based on earlier-found death certificates, had been obtained from the same East Coast county records office on the same day. The way the FBI had plugged into that batch became clear in retrospect. In December 1970, an underground militant had been arrested, spotted by an FBI agent in a movie theater. She didn't lead to anyone and there were no houses or cars under that ID. She wasn't wanted for serious charges, so she was released, and soon making a strong contribution to the aboveground movement. At the time, the organization considered her bust an isolated and contained incident. No one involved thought about the implications of the fact that her ID was based on a birth certificate obtained at the same time as several others. But the FBI, with the WUO as a top priority, showed dogged thoroughness on following through to where each of those certificates led. We later found out that the Western Union stake-out came from another source—someone indiscreetly bragging about his contact with the underground to a "movement" friend who was actually an infiltrator.

Within three months of that December bust, the FBI evidently had made enough progress on mapping IDs to assure President Nixon that they were about to catch us. Within days of his "most dastardly act in American history" remark, we were feeling scorched by the heat all around us.

Once we figured out the group of suspect IDs and charted everything directly and indirectly tied to them, we could see that a large part of our Bay Area infrastructure had been blown or was in danger. We had experienced a series of prods, rather than an initial quick raid, because the FBI evidently was working to draw a net around the whole organization before snapping it shut. They had come breathtakingly close to doing so. We dubbed the situation "the encirclement," which underscored that patchwork defenses wouldn't suffice. We decided to make a complete strategic retreat from the Bay Area.

A carload of us driving north finally gave in to the Oregon rain storm to stop for the night at a cheap motel. Two people rented the room and then the other four slipped in. Huddled together with little property and no clear plan, we turned on the TV, only to be barraged by commercials. Bernardine answered back, "After the revolution, advertisements will be abolished." It may seem ridiculous—six fugitives, powerless and with only a few dollars to our names, making such proclamations. But I relished her defiance and the values expressed, and I fully believed there would be a revolution that would replace the dominant commercial culture with one that cherished the lives and potential of all human beings.

Once we got to safer ground, we had two priorities: to identify the mistakes in order to avoid repeating them, and then to start rebuilding infrastructure. Most of the analysis and initiative came from the CC, who had the best overview of what had happened. As a result of my earlier argument for clearing out of Pine Street, I acquired a reputation for being "good on security." Since that position hadn't been implemented, it hadn't done any good, but earlier I had won a less pressured debate that had made a difference. When we first rented the apartment, we had to decide whether to get a telephone. No ID was required but movement people at the time felt that government wiretaps were extremely widespread. Some comrades worried that a random listening sweep might catch an indiscreet phone conversation, which would lead to the apartment. I argued that a tap on an unknown phone was unlikely, that we could be disciplined about the language we used (in practice we weren't), and that a phone could prove critical if needed for immediate, emergency communication. So I got some credit for the phone that got us out of Pine Street in the nick of time.

I was pleased to receive such recognition, but I was pretty sure I wouldn't become our security specialist. Early on in a new endeavor like armed struggle or functioning underground, one or two successes can prematurely lead to "expert" status. But over the long haul, I didn't prove to have any special flair for that line of work. Like all of us, I tried to regularly and intelligently engage in ongoing security evaluations, but it did not become my main area of responsibility.

Clearly we would never again acquire IDs in batches. The more general lesson was the imperative, whenever any setback such as the December 1970 bust happens, to systematically chart everything else it could lead to, to draw a tree of the most immediate and then more outlying connections. And to never again underestimate the FBI's bureaucratic thoroughness in following the links on a chain.

Clandestinity

The positive, proactive program to prevent such linkage was "compartmentalization," which we later learned from studying the Tupamaros, the urban guerrillas in Uruguay. The analogy came from the way submarines are built, with separate watertight compartments, so that a breach in one wall won't lead to flooding throughout the ship. The idea is to structure the organization so that the loss of a cadre or safehouse won't lead to others. The more, and more varied, the IDs, the more ability to separate things. Communication was also a major area of concern, but a complete wall wouldn't do because regular exchanges to develop political unity and forge strategy are essential. In this arena, precautions involved finding secure means of communication that didn't lead to anything else. (The Tupamaros, several orders of magnitude ahead of us as a revolutionary force in their country, were eventually crushed. From what I could tell, the Uruguayan military and police engaged in widespread round-ups and torture of legal activists to find and then break the few who had contact with the underground.)

In our culture, movies often shape our senses of reality more than actual experiences. The way the encirclement played out was striking in how it diverged from the ubiquitous spy novels and films of the day. Both James Bond and his antagonist were always technologically dazzling and technically brilliant. In the long and intricate conflict, the enemy would make just one mistake, allowing the perfect Agent 007 to prevail. In real life, we had made several mistakes, but the FBI had made one or two more. And "luck," or unpredictable contingencies, played a role too. Certainly it is critical to reduce mistakes—you never know which one will bring you down. Nonetheless, the real process is complex and varied. Broad strategy and intelligent adjustments to setbacks are usually more important than clever techniques; the human element—political consciousness and psychological strength—often trumps technology.

The guideline for clandestine practice most often adopted from the movies was that information should only be shared on a "need to know" basis. That was a fine principle for details, like person, places, things, that can lead to busts, but, in my opinion, would have been a wrong basis for building a political underground. Such specifics as what types of actions to consider, whether and how to try to influence the mass movement, how many resources to allocate to aiding other anti-imperialist fugitives, whether to develop a clandestine press—all express important political decisions. Widespread and lively political discussions are needed to forge direction and strategy—both to be democratic and because cadres putting life and liberty on the line need to have a clear understanding of why the risks are being taken. Too often the freighted term "security" can be used to restrict needed political struggles; at the same time, compromising details can be bandied around too loosely, even become a kind of currency of power, to be selectively shared with the individuals in favor with those in the know. While in the WUO, I came to see it as both necessary and possible for a clandestine group to develop a dialectic of strict and objective limits on compromising details, while still finding ways to open up and promote broad political and strategic debate throughout the organization.

While the CC members and Sonny's driving heroics that night had played a dramatic role, our overall success had been built on a much broader and stronger foundation: popular support, which meant that information flowed away from the government and to the guerrillas. The FBI evidently believed, based on traditional police work, that the IDs would lead to the addresses that would enable them to draw a net around our whole operation. But there was a layer of insulation between the addresses they found and the actual fugitives. My friends were an example of the many conscious supporters who could be counted on both to tell the police nothing and to alert us. In other cases, to have enough addresses, IDs had been mailed to hippy cultural centers—like rural communes or urban health food stores. An important principle is that the level of risk taken must be commensurate with the person's level of political commitment. However in such settings—where all kinds of people came and went and received mail, we felt there was no significant legal liability for the leaseholders. Even in these situations, because the prevailing youth culture was so anti-war and anti-police, those questioned generally provided no descriptions or other details to the authorities, but did their best to alert us to the heat if we called in. No one cooperated to try to draw us into a trap to be busted. In one instance, an agent told a young woman that it was urgent that she cooperate with the FBI because her name and address had been found with some dynamite set to blow up a bus filled with schoolchildren—but there was no way she would believe such a story about us.

Regrouping

During our period of retreat in the Northwest many of us burrowed deeply into youth culture as a refuge. We could easily drift into such communities without providing detailed job or residential histories, and we fit in with and emulated others trying to live simply and cheaply. With our ability to contact our supporters now constricted, our funds were extremely limited, but it didn't yet occur to me to get a job. I made yogurt, ate tofu, and bought produce at low-priced farmers' markets. When money got desperately low, I discovered three-day fasts (although with juice), which cleaned out my system and left me feeling great. I learned how to tie-dye T-shirts, both for gifts to those who had shown me hospitality and to occasionally sell for a little cash. I also managed to meet and work with some contacts who became long-term friends and part of our support network. (And this was the period when I got to read Doris Lessing's iconic novel about an earlier Left, the communist movement in England in the 1950s. *The Golden Notebook* vividly describes how Left men, despite their formal politics on equality, are sexist—emotionally withdrawn and manipulative with women. Ouch!)

In my memory this Northwest retreat seems like a year, but that sense must reflect how quickly I plunged into youth culture there and my relative passivity to the tasks of rebuilding the organization. The chronology shows we were back in the Bay Area, secure and functional, in five months. On August 28, 1971, the WUO bombed California Department of Corrections buildings in San Francisco and Sacramento. Seven days earlier the guards had shot and killed the charismatic prisoner activist George Jackson. Jackson had entered prison as an eighteen-year-old sentenced to one year to life for a secondary role in a seventy-dollar robbery. As often happened with a Black prisoner who showed any self-respect and defiance, ten years later he still had no prospect of parole. In the interim he had transformed himself into a well-read and extremely eloquent advocate for Black Power, social justice, and revolution. His book, *Soledad Brother*, was one of the most moving works of the time and is still inspiring people today. Jackson was a field marshal in the BPP, and he was considered the leading national figure in—the spearhead of—prison resistance. Clearly the authorities wanted him dead, and regardless of the different versions of how events played out that day, they fulfilled their wish on August 21, 1971. My personal response was so emotional that a long poem—and I was someone who virtually never wrote poetry—simply erupted out of me. The WUO, which had barely escaped getting wiped out in March, bombed two different CDC offices in two different cities in August.

Action

Our past experience hasn't eliminated the jitters, and the tension is thick as the three of us, all guys this particular time, head to the action. The driver is so nervous and overcautious that he stops for a green light. I'm thinking, that it would be healthier to openly admit our fears, but men generally don't do that. Looking for a diplomatic way to break the ice, I say, "I wonder how long it will take before we have nerves of steel." My buddy, the most macho of us three, shoots back, "Right now I'd settle for nerves of jello!" He's serious, but his remark gives us a chance to laugh, relax a bit, drive through the green lights, and focus on the work ahead.

George Jackson's death proved to be the catalyst, 2,500 miles away in Attica, New York, for the biggest and most dramatic prison uprising in

U.S. history. Prisoners had already been organizing there against the brutal and demeaning conditions, but it was the murder of the greatly admired Jackson that pushed activity into high gear. (For a full account of events see Tom Wicker's *A Time to Die*.) On September 9, 1971, about 1,500 prisoners took over the D-block yard, holding about forty guards hostage as a protection against attack. They developed a list of fifteen practical proposals about ending the prevailing racism, brutality, religious persecution, and lack of constructive programs. Later they added five broad political demands such as being allowed asylum in anti-imperialist countries. The twenty-one-year-old L.D. Barkley stated the central theme most eloquently: "We are men! We are not beasts, and we do not intend to be beaten and driven as such." The prisoners called in a number of respected outsiders, such as BPP Chairman Bobby Seale and radical lawyer William Kunstler, to act as mediators.

Underground, we followed the unfolding takeover for those first three days with intense interest and high hopes. The civil rights and then Black power movements had created a context to finally expose the inhumanity of prison conditions in the U.S. The rebellion exemplified how Black Power could be a spearhead to unite all the oppressed, as Black, Puerto Rican, Native American, Asian, and white prisoners stood up together. Believing the level of public scrutiny was a shield against mass murder, I was hopeful for a positive resolution with significant reforms.

But New York Governor Nelson Rockefeller calculated that his ambition to become president would best be served by a tough-on-crime stance. He refused to come to Attica to negotiate and ordered state troopers to retake the prison by force on September 13. That all-out assault left thirty-nine men dead—twenty-nine prisoners and ten guards—and another eighty-nine wounded. Recognizable leaders, like L.D. Barkley and Sam Melville, a white anti-imperialist in prison for bombings that had preceded the WUO, were killed. Since a guard and three prisoners had died earlier in the takeover, the overall death toll was forty-three. (Later, Attica was regularly referred to as 'the largest killing of Americans by Americans since the Civil War.' However, that grim title was awarded only because the mainstream media and history obliterated memory of an even more heinous massacre: On June 1, 1921, in Tulsa, Oklahoma, white rioters backed by the national guard and police killed an untallied hundreds of Black citizens.)

The news of the police assault and thirty-nine deaths was shocking and sickening. I was furious at the state's violence, but also at the media's lies. Headlines initially screamed that the inmates had killed the ten hostages by slashing their throats, and some of those murdered guards had been castrated, with their private parts stuffed into their mouths. The next day the autopsies revealed that not one hostage was killed or in any way cut with a knife; all ten had died from state troopers' gunfire. Meanwhile the prisoners, who had treated their hostages humanely, were being tortured, quite literally, with kicks, broken glass, and cigarette burns by the authorities who retook the prison. But that didn't make the news.

We felt an absolute imperative to express solidarity with the prisoners and to highlight, for white youth, the central importance of Attica. On September 17, the WUO bombed NYS Department of Correctional Services (DOCS) headquarters in Albany. While many prisoners felt buoyed by the action, we also received feedback that some questioned the limited nature of our response. Why did the WUO make a point of bombing DOCS offices at a time when no one was there? This implicit criticism of our purely symbolic action was completely understandable. Prisoners had been murdered wholesale, without any firearms to fight back, and continued to be tormented, yet the authorities responsible had paid no price at all.

I felt that the criticism was righteous, but, nonetheless, that our strategy was right. In a way we felt caught between two contradictory poles for assessing armed action. The politics of solidarity with Third World peoples meant pushing ourselves toward fighting at their level; yet the need both to have adequate support and to still influence a mass movement militated against severing ourselves from our base of support. To me the bigger error was expressed by the large sectors of the white Left that argued against any armed action before the (predominantly white) "masses" or "working class" supported it. Given the history of racism in America, the majority of white people would never be ready for revolutionary action without a Left leadership that promoted identification and solidarity with Third World struggles; and even then our goal couldn't be a majority but rather a significant mass base. On the other hand, the killing of ruling class individuals or their armed enforcers, no matter how justified by the bloody war they waged on the oppressed, would be hard for those who hadn't experienced the repression directly, even radical white youth, to accept. If our mass support evaporated, we wouldn't be able to sustain armed struggle on any level.

Measured by either standard—full solidarity with the Third World or support by a majority of white people—the WUO was a failure. But we were trying to be a bridge between those two poles. As I understood it from our internal discussions, our strategy of armed propaganda had five main aims: 1) draw some heat so that the police and FBI couldn't concentrate all their forces on Black, Latino/a, Native, and Asian groups; 2) create a visible (if invisible!) example of whites fighting in solidarity with Third World struggles; 3) educate broadly about the major political issues; 4) identify key institutions of oppression; and 5) encourage white youth to find a range of creative ways to resist despite repression. These considerations may seem abstract today, when armed struggle is not on the agenda for the anti-imperialist movement in the U.S., but they resonated and even had a certain urgency at a time when revolutionary struggles were raging throughout the world. In any case, the centerpiece is not any particular set of tactics but rather a politics of creating an example and presence of solidarity with people of color, which is also the essential step for developing any kind of revolutionary movement worthy of that name among white people.

Even good politics can get mixed with more self-serving motives. An organization can do actions more to establish its leadership than to advance the struggle, and individuals can feel driven to achieve status within the organization. Two examples of the latter problem caused me some anxious moments. In both cases cadres who were not yet established leaders in military work courted danger because they became overly eager to prove themselves.

I was working for the first time as a team with two women whose judgment I greatly respected. There was a major problem: the only reasonable spot we found for the device was not a good hiding place, so we were worried that the device could be found and disarmed. My coworkers proposed dispensing with our usual warning call for this one action. I felt they got caught up in their fear of looking like a failure to leadership if the action didn't work. But, making sure there were no casualties and showing our care on that matter was always the priority. I insisted, and they quickly came around, on the warning call. In the event, the action was a success.

In another situation a cadre who was seen as a potential emerging leader for military work realized, only after the device had been placed, that he'd not rewound the watch in the timing mechanism. Fearing that his device would fail to go off, he implored me to go to the site and recover it so that it could be rewound. I reluctantly acceded—and was dead wrong to do so. Such a recovery effort was very dangerous in terms both of getting caught and of rehandling an explosive device. When I got there, I was relieved to find that conditions made the retrieval impossible. To be safe, we still made the warning call at the appointed time. The next morning's news told us the bomb had gone off, but two hours later than planned. (Evidently, the watch kept going but slowed considerably as it wound down.) Thankfully, two hours late was still before anyone had arrived for work. (This example shows that there was some luck involved in our proud record of avoiding casualties.) The news accounts confirmed my suspicions that the police, despite their claims, did not make the effort to clear buildings or defuse bombs. As always, the media described how the police, upon receiving the call, were preparing to rush in just as the bomb went off, but we knew that they had received the warning long before detonation.

These two worst examples from my experience did not lead to any casualties or setbacks. Given the culture we come from, ego, status, and prestige are bound to rear their heads in any challenging endeavor. Our shortcoming, in my retrospective view, was not that these forces were in play but rather that we did not develop an open way to talk about and struggle with them. Nonetheless, given the context of the time, our actions (except for the Leary escapade) were well conceived and politically effective. Our political problems were revealed more in the times we didn't act. Ego and self-aggrandizement later proved to be corrosive, not so much in the actions themselves but instead in eating away at the very undergirdings of the organization.

A month after Attica, the all-women Proud Eagle Tribe of the WUO carried out another successful action against war research, this time at MIT. After the U.S. mined North Vietnamese harbors and bombed Hanoi in 1972, the WUO responded by bombing the Pentagon on May 19 (the birthday of both Ho Chi Minh and Malcolm X). But then a one-year hiatus followed, more than twice as long as the inaction after the encirclement. This time we weren't on the run. Our problems were internal, and our metabolism was slowing down toward paralysis.

Status and Hierarchy

Our collective gathers with a visiting member of the Central Committee for a meeting to assess direction and strategy. We also have a specific piece of business. By mutual consent the trial period with potential recruit, Janie, hasn't worked out. She's not a fugitive, and we will formalize agreement for her to resurface. I haven't met her before, but Holly, the cadre working with her, was sure from the beginning that Janie wouldn't make it and therefore went to great lengths to keep her from knowledge of our compartmentalized support structure.

Janie addresses the collective: "These two months have shown me that I'm not suited for underground work. Under the stress, I became literally paranoid. Once when I returned unexpectedly and rang the bell at the safehouse, I was sure I heard people whispering and then someone hustling out the back way. But when I asked the comrades there, they assured me that nothing like that had happened. It seemed so real to me; I must be paranoid."

Everyone in the collective is nodding and smiling, relieved that there will be no acrimony involved in their decision on Janie. But my heart is pounding because, even though I wasn't there at the time, I know that the incident did happen; several supporters had been hustled out the back. Despite the demands of security, it's just too cruel, and I blurt out, "You're not paranoid, Janie, the incident you perceived really happened." She screams, "How could you do that to me?" and, crying, flies out the door. I've never before felt so much tension in such a small space; a searing electric current seems to fill the room, as the whole collective turns on me for causing such a potential breach in security. "Look what you did!" "How irresponsible!" and more. The wave of vehemence is so intense that I can't find my voice to defend myself. I'm sure my position as leader of the collective is finished. The CC member, himself somewhat intimidated, takes a deep breath and then quickly deflates the attack. "Don't blame him for being honest."

After the encirclement, the CC decided we shouldn't keep our forces concentrated in any one area. As we diversified geographically, I found myself, in kind of reprise of Denver, leading a small collective in a city without a day-to-day CC presence. Once again that meant missing some of the key political debates, but it afforded a greater range of initiative. A big and welcome difference from Denver was that this time I had a coleader, a woman whose politics and organizing work I admired. Our gender balance reflected the organization as a whole. Of the five CC members, two were women, with Bernardine Dohrn identified as "first secretary" and primary spokesperson. On the next level, regional leadership was generally shared by a man and a woman.

Such parity was almost unheard-of in Left organizations of the day, where men always heavily predominated. Our difference was more a tribute to the women's individual assertive efforts to build anti-imperialist politics than to any organized program against sexism. The weakness was that women in leadership tended to be part of a leading heterosexual couple, and women aspiring to leadership felt some social pressure to do so. The lesbians and women-identified women who argued for more of a feminist program usually weren't seen as leaders. (For a fuller account of WUO struggle around feminism, drawing on unpublished internal documents, see Dan Berger's *Outlaws of America*.)

After two years underground, now in my late twenties, I began to yearn for a more serious, committed relationship. My new longing and complicated circumstances hit me with a double whammy as I fell in love almost simultaneously with two different women, one under and one above, in my compartmentalized world. Of course such a situation was untenable, and organizational standards, although not always scrupulously followed, required that each woman be told about the other and that we resolve the situation. Otherwise secrecy could impose a whopping power imbalance. The initial excitement with the under comrade wasn't, I soon realized, so much a romantic spark as a vibrant personal connection; we were able to define and build our relationship as a strong friendship. Meanwhile any above/under romance has its own complications, which made it essential to designate a woman cadre to work closely with Laurie so that her political relationship to the organization wasn't solely through her boyfriend, me.

Before long, I moved in with Laurie. We considered that secure because she had no history in SDS and no known personal connections with Weatherpeople. Although her politics on the war and racism were clear, she'd never played a visible public role. Living together provided a more passionate and consistent love life than either of us had experienced in our more freewheeling days. But beyond the personal chemistry, there was another whole dimension to the relationship: her kids. A few years older than I, Laurie was young when she had children, so they were already school age. I couldn't kid myself that I'd in any way become a full-fledged coparent, but I was crazy about them. Even though my underground status meant that I shunned certain public scenes and that I might have to flee the home on a moment's notice, we had lots of fun together. In a way, I enjoyed the great benefits without the burdens, as I lived many of the joys of parenting without the awesome responsibilities of financial support and long-term stability—and what would it mean for the kids if I had to suddenly disappear? (As it happens, even well after Laurie and I had broken up, I was able to help the eldest child, then a teen, work through a crisis in a moment when mother/daughter communications had broken down.)

Laurie was a working-class woman who had long ago divorced her abusive husband. Living with her I learned for the first time what an incredibly demanding as well as rewarding job it was to be a single mother. She was also the survivor of a brutal rape, which had happened before the women's movement began to challenge the way victims were treated. Laurie tearfully told me how everyone, family and friends, had blamed her, even though the rapist came in through a second story window and held a gun to her head. After that she was further humiliated when the police convinced her to identify a suspect who turned out to be innocent.

Laurie became increasingly feminist in the course of our relationship. She generously credited me with providing the respect and support that helped her bloom in this way. But there were also growing frictions in the situation. The status imbalances of under/above and more/less politically experienced compounded society's preexisting male/female power disparity. And Laurie was not part of a collective with a women's caucus that could serve as a counterweight to the male dominant inertia of the traditional couple. She became active in the local women's center, where people were understandably skeptical of the phantom "supportive boyfriend" who never showed up at the center to help. Our relationship as a couple ended (on good terms) after a little more than a year, but in that time I learned a tremendous amount about life and politics from Laurie, about raising kids, and I guess about my own values. My next relationship grew to be a lifetime bond.

Another rewarding aspect of underground life was reconnecting with nature. Although I had gone camping since I was one year old, outdoor life was just beginning to catch on in a mass way in the early 1970s. Campgrounds were still cheap; wildernesses still unpopulated. Laurie and the kids and I spent a week camping on the wild and lovely southern Oregon coast. In later years, I went backpacking by myself. On one three-day trip I hiked in the spectacular High Sierras; on another, I walked (and swam) along the gorgeous shoreline of Olympic National Park. The reflowering of a love of nature within Weather helped us respond positively to the emerging environmental movement, even if we hadn't yet fully incorporated it into our politics.

But the human dynamics in the WUO were mixed, at best. Many Weather folks looking back feel the problems of hierarchy the most intensely. What I felt at the time, and what I miss, is the strong, positive sense of community, built on the basis of our common purpose and reinforced by our interdependence for safety and survival.

Democratic Centralism

Our organizational model was democratic centralism because we aspired to become disciplined and successful revolutionaries, like those in the struggles we so admired. But we didn't have a conscious critique or effective practice to ensure that the structure didn't get co-opted by ego and hierarchy.

In the Chinese Revolution, Mao led breakthroughs such as basing the revolution in the peasantry, carrying out needed democratic reforms as a basis to go on to build socialism, recognizing that class struggle continues even after the seizure of state power. According to the official Chinese version of history, Mao was singularly right, usually contravening the conventional wisdom, at every crucial turning point. When someone has a record like that, how do you ever disagree with him?

On a much more modest scale, I had a similar problem with the leadership of the WUO. I had veered off course into militarism while the current central committee had guided us through the earth-shattering crisis following the townhouse. After that turning point, they had the confidence and ability to build a secure underground apparatus, while I was still recovering psychologically. So, when a disagreement arose, I tended to assume the CC was right and I was wrong.

But it wasn't just my problem. In fact, pretty much all democratic-centralist organizations—certainly in the white Left but also throughout the Third World—became too top-down, as the legacy of millennia of hierarchical societies weighed far too heavily on our consciousness and practice. Being underground created additional pressures. The danger of being captured and the demands of armed actions put a premium on discipline and cohesion, while clandestinity and compartmentalization made open, organization-wide debate difficult.

We could have done more to clear this second hurdle. We could have developed an internal newsletter (to be destroyed after reading) where cadres from different sectors of the organization, using code names, could argue positions on the key political and strategic issues we faced. In practice, while there was some travel and direct exchange among collectives, a lot of the communication went through the CC, the only ones in regular touch with all regions. I remember asking about comrades in other regions and getting answers like, "She's great," or, "He's having a rough time right now." That kind of personal, subjective characterization often masked political differences that should have been argued out more explicitly and fully. Sally, who is described as "messed up," may in fact be challenging the prevailing political line, but if I don't know that, I can't join the debate.

This problem piggybacked on the broader one of status consciousness. We deemed armed clandestine work as the most important, as being "revolutionary on the highest level." But there was little or no prospect of accomplishing that as a lone individual. So, many of us were reluctant to risk arguing positions that might put us at odds with the leadership and possibly even jeopardize our place in the organization.

Additionally, such a close-knit and restricted world made any implicit threat of social isolation especially intimidating. If one became an outcast, he had almost no place to go and no way to function as an activist. (As I later learned, even "nonhierarchical communities," including feminists and anarchists, can also shun open political debate and instead use social ostracism as a powerful club against dissent.) I certainly didn't want to get labeled as "messed up" or "unreliable."

Regional leaders and local cadres tended to ape the same power dynamics toward those below us in the organizational structure. Differences were discussed but tended to get resolved by the weight of leadership or the prestige of being under. Above supporters often didn't know about others who might be raising the same issues. "Need to know" too often meant "don't ask." Overall, political discussions and even debates happened all the time, but the boundaries were too narrow and the playing field too tilted.

Some supporters educated me about a basic power differential on a more practical level. I knew how to contact them but they had no way to get in touch with me. That procedure was reasonable in terms of protecting the clandestine core, but it left them feeling passive and powerless to take initiative or to raise issues with me. On occasion, I would go for a long time without being in touch. Because I knew it was wrong to ask for support without political agreement, I would put off calling until I had time to meet them for in-depth discussions. But the long break left the supporters worried about my safety and security. They taught me that it was much more considerate and empowering to call in often, even if I didn't have the time for a meeting, to let them know I was OK and to see if they had some concerns that I needed to prioritize.

The incident when our collective almost convinced Janie she was paranoid and then vehemently turned on me was a most dramatic one, not a typical example of the power dynamics. Overall, the higher we were in the hierarchy, the more responsibility we had for perpetuating the pecking order. But sometimes the leaders who have set the prevailing terms feel confident enough to challenge the more outlandish instances. In this case, the cadre who had disparaged Janie had herself been similarly put down at an earlier time as "shaky" and "having a hard time." Once she was back in good graces, she exercised that same kind of power on a new recruit. Terms that characterized people by personality or psychology—very similar to the in-crowd/out-crowd mentality of junior high school—often preempted sorely needed open and vigorous political struggle.

In Janie's case, the personalized put-downs were all wrong. She had the courage to return to the meeting and confront us in a direct and determined way about how she had been treated, and she went on to make an invaluable and ongoing political contribution, both inside the WUO and long after its demise. At the time of the incident, internal status consciousness had probably been intensified by how little the organization was accomplishing in the world.

The Doldrums

The WUO is ailing and in danger of dying. The sense of purpose and even some of the cadres are drifting away. Our small collective holds a series of discussions to try to thrash out goals and strategy in a period when the revolutionary impulses of youth culture have drastically receded. Lionel throws out a bold challenge: "We've lost touch with reality by living underground. The majority of people don't support, they actually oppose our bombings. We need to develop roots in the working class." I retort, "The white working class that you're talking about is a part of reality—an about 4 percent part if our standpoint is humankind. Solidarity with Third World people is still the cutting edge for forging any revolutionary politics worthy of that name among white people."

The full list of Weather actions is impressive. The inactivity from May 1972 to May 1973 should be equally striking. That year includes these events, with no public WUO response: the Christmas bombings of Hanoi; the January 1973 assassination of Amílcar Cabral (who was not only the leader of Guinea-Bissau and the Cape Verde Islands' struggle against Portuguese colonialism, but also an invaluable revolutionary theorist worldwide); the rocking of the country in February by the Native American occupation of Wounded Knee and the FBI's violent military siege on it; fierce and costly battles between the BLA and police forces. Where was the WUO?

At the time, the year felt pretty much like any other: lots of meetings to maintain our support network, travel and living in the counterculture, and political study sessions. One change after the encirclement was that most of us had part-time jobs for money. I worked bagging groceries, and the union medical plan afforded me some long-neglected dental work. The twenty-five hours a week at the job had the benefit of talking with, and learning more about the lives and ideas of, other workers. Our collective also held our first group discussions of the politics of sexual orientation, as lesbian and gay members explained that they felt little support inside the organization for lesbian/gay culture and politics.

When circulating among hippies, I sensed a gradual shift in sensibilities. On a couple of delightful occasions in 1970–71, I met folks while hitchhiking who exulted to me (by all appearances just another anonymous hippy) about the most recent WUO action. Opposition to the war and a vague sense of "brotherhood" (as opposed to the most blatant forms of racism) had been the common denominators. Now there was a growing emphasis on communes and spirituality—the latter both in the progressive sense that we're all one soul and in the more mystical way of looking to various supernatural forces for the answers to our problems.

The communes impressed me as a wonderful effort to live more cooperatively and more in harmony with nature. They also resonated with my 1968 critique of consumerism—but that had only been theory; these people were creating real-life alternatives. The display of culture, crafts, and colors at the many "Renaissance Faires" was mesmerizing. In my view, the communes also offered a potential model and even nucleus for responding to the future crisis of imperialism. As the colonies liberated themselves from exploitation, the lavish and wasteful U.S. economy would unravel. In the deep depression that ensued, reactionary forces would do their best to mobilize masses of white people on a virulently racist basis to reconquer "our" wealth and resources around the world. (Such a racist mass mobilization to gain or regain empire is, in my opinion, the heart of fascism.) Any humane alternative would have to be based on solidarity with the rest of humanity, but also would have to offer a realizable alternative to plunder by showing white Americans that there were less prodigal, less destructive, more sustainable and more satisfying ways to live. So the communes could be the seeds of an ecologically sound, homegrown socialism that allied with the Third World peoples who were reclaiming their own lands and natural riches.

But by mid-1972 the communes were becoming more about re-treat—not just to the countryside but also from opposing the system. That growing undercurrent was expressed in a proliferation of theories on how to achieve change without struggle—beliefs that a new consciousness would sweep the nation or that a new astrological age was dawning or that we could change the world by living in harmony with the spirits of nature or with the feminine goddesses. In a way, youth culture as a whole was reprising the sense of crisis and retreat into magical thinking that had afflicted the New Left four years earlier, when, finding out that it was up against a colossal and ruthless power, much of the Left retreated into a form of magical thinking: a recitation of Marxist dictums on revolutionary agency as a substitute for the concrete analysis of our actual conditions.

The turning point for the broader counterculture came in the wake of Kent State. The first response was massive protests and heightened militancy. But after a while, especially when that outpouring didn't pro-duce instant change in who wielded power, the reality sunk in that the government was willing to kill white kids too, and over the next couple of years many youth shifted away from political struggle and into utopian communities and forms of magical thinking. After I came to this analysis of the impact of Kent State, I regularly chafed at the oft-repeated and way oversimplified Left slogan, "Repression Breeds Resistance." It can—but it also can produce demoralization. As activists, we can't fool ourselves that the process is automatic. We have to find ways to show that resistance can continue and even grow in the face of repression—in fact that was one of the main reasons we went underground in 1970.

The companion and bigger factor in ebbing militancy was that white youth felt less directly threatened by the war as the draft ended, as Nixon shifted casualties to the (U.S.-created) South Vietnamese Army still backed by a ferocious U.S. bombing campaign, and as peace negotiations inched forward in Paris. At the time, I scoffed at the idea that fear of conscription had propelled the movement. Hadn't the anti-war activism started at colleges campuses, where students enjoyed draft deferments? To me opposition had an idealistic basis, but the end of the draft did correlate with a receding movement.

None of this changed our sense of ourselves, at least not consciously. We avidly followed every major battle in and the peace negotiations for Vietnam. We were also excited about Chile from 1970 to 1973, after Salvador Allende was elected president. We embraced his hope for a peaceful path to socialism, since the U.S. was so bogged down in Vietnam that it could not readily invade Chile. We also were learning about various African liberation movements and deepening our sense of solidarity with the Palestinian struggle, which I felt was a completely consistent and necessary companion to my history of opposition to anti-Semitism.

A few cadres got tired of being under, didn't see the purpose in it, and drifted away. After my debate with Lionel, I doubted that he was a sudden, heartfelt convert to the traditional Left politics on the working class; instead, he seemed to be looking for a justification for leaving the underground. We grew up in a competitive, macho culture, which made it hard to admit it even to ourselves, let alone to others, when we didn't feel capable of continuing valuable but dangerous work; instead one would feel a need to question the work itself. The lesson to me was that peer pressure or daring people into high-risk activity was not only wrong but also counterproductive. To be sustained, such a demanding commitment had to come from the heart; otherwise people who wanted to get out but couldn't say so openly would unconsciously make costly mistakes or seek to discredit the whole enterprise.

Although a few people left, the organization was still intact and reasonably safe from the FBI hunt; we certainly had the capacity to act. Since I wasn't someone who generally played the role of initiating actions, I was passive to their absence—didn't really feel it until Wounded Knee, and even then took some comfort in being told that some of our aboveground members had taken daring action to get supplies into the besieged Native Americans. Looking back now, I think we were too much a part of youth culture and swept along in its drift away from struggle. That could happen because we hadn't accomplished nearly enough of our historic task of developing the widespread anti-war sentiment into a deeper anti-racist and anti-imperialist consciousness. As the anti-war movement receded, we did too.

The Black liberation movement had been our most direct source of inspiration and political leadership, but underground we had much less contact—for most of us it was none at all—with revolutionary Black groups or with Native, Latino/a, or Asian organizations either. In the wake of the withering COINTELPRO attacks on revolutionary nationalists, and especially after the split of the Panthers, the spearheads for radical change and activism throughout U.S. society had been considerably blunted. The people we most admired, the BLA, were now getting gunned down by the police and were on the run.

When I asked a member of the central committee why the BLA was taking lots of busts while we weren't, the answer (which I didn't openly question) was the quality of their clandestine technique compared to ours. The discussion didn't delve into the decisive differences rooted in racism: we could raise money from middle-class friends, while the BLA took its greatest losses doing robberies; we could blend into a much larger and less harassed population; and we were much less prone to routine police stops, and when they did happen, we could talk our way out of them, while Black people faced frequent, hostile stops which, for underground cadres, often led to shoot-outs.

Our complacent discussion about the BLA's far more dire straits crystallized how our 1972–73 doldrums resulted from an opportunism, a sliding on principles that had emerged earlier, even while we were doing more actions. We hadn't deigned to answer, or even to seriously consider, the Panther 21's on-point criticism of our "New Morning" statement of December 1970; and we hadn't grappled at all with the BPP International Section's discomfort with providing refuge for Timothy Leary. Our unwillingness to be accountable to revolutionary Black forces and our pandering to white-centered, prodrug, and nonstruggle elements of youth culture allowed that initial infection to spread to near-paralysis two years later.

In our own way, we were repeating the historic failures we had so trenchantly criticized in the white Lefts of earlier generations. Almost all the promising radical movements among white people—populism, women's suffrage, trade unions—had lost their revolutionary edge by accepting immediate benefits for themselves at the expense of people of color within the U.S. and around the world. The most immediate and galling example was the way the AFL-CIO had acted both to exclude Blacks and women from the best-paid jobs and to actively support imperial interventions throughout the world. (For a more developed and insightful study of the broader history, see Robert Allen and Pamela Allen, *Reluctant Reformers: Racism and Social Reform Movements in the United States*; also, J. Sakai, *Settlers: The Mythology of the White Proletariat*.) Now we had started down a similar path with youth culture: we found a promising radical base among white people without fully engaging the difficult but historically crucial job of transforming that into a revolutionary movement, a staunch ally of people of color. A serious attempt to do so would have involved: 1) also relating to and learning from the women's movement; 2) making more effort to reach working-class youth; and most importantly, 3) being more consistent and thorough about forging anti-war consciousness into a deeper anti-racism by fostering situations where white youth worked in alliances with and learned from people of color. Instead, we floated along as youth culture ebbed back from political struggle to counterculture niches—even as ferocious wars were still being waged against Third World peoples from Angola to Guatemala to Harlem to Palestine to Wounded Knee.

I didn't understand all that in 1973, but I did become increasingly uncomfortable with our inaction and drift. Since our birth, Weather had proclaimed ourselves to be revolutionaries, anti-imperialists, staunch allies of Black liberation. But now, at a time when so much more needed to be done, we were acting like we had been nothing more than the militant edge of the now receding anti-war movement.

Kathy Boudin

During this period, what had been a warm and cherished friendship blossomed into something more. There had been no romantic spark when Kathy Boudin and I first met in 1969, which perhaps made us less self-conscious in developing a lively exchange of ideas and ideals and in enjoying a common love of nature. The depth of that friendship provided a solid foundation for a love that grew into our becoming long-term life partners who eventually went on to the miraculous experience and incredible bond of having a child together.

I won't attempt to integrate this central relationship into the narrative. I don't want to be misinterpreted as speaking for her. Another major obstacle to writing about us is that we, and Kathy in particular, have been the objects of reams of grotesque slanders, generally farther from the truth than the most outlandish science fiction and designed to discredit us as human beings. To try to respond to or answer the misinformation would take a book in itself.

Here I'll just take one of the countless, purposeful examples of slander. The "authoritative" book on the "Brink's case," *The Big Dance*, stated as solid fact that I opposed Kathy's breast-feeding of our baby because that was a form of inequality between the sexes. You can just hear the subtext echoing: "This radical is so vile that he's not just against God and country but he's even against motherhood!" In reality I was, of course, totally and enthusiastically for breast-feeding, which was never even a question between us.

The ways that Kathy has been so pervasively mischaracterized and maligned are especially unfair. Here I'll just briefly say that the public demonization of her is a total opposite of the real person. I fell in love with Kathy because she is an incredibly compassionate, talented, and thoughtful woman from whom I learned a tremendous amount and who challenged me in our joint effort to build a loving relationship consistent with our belief in equality. We certainly weren't free of the problems couples often have, including separations. But I deeply feel that we always treated each other with a tremendous amount of mutual respect. And the ecstasy and fulfillment of having a child together has created a most cherished lifetime bond.

Prairie Fire

The sense of purpose and the cadres themselves seem to be drifting away. With a CC member visiting our region, I'm excited to have a strong leader as an ally in my push for rebuilding the organization. One of our members repeats her question from our earlier discussions: "Why do we need an organization?" I'm about to answer, as I have before, "So we can fight imperialism," but before I can open my mouth I'm taken aback by the CC member's immediate response: "So we can lead everything."

As the organization floundered in 1972, Bill Ayers began what turned out to be a wonderful initiative: writing a book-length statement of our views and analysis to reconsolidate the organization, to articulate why our purpose went beyond just stopping the war, and to have a basis for dialogue with the thousands still left in the aboveground movement. I liked his idea but never imagined that a writing project would galvanize the WUO, a group that always distinguished itself by action. As Bill wrote away, with one or two other people making major contributions, I was supportive but had no direct role. But once the draft was completed, the entire organization became engaged and animated in discussing it. We eventually named the book *Prairie Fire: The Politics of Revolutionary Anti-Imperialism* (PF). The title came from Mao's famous saying that "a single spark can start a prairie fire"—meaning that under certain conditions a timely initiative can set off massive and intense revolutionary struggle.

The process around the book was amazing, the one time that democracy flowered in the WUO. Every under collective as well as above members and close supporters read the draft, and we were all encouraged to criticize and propose changes. The section that most surprised and impressed me was the chapter on U.S. history. In the past, movement debates on the relationship of race and class had been waged by trotting out competing quotes from Marx and Lenin. One side would cite the Marxist truths that the proletariat is the only revolutionary class. The other would stress the analysis of a bought-off labor aristocracy under imperialism and the importance of "the national question." *PF* moved past that approach of arguing by authority and plucking quotes, to using a truly Marxist method in looking at how the actual formations and struggles had developed in the U.S.; history was our best tool for analyzing race and class.

PF as a whole was breaking new ground for us in paying more attention to class, in seeing the working class as central among the whites we needed to reach and organize in an anti-racist way. The revolutionary youth movement had been a good first step toward deepening our class base, but it certainly wasn't adequate and it was losing momentum, so we had to figure out how to move forward.

While I welcomed greater attention to class, some aspects of the draft bothered me. Much of the language, especially outside the history section, slipped back into or borrowed from traditional white Left formulations. There were too many places where class could be read as subsuming race, denying or fudging the independent and leading role of the national liberation struggles within the U.S. Two comrades and I took on the job of going through the text systematically, not to delete class but to make sure the relationship between race and class was clear and sharp throughout. While in the past those criticizing leadership ran the risk of disapproval and ostracism, in this case our reworking of the text was welcomed and most of our changes were incorporated. Both the content of and the process around *PF* left me energized and optimistic about the future of the WUO.

After thorough discussions of the working draft, each collective elected a representative who, along with selected aboveground members, attended a small national meeting (which required careful security preparations) for final modifications and ratification. For Weather, this exercise in democracy was unprecedented. Elected by my collective, in part to argue the position on race and class, I found the national get-together to be a place for lively political exchange. One question of the day was what position to take on the Sino-Soviet split. With the communist parties of

China and the USSR locked in a bitter dispute, communists and other revolutionaries around the world lined up behind one or the other as the leader of the Left worldwide. The dispute involved major ideological differences, and there was also a lot at stake in terms of material aid. Aid wasn't an issue for us, but for guerrillas getting carpet-bombed every day, access to surface-to-air missiles could make a big difference.

One or two members argued strongly for alignment with either side, but most of us felt mixed. We had long been alienated from the USSR as bureaucratic and repressive, and we had welcomed the Chinese Revolution because it had happened in a Third World country, mobilized the peasantry, maintained a more militant line against imperialism, and recognized the need to continue class struggle even after seizing state power. But the USSR, even if its motives were based more on competition with the U.S. than on principles, was providing valuable material aid to most of the leading national liberation struggles. The Chinese, in their sectarian elevation of "Soviet Revisionism" to "number-one enemy," had actually blocked a trainload of Russian supplies headed to Vietnam, and they also backed the CIA-sponsored guerrilla group (FNLA) that was fighting against the national liberation movement, led by the Soviet-backed MPLA, in Angola. "Foreign policy" *should* be a reflection of the revolutionary character of the home government—but in this situation we saw a major divergence. As I remember it, *PF* noted this mixed reality, mentioning both the advances of the Chinese Revolution and the importance of Soviet aid to national liberation, without aligning with either—a most unusual position at the time.

The full political content of that position was crystallized for me later by a comrade's comments. After the national meeting we dispersed in pairs to bring the ratified version back to the collectives. I was teamed with a leader from another region. When we were asked about this section, she fielded the question: "The point is, we're not taking the Sino [China] side and we're not taking the Soviet side. We *are* firmly rooted in a *pronational liberation* position. What that means is that we, unlike most communist parties, do not base our support on which side they align with. Instead we look at the national liberation struggle itself. We support the group that is fighting hardest against imperialism and that has the greatest mass support within their nation."

Without the benefit of rereading *PF*, my memory is that overall the book was a valuable statement of revolutionary anti-imperialist politics. One advance for us was doing at least a little self-criticism, including of our earlier failure to respond to the open letter from the Panther 21. The book also had major gaps and weaknesses. It talked about women's liberation, and had some discussion of the oppression of women in jobs and by welfare agencies, but I don't remember much programmatic substance beyond mobilizing women to fight imperialism, or any self-criticism for our failures to support the women's movement; there was only minimal mention and support of lesbian/gay/bisexual/transgender (LGBT) issues or politics. And I don't remember any serious assessment of the Revolutionary Youth Movement, which had been our main strategy since 1968. What had been right and wrong about RYM? What were the potentials and shortcomings of youth culture in 1973? The book also had some other strengths—like an in-depth assessment of the Vietnam War and its role in history, and a highlighting of the democratic effort to build socialism in Chile. (*Prairie Fire* is included in *Sing a Battle Song*, edited by Bill Ayers, Bernardine Dohrn, and Jeff Jones, Seven Stories Press.)

1974 brought an unanticipated but exhilarating boost to the politics of revolutionary anti-imperialism. On April 25, the dictatorship that had ruled Portugal with an iron hand since 1932 was overthrown. Popular discontent had been central, and radicals, including socialists and communists, were major forces in the new constellation of power. The new government soon ceded independence to all of Portugal's remaining colonies. The series of colonial wars in Africa had drained Portugal's resources and economy, and that created the conditions for radical internal changes. We saw the relatively poor imperial nation of Portugal as possible small-scale model of what could happen to the far more powerful U.S. after a protracted period of economic loses and strains brought on by "two, three, many Vietnams." The costs of a series of imperial wars could crack open the potential of radical change within the home country.

The work on the book served as a vital tonic to revitalize the organization, and we became active again in 1973 in a number of ways, now with more focus on helping to build the mass movement. I worked with a comrade on an article about the aspirations and treatment of Mexican immigrant laborers that we placed (under a pseudonym) in several college newspapers. We carried out a number of political spray-paintings and later two stink bombings at public speeches of abusers of human rights: Nelson Rockefeller for his role at Attica and for his draconian drug laws, and a Chilean general being feted here for the bloody coup against Allende. One action took a page from the Sam Greenlee novel, *The Spook Who Sat by the Door*. Two of us dressed up as janitors and walked unnoticed into the heart of a major corporate center, with a tarp rolled up under our arms. We attached the tarp to lobby railing and split. Five minutes later (as a timer burned the twine that held it) the large banner unrolled revealing slogans against the exploitation of farm workers. A photographer was in place and the pictures appeared in a couple of alternative papers.

Obviously it would be uncool for underground fugitives to regularly risk getting busted to do spray-paintings or hang banners. Our idea was to provide a few examples of creativity and militancy for the aboveground movement. We may not have been needed for that and probably had little impact, but thinking about a more dynamic interaction with the mass movement was a healthy step forward for us. From that orientation we undertook what was perhaps our most ambitious underground project: setting up and running a clandestine print shop. Personally, I had little relation to this project located in another region, but I was awed by what they accomplished. By July 1974, they produced two-thousand fingerprint-free copies of our 150-page book. After that, the print shop went on to produce the WUO's quarterly journal, *Osawatomie*, and other literature. The ongoing publishing effort accelerated our working with the mass movement. Aboveground activists who agreed with the politics formed a Prairie Fire Distribution Committee to promote circulation and discussion of the book.

Our internal mobilization around the book got us going again on armed action well before *PF* was published. In May 1973, the WUO bombed a NYPD precinct after police shot and killed an unarmed Black child, Clifford Glover. (Regrettably, we didn't make this or any other action explicitly in solidarity with the BLA, which was under heavy police attack at the time.) Then, on September 11, we were horrified as the Chilean military, following a CIA-orchestrated three-year destabilization campaign, overthrew the elected government of Chile and murdered President Allende. They went on to torture, disappear, and murder thousands of people in order to impose a military dictatorship backed by U.S. business. Later that month the WUO bombed the multinational corporation ITT for its role in sponsoring the bloody military takeover and did similar actions against other implicated companies on each of the next two anniversaries of the coup. On March 6, 1974, the Women's Brigade of the WUO bombed an office of what was then called the federal government's Department of Health, Education, and Welfare, demanding women's control of daycare, birth control, and their health care, as well as an end to the forced sterilization of women of color. A couple of months later we hit Gulf Oil for its role in supporting and profiting from Portuguese colonialism in Africa. (Most of the Weather communiqués are reprinted in Ayers, Dohrn, and Jones, *Sing a Battle Song*; a fuller list of WUO actions is contained within the timeline in Berger's *Outlaws of America*.)

The WUO was on the move again, even as the mass anti-war movement receded after the U.S.-Vietnam peace pact was signed in January 1973. But although we were humming along on all cylinders, our engine was about to throw a rod. One problem had been foreshadowed by that earlier divergence on whether the primary purpose for our organization was to fight imperialism or to lead the entire movement—with the latter theme echoed in *PF*'s strong criticism of "anti-organization tendencies." The only successful model of the time was that of the vanguard communist party, so I'd seen our two different statements as a question of emphasis between political goals and the organization needed to accomplish them. I didn't yet realize how the drive for leadership could lead to subverting the proclaimed political principles.

Organization Man

We're wrapping up the second cadre school. It's been a big success, and I feel great. I love educational work, and I'm also pleased with the praise I've been getting for my role—my highest level of responsibility in the organization so far. But as we summarize our new synthesis on race and class, Meryl, a relatively new and unsophisticated cadre, still doesn't get it. "If we now say the multinational working class will make the revolution, doesn't that undercut the independent and leading role of the national liberation struggles within the U.S.?" All the top cadres are chiming in to answer. With her both new and outnumbered, I don't want to browbeat her, but I do want to show that I'm taking responsibility to promote the new line. So once again I patiently explain that our emphasis on class doesn't eliminate support for national liberation, but that we have to realize that we can't make the revolution without organizing the majority. At a certain point Meryl, overwhelmed, stops arguing…although she clearly does not agree. We finish our wrap-up session, which assesses the second cadre school as a great advance in deepening our understanding of Marxism and moving the WUO toward a fuller, more mature politics for leading a revolution in the U.S.

The writing of *Prairie Fire* provided fertile soil for a new, and to me lovely, flower to bloom: a serious organizational interest in political education. Underground we had always read a lot, and even conducted occasional study groups on specific issues, but now the CC wanted more systematic study of Marxism-Leninism (M-L). They made a bold proposal: a two-week cadre school over the summer. The CC would select students from different sectors of the organization, and the school would bring together the largest-ever gathering of WUO cadres. With a CC member designated to head the project, the leadership team would also include myself and an aboveground activist with a long history, going back to the 1930s, and a deep grounding in Marxism.

While I was enthusiastic about in-depth education, my first reaction to the CC proposal was a warning: Every time I'd seen white radicals get heavily into M-L, I'd seen a shift to elevating the predominantly white working class over the national liberation struggles as the main force for revolution; and, along with that, a "glossing over" of the problems of white supremacy and imperial privilege in order to seek a ready base of support, which nonetheless was never achieved, in the working class. The CC's response was that my awareness of that problem made me a good person to help lead the school.

I understood that the problem wasn't theory per se but rather the deep history and powerful material impact of white supremacy and benefits from imperialism. The repeated drifts into white opportunism also characterized movements that didn't invoke M-L at all, such as populism and women's suffrage. Theory wasn't the cause but rather the rationalization for groups that wanted to claim the mantle of "revolutionary" without staunchly standing by the side of people of color under lethal attack. We were different, I told myself. Most of our inspiration and theory came from Third World Marxist-Leninists, who led revolutions in Vietnam, Cuba, China, Angola, and elsewhere, and who were among the leading forces of Black and other people of color struggles within the U.S. I agreed that we needed to do more to incorporate class into our analysis and organizing—we just had to do it without repeating the classic opportunist errors.

With a combination of mild trepidation and major excitement, I proceeded to work with the others on a curriculum. The process felt much more collegial than top-down. The school promised me an opportunity to help correct the almost universal distortion within the U.S. of Marx's broad analysis as sketched in *The Communist Manifesto*. To the degree Marxism was mentioned at all in academia, the standard summary stated that Marx claimed that the proletariat would make the revolution because they would become increasingly impoverished under capitalism. The smug rejoinder was that Marx was obviously and completely wrong as proven by the increasingly high standard of living of the workers (in the U.S., Europe, and Japan). Many leftists accepted those terms but then tried to prove that even highly paid union workers were being pauperized.

But Marx's model was never simplistically about oppression—otherwise it would have been the peasants, rather than the bourgeoisie, who had triumphed over feudalism. Instead, Marx saw that as a mode of production, a social and economic system, developed it generated contradictions—major stresses and tensions. The strains between emerging new forces of production, how labor was organized and the tools and machinery used, and the old ways of ruling society eventually approached a breaking point. That systemic crisis could only be positively resolved by the class in the best position to organize production and society on a radically new basis. For capitalism that contradiction was driven by how production became increasingly *social*—with giant concentrations of labor, materials, and machinery—while control of the system was *private*, with a handful of owners and managers making the key decisions, based only on maximizing profits. That social/private tension led to all kinds of irrationalities in society and a range of economic and social crises. Only those in the position to reorganize the control of production on a *social* basis, the proletariat, constituted the revolutionary class.

In modern times, with capitalist production organized on a global basis, the vast majority of those who work to enrich capital have indeed become terribly impoverished—the peasants and workers in the Third World. But more to the point, the total breakdown of the economies in those countries constitutes the most palpable example of the irrationality and inhumanity of capitalism—which can be transcended only by the exploited classes reclaiming and socializing their national economies, which would be a crucial step toward overturning the world capitalist system.

In addition to Marx's critique of political economy, our cadre school curriculum included Lenin on imperialism and his theses (along with Comrade Roy of India) on the national and colonial question. This analysis was supplemented by modern "development of underdevelopment" theory—how it was the very drains and distortions caused by the penetration of Western capital that prevented Third World economies from taking off. That laid the basis for us to study what various Third World communist parties called the "national democratic revolution" or "new democracy": given that these countries were blocked from the political and economic transformations Europe had experienced, they needed revolutions led by the workers and the peasants to break from imperialism in order to achieve democracy and development, and to do so in a way that laid a basis for building socialism. We also made use of Mao's essays "On Contradictions" and "On Practice" as a less abstract, more real-life way to present dialectical materialism as a mode of analysis.

The first cadre school (CS-I) was held in the summer of 1974, right around the time *PF* was published, and was centered on deepening an understanding of and an ability to defend our book. The security for this gathering was more challenging and daring than the meeting to ratify *PF*. That gathering had involved less than a dozen, mainly under and all experienced; the cadre school numbered into the twenties, with a lot of above and newer members. Summer provided better excuses for people to be away from their home scenes for a week or two. But a range of above activists had to be brought under safely, and we needed a really good cover and an appropriate venue for such a big and intense gathering.

Once there, I was delighted by the warm sense of community, with such a large gathering unprecedented for us, and by the lively engagement in education and theory, with everyone actively participating. We complemented the education with some fun cultural activities—old songs of struggle and dramatic skits, usually scenes from Bertolt Brecht plays. The latter allowed me to once again express the ham in me, which hadn't had a chance to shine since the days of guerrilla theater at Columbia.

The political line of the school was more problematical. Basically we had slipped back to the first draft of *Prairie Fire*—there was still a lot on national liberation but it was becoming overshadowed by traditional formulations on the "multinational working class." My earlier warning notwithstanding, I was now on board in organizing, or "educating," for that approach.

The same team of three led the second school a year later. The one criticism in the otherwise positive evaluation of my work at CS-I was that I hadn't taken responsibility for the complicated and crucial logistics; this time I was put in charge of that. My smartest move was to recognize from the outset that I couldn't be completely on top of it by myself, so I got permission to pick two excellent cadres, one under and one above, to work with me. They really shone in response to my belief in their abilities and grew to take a lot of responsibility. The result was a top-flight job on security and logistics, except for one notable oversight. It never occurred to me, or for that matter the above cadre, who herself had kids, to make any provisions for childcare. By 1975 the feminist movement must have been conscious of this need for events and gatherings, but I don't think it had yet penetrated into much of the mixed Left, and certainly not to the underground, where none of the cadres had kids. While it hadn't been raised for CS-I, childcare became a pivotal issue for a few of the above cadres attending CS-II. After a last-minute scramble, a CC member dropped his work for those two weeks to run a mini-daycare center at our school.

To me, CS-II felt a lot like the first, with a warm sense of community, a creative cultural component, and lively discussions of texts. This curriculum put even more emphasis on Marx's works such as "Wage Labor and Capital" that stressed the central role of the proletariat, Marx's focus as he lived and wrote in nineteenth century Europe. Most important, the sturdy shoots of opportunism at CS-I came to full fruition at CS-II. The new CC political line was now developed and explicit: our historic task was to help lead the working class to seize power and build socialism. The real purpose of the school was to organize the cadres—many of whom had joined Weather to *oppose* that predominant position in the white Left—to accept the new class stand. That job proved remarkably easy, mainly because of the great respect for and excessive deference to leadership, but also because of the context. We were anxious to find new sails to raise in order to catch a wind that could move us out of the post-Vietnam War doldrums for radicalism in the U.S.

I proved to be especially effective. As many expressed in our evaluation session, I exuded an infectious love for the study and taught with a patient and encouraging manner. That style, combined with my long history of arguing for anti-imperialism, gave credibility to the formal position that the WUO's new line on class was a deepening of rather than a retreat from the politics of solidarity. At the time I believed it myself—but how could someone who had warned so explicitly against this danger in the study of M-L now become an active advocate for it? Despite the problems with political struggle in the organization, I hadn't hesitated in 1973 to systematically critique the rightward drift in the first draft of *PF* toward subordinating the fight against white supremacy to a romanticized view of the U.S. working class. Now in 1975, infatuated by a fantasy of emerging as an organization-wide leader, I became a major proponent of that same opportunist line. By the end of CS-II, only the inexperienced and powerless Meryl objected.

Cadre school was just one horse in a team of four pulling us fast and hard to the right. The other three powerful stallions were the organization's journal, *Osawatomie*; the proposal for "inversion," to bring most of the underground "up" to lead mass work; and most fatefully, the work on the January 1976 "Hard Times Conference."

Hard Times

"You're denying us the one thing we've been fighting for for 400 years—self-determination."
—Black Caucus, Hard Times Conference

The value of *Prairie Fire* went beyond a fuller and more accessible statement of the politics of revolutionary anti-imperialism. The book also was meant to offer a hand across the unfortunate divide between the under and aboveground movements. In 1970, in the frantic and daunting effort to build an underground, we had forfeited our ability to be a force or even a direct presence in open political work. In the heat of the moment, we and movement groups opposed to us created a bitter sectarian divide that pitted armed struggle against mass organizing. Now that we had successfully secured an active underground—one defined more by politics than tactics—we could try to repair that breach and build toward a more mature model, like that of the IRA and Sinn Fein in northern Ireland, with both armed and legal formations that had broadly similar politics. About a year after the book was published, the Prairie Fire Distribution Committee became the Prairie Fire Organizing Committee (PFOC), an open, legal group in agreement with the politics of the book. Now activists and those newly awakened to the struggle could find, talk with, and even join a group based on revolutionary anti-imperialism. The WUO, which had provided the broad initiative for this direction, also had a few aboveground members directly involved in the process. I wasn't personally working with those cadres and didn't have direct responsibility for this area of work.

Meanwhile, within the WUO, the CC broached a totally radical change: "inversion." The idea was that in the post–Vietnam War phase, building a communist party and leading the mass movement were the most pressing tasks. Therefore we should surface most of the organization to provide direct leadership for that process. Legal obstacles were not seen as insurmountable. As far as we knew, no bombing could be pinned on any individuals. Pending charges were for such offenses as "rioting," and the prosecution of these cases would be tainted by the government's more serious illegal acts against us and our supporters. The CC also expected that, since public opinion had turned against the misadventure in Vietnam, there would be considerable sympathy for us as the militant edge of the anti-war movement. We were reassured that while the CC and most of the organization would surface, we would retain a small clandestine capacity.

The notion of a token section remaining under struck me as a sop. Functioning underground was challenging work that required considerable leadership and resources; a small clandestine branch would soon wither and die. Personally, I had no special flair for military work; my own talents lay more in the fields of education and organizing. But I also understood that armed struggle required a high level of commitment and experience, which was why I had felt responsibility to take on that work. Jettisoning what we had so painstakingly built would mean losing that capacity for a long time to come.

Inversion was presented as a proposal, nothing more, but the process felt just like past organizational shifts where the CC had already made the decision and then worked to organize the cadres. So I had a fatalistic sense that the battle was already lost as I argued that the inversion idea had a couple of fatal flaws. First, even at a time when open work was primary, armed propaganda played a valuable role, especially in this post–Vietnam War period when we needed to expose the wider government and corporate role in exploiting resources and suppressing liberation struggles in Africa, Asia, and Latin America. Second, even beyond the question of various forms of struggle, clandestinity itself was a valuable asset. The government had shown its willingness to frame and even assassinate key radical leaders. Given the nature of the state, we needed to keep some revolutionaries and capacity to function out of the sight and reach of the state.

My criticism, though, didn't get to the political roots of the problem. The impetus toward and role of armed struggle had always been intimately linked to how close we felt to Third World struggles, especially to the Black struggle within the U.S. And that was changing fast. The evidence of the WUO's shift to a more white-centered view of the world came rolling off our own printing press every three months in our journal *Osawatomie*.

While I wasn't involved in editing or producing the journal, I occasionally wrote for it. My most worthwhile article was a review of *Longtime Californ'*, a book on the experience of Chinese immigrants in the U.S. The impetus came from Shin'ya Ono's earlier friendly criticism of Weather's failure to address anti-Asian racism. The journal, which was distributed by PFOC, had a regular feature called "The Toolbox" that tried to present brief and understandable explanations of basic Marxian concepts. I did a couple on political economy—I'm sure in keeping with the flawed line of CS-II, the second cadre school.

Overall, as I remember it, *Osawatomie* is where the new opportunism had its fullest, clearest expression. Ironically, the magazine was named after a Kansas battle fought by abolitionist John Brown, an early and exemplary ally of the Black struggle. We still wrote a lot about racism, and a major focus of our organizing and writing in that period was about standing up to the racist backlash against school busing in Boston. But every single major arena of struggle, from fighting racism to women's liberation, now became at its heart a "class question." Of course class is fundamental and important in all social arenas. But in defining all those issues as primarily—often it sounded like wholly—about class, the analysis wiped out the real legacies and ongoing fundamental structures of white and male supremacy, as well as undercut the basis for the oppressed to have independent organizations and to lead their own struggles. The new line was also a form of denial about how thoroughly white and male supremacy permeated the U.S. working class; yet, revolutionaries couldn't have a meaningful class strategy without fully facing that reality.

The "everything is class" mantra reached such an extreme that even a loyal cadre like myself was shaking my head when the article on the criminal justice system asserted that "prisons are a class question." Well, yeah, prisons are tools to maintain capitalist rule and those inside them are overwhelmingly poor. But, with the Black imprisonment rate something like six times that of whites, and especially with the role massive incarceration was playing in the government's counter-attack against the 1960s upsurges in the Black and Latino/a communities, prisons were also, first and foremost, a colonial question.

Still an organization man, although mentioning my qualms to the author, I rationalized the ridiculous—telling myself that inevitable exaggerations always happen when the pendulum swings back, in this case to correct our past error of inadequate attention to class. I was confident we'd soon get the balance right—a mature politics with our clear understanding of national liberation as the leading revolutionary struggle, but with a fuller sense of how to develop a class base for organizing large numbers of white people to join the revolution.

In my role as educator, I was most conscious of the discussions of political line, on class, race, empire, and gender—and that's where my divided loyalties between our formative politics and my desire to rise in leadership played out. But there was another disastrous theme running through our changes, and I should have seen it way back when the CC member said we needed an organization so that we could "lead everything," and then especially when it became a recurring refrain in *Osawatomie*.

We were not alone in this, of course. The main Left response to the receding of the militant anti-war movement in the 1970s was the development of the "party-building tendency," which held that the key to moving forward was to forge a vanguard communist party. Formerly militant groups were all wrapped up in increasingly rarefied discussions and debates on theory and political line. In my opinion this tendency was a tremendous setback for the Left, a retreat from organizing new people and from struggle against the state. In theory, theory can illuminate the way forward; in practice these groups, each driven by the competition to become the leader, were expending incredible energy, and often engaging in bitter battles, on secondary and often irrelevant ideological fine points.

But I didn't apply that criticism of the prevailing party-building tendency to the WUO; after all, hadn't we distinguished ourselves both by militancy and by recognizing that people of color would lead, both globally and within the U.S.? However, the new class line in *Osawatomie* was accompanied by frequent calls to build a communist party to lead the struggle. The shift to now saying that the multinational working class would make the revolution also served to bestow legitimacy on us to emerge as key overall leaders in the whole U.S. revolution. In our own way, we were playing out the presumptuous pomp and pretense of the prevailing party-building tendency—both in denying the lead of national liberation and in promoting ourselves as leaders. It may sound apolitical to say this, but such mistakes cannot always be understood solely on the basis of analysis and line. Plain old ego can play a hell of a role, even when we start out with the best of intentions.

The various strands of the changes we were going through in the mid-1970s—our new class line, the inversion proposal, the shift toward party-building—got woven into a big, bright tapestry boldly put on public display at the Hard Times Conference of January 1976. This ultimately disastrous endeavor seemed at the time like an exciting and promising effort to bring together an impressive range of radical organizations from the different nations and nationalities within the U.S. PFOC made the initial call, but the impetus and leadership came from the WUO. Since I wasn't working with any key aboveground members, I didn't have direct responsibility for or detailed knowledge of this project, but I was certainly involved in organizational discussions of the strategy.

What seemed both healthy and exciting was the effort to respond to some dramatic changes in the world and for our movements. 1) The war in Vietnam had ended and the radical surge among white youth had ebbed. 2) At the same time, the U.S. had gone into a serious economic recession, partly as a result of setbacks to imperialism such as higher oil and raw material prices and also a new worker militancy at home. We overprojected, as leftists often do, a deep and long depression, but we were right that the post–World War II golden era of unfettered capitalist expansion had come to an end. 3) The Puerto Rican independence movement had risen to a high tide, both on the island and on the mainland U.S., and the Puerto Rican Socialist Party was planning massive anti-colonial demonstrations to counter the U.S. bicentennial celebrations in July of 1976.

So lots of it made sense. I noticed but didn't really complain that the name "Hard Times" had a kind of 1930s ring to it—a period in which the Left made tremendous strides in labor organizing, but with the cost that most unions excluded Blacks and women. But by this time I was already rationalizing away *Osawatomie's* increasingly exclusivist, and therefore predominantly white, way of subsuming every issue into class.

The WUO, having been distinguished by explicitly challenging white privilege, certainly couldn't pretend the problem never existed. Instead our position was that now, as the decline of imperialism brought recession to the U.S., those white privileges were being eroded. The Sojourner

Truth Organization (which didn't seem to have an overall anti-imperialist program, but placed a strong emphasis on opposing white supremacy) published a criticism of the Hard Times literature, arguing that while *absolute* privilege, in the sense of overall standard of living, might be declining, *relative* privilege, the gap between white and Black, was intensifying because Black people disproportionately bore the brunt of the recession. In most ways the white/Black differences were increasing, making principled class unity even more of a challenge.

Their criticism rang true with everything we had understood and argued, but inside the WUO we discredited their position as "Left sectarian." My own approach in that discussion was to take it on faith that our organization, which had been outstanding on these issues in the past, was continuing to blaze the trail to revolution on today's new terrain. The exciting momentum toward the conference seemed to vindicate that faith. PFOC's political association with the WUO gave the project a level of credibility among a range of people of color groups, including revolutionary nationalists, that wouldn't have been afforded to any other organization in the white Left. Two thousand people, twice the expected attendance, gathered in Chicago for the Hard Times Conference on January 30, 1976, with an impressive array and range of groups and outstanding activists. The promise of sustaining the momentum was palpable, with the plans for the Puerto Rican independence "Bi-Centennial Without Colonies" protest already in motion for July.

It pretty quickly all went south. It began with the statement by the Black Caucus. Critical of the shift from support for internal national liberation to the multinational working class as the agent of revolution, they asked for an unscheduled chance to address the plenary. When that request was rejected, their spokeswoman denounced the Hard Times leadership for denying self-determination. A women's caucus made a parallel criticism for being denied their own independent voice.

The conference was large and complex; many different Third World forces, with a range of positions on race and class, attended. There were also a number of sectarian Left groups, some of which may have raised the valid self-determination challenge as a competitive maneuver to establish themselves as leadership. But we didn't need to sort out every little in and out to know that the heart of the criticism was on-point—we didn't have to look any further than *Osawatomie* to see the deterioration of our politics into a more traditional white Left line. For the WUO and our supporters, given our reason for forming in the first place, such an explicit criticism by the Black Caucus was shattering. It had the same explosive impact on PFOC, with the added dimension that some felt manipulated by PFOCers who were secretly members of the WUO.

Underground, the tremendous deference to leadership had served as a lid on any major expressions of discontent. With that lid now cracked apart, all kinds of repressed vitriol came bubbling up. Previously enthusiastic cadres expressed bitter resentment toward those above them in the hierarchy. While we all felt we were in a dire crisis, people had different positions on the source of the problems. We were engaged in a mad scramble to both correct errors and keep the organization together—but the center would not hold.

Things Fall Apart

Linda, a cadre who had been a rung below me, has been leading in criticizing the old CC. She and her allies have been crystal clear in articulating that the basis for what went wrong is white and male supremacy, and they also have denounced the top-down way the organization was run. I now look to her as a leader as we prepare to meet with supporters to explain what's happened with the WUO. With considerable deference I ask Linda, "How should we open our self-criticism?" As she looks at me blankly, I stammer on, "You know, how you and I played out the organization's wrong line and top-down approach in our work with them." Linda responds, "What in the world are you talking about?"

While the underground may have been the starting point for this disaster, there was a time delay before we felt the full impact; it was as though the aftershocks, rather than the earthquake itself, took down our structures. The initial reports I heard about the Hard Times Conference were mainly positive, emphasizing the size and range of the turnout. But the criticism by the Black and the women's caucuses couldn't be avoided. PFOC was directly confronted and risked being discredited if they did not respond fully. Some underground cadres with close ties to public activists felt the earth shift and transmitted the tremors to the rest of us. With the CC's previously unchallenged leadership now in question, all kinds of repressed discontent and resentments emerged.

The result was an organization-wide rectification campaign, similar to what various Third World communist parties had undertaken when they had to correct and recover from major wrong turns. The process was severe and systematic, going beyond individual errors to look at the organization as a whole and emphasizing political line and strategy. At this point, we understood rectification as a vital democratic process for correcting major errors, but we weren't yet aware of how it had also been misused, in China and other places, for internal power struggles. Also, in the examples that had inspired us, rectification had been guided by the top party leadership, whereas now the role and the continuation of our CC were in doubt.

On the West Coast I was chosen with two women, who were also seasoned but non-CC cadres, to form an interim leadership. The impetus came from younger members who felt that the CC could not be trusted to lead the process. I think I was picked because I had criticized some of the "Hard Times" trends in the first draft of *Prairie Fire*, and more recently had opposed inversion. At the same time, my role at the cadre schools showed that I was far from a consistent champion against opportunism, so my leadership role was clearly provisional.

Rectification involved several related efforts. There was a certain amount of debriefing needed, to get a fuller picture of how positions on and work for the Hard Times Conference had developed, but the heart of the process was defining the terms politically: what had been the political line that had led to the setback, and what were the political terms for regaining a revolutionary direction? Those on the West Coast pushing for rectification argued that the WUO's fundamental problems were the same that had historically stymied the U.S. Left—white and male supremacy. Another collective asserted that the organization's central shortcoming had been the lack of internal democracy, the failure to actively involve all members in shaping policy. A few still believed in the Hard Times direction and felt that what we most needed were deeper roots in the multinational working class. The circulating papers diverged so much in analyses and solutions that it almost seemed that we were a set of independent collectives, in touch with one another but not part of the same organization.

The way I fulfilled my responsibility as an interim leader was basically bureaucratic, in that I didn't initiate a position on political line but focused on keeping the organization together until we could complete rectification. Disarray and fragmentation entailed special dangers for the underground, because a breakdown in fundraising, support structures, and security could easily lead to us all getting busted. A lot of my time was spent at restaurant meetings with aboveground activists, struggling to maintain continued material support during that stormy period.

Politically, the critique of white and male supremacy was the position that resonated with me—but I didn't feel that the fault lines were as deep or the changes needed were as profound as many were insisting. I compared our errors to the first draft of *Prairie Fire*: there had been a slip backward toward a white-centered politics, but our origins and history were solid enough that, with focused political struggle, we could set things right. I still had tremendous respect for the old leadership and didn't envision anything as radical as expelling them. Instead, I thought we would end up with a restructured CC, perhaps with one or two members removed and with a handful of cadres who'd had a better line (possibly including myself) added.

My moderate sense of the changes needed was not equal to the task, as the shock waves gathered strength and speed and the disarray of the organization spiraled out of control. Our small interim leadership group gave way to a self-named Revolutionary Committee (RC), none of whom had been on the CC or in regional leadership. I was soon purged myself—and none too politely. I even agreed. I hadn't grasped the depth of the opportunism; I had promoted the wrong line at the cadre schools; my approach to rectification had been reformist when radical changes were needed. Now completely unsure of my own judgment, I looked to the RC to lead us back onto the path of revolution.

With this overriding need, I was willing to overlook their arrogance and contempt in dealing with old comrades, as well as their personal failings. Some of those in the RC must have felt overwhelmed themselves. I remember the meeting where a key underground RC leader was drunk. An internal voice told me it was time to walk away, but like the others at the meeting, as we rolled our eyes at one another, I just accepted the situation as a momentary lapse.

Initially the RC concentrated on interrogating the old CC members in our area. The reasoning was that we needed a full account of their errors in order to understand the mess we were in. But also, as often happens in battles within the movement, a new leadership seeking to establish itself sought to discredit its predecessors. My main concern was to prove myself politically sound and useful to the RC—I had sort of leapfrogged from being a loyal lieutenant to the CC, to striving to be a loyal lieutenant for the RC. While they didn't trust me enough to bring me into those criticism sessions, I could tell that they lacked the sense of humanity with which even errant comrades should be treated. The passion to thoroughly root out opportunism spilled over into a vehemence that disdained everything that had been done; the determination to overturn an entrenched leadership turned into a seething contempt. In providing background information to the RC, I abetted these cruel interrogations.

In a way there was a similarity here to our earlier, broader "exceptional whites" error. By making others the personification of all that was wrong, we not only wrote off potential allies but also missed the ways we had to struggle with the same powerful forces within ourselves. Thus Linda, a sincere and committed militant, could be so clear and cogent in critiquing the CC's use of authority to block political struggle, and yet be oblivious to how she and I had done the same thing with our supporters. (At that moment, I swallowed hard at her inconsistency but didn't push the point.) For me, living in a world where millions of children died every year from malnutrition and disease and at a time when revolutions were raging in the Third World, my overriding passion and need was to be part of the revolutionary process. Yet in 1974–75, I had readily rationalized away compromises in the politics to continue to work with what I saw as the vanguard among whites, the CC of the WUO; now in 1976, I was overlooking clear signs of a harshness in internal struggle that contradicted our underlying humanism in order to continue working those who now appeared to carry the red flag, the RC.

I felt extremely unsure of myself and unsteady because of my inability to fully grasp the sources and scope of what had gone so wrong—with an organization that not only expressed my politics but in which I lived my life. The way that shock put me out of touch with reality was revealed in my response to a proposal from the RC. They were considering sending me and one or two other well-known members of the WUO back aboveground to present and give credibility to the politics of rectification. I was pleased with their apparent confidence in me, but as I tried to picture how to do it, one aspect of the plan threw me for a loop: I'd have to turn myself in. Dealing with legal charges and possible, but probably short, jail time was manageable. The sticking point for me was that inversion had been a centerpiece of WUO opportunism. I didn't want to send the wrong message by turning myself in peacefully to the FBI, which had direct responsibility for assassinating Fred Hampton and other Third World militants. Physical resistance, however, would be both futile and beside the point when submitting myself to arrest. After obsessing about this dilemma, I came up with a proposal: when I turned myself in, I would carry out a symbolic but dramatic gesture, like spitting in the FBI agent's eye. The RC folks just looked at me without saying a word, and the idea of my surfacing to be a spokesperson was never raised again.

Meanwhile, our fundraising sources were drying up. Without being in the RC, I couldn't make a claim on the limited money available. So I had to look for a job, something I hadn't done for a couple of years. Through a local temporary labor agency, I got hired out on a daily basis for unskilled construction or janitorial work. In those days, such crews were all male, and in this neighborhood almost all Black. Although the mix of individuals varied considerably from day to day, we enjoyed considerable camaraderie. We were all down and out, and we all tried to be attuned to one another to maintain a communal rhythm—no one would go so slow as to shift work to others or so fast as to make others look bad. We talked a lot about what was happening in the world, but without the high personal stakes or intense self-consciousness of an organizational rectification campaign.

Jackie went out on the same crew with me several times. Despite a missing front tooth, his smile radiated sunshine, which went with his personality. Although he said he had a drinking problem, I could tell he had solid, decent values. I really liked the respect he expressed when talking about his wife, Ruby. Meanwhile our underground financial situation got so bad that my love and I had to give up our apartment, while limited resources and security considerations meant we couldn't just jam into the RC safehouse. Jackie, without knowing the exact reasons, saw that I was on the verge of being homeless and invited us to stay with them. Jackie and Ruby never expressed feeling imposed on in any way as they made room for another couple, whom they didn't know that well, in their small apartment. They lived in the projects in the heart of the ghetto, where my partner and I were the only white faces in sight.

It only lasted a couple of weeks, but as it happened, almost miraculously, the timing of our brief stay meant we shared in a most amazing national phenomenon: the TV broadcast of Alex Haley's *Roots*. Haley was the coauthor of *The Autobiography of Malcolm X*, perhaps the most moving and influential book for the generation coming to consciousness in the 1960s. His next project had been to trace his own family's history, all the way back to Africa. This powerful book had been made into a film for television, to be presented in one-to-two-hour segments for a week. The whole country, including tens of millions of white Americans who generally lived in a state of denial about U.S. history and racism, was gripped by this epic, with everyone talking about Kunta Kinte's attempted escape or Chicken George's struggle to keep his family together.

Ironically, if I hadn't lost my apartment I wouldn't have seen the series because I never owned a TV. Watching the unfolding drama with Jackie and Ruby, discussing episodes late into the night, picking up the buzz and chatter about it in the street was a magical moment. I even had hopes that the TV presentation of *Roots* would make a major dent in white supremacy, that many white viewers would become aware of racism, but any such effect was short-lived.

This unexpected experience of living in their home helped save my sanity and soul. Political struggle within the Left is necessary to correct errors and to respond to changing conditions. But the danger is that it can become too internalized, too narrow, and often too vicious. And the personal stakes can become excruciatingly high for those of us who have dedicated our lives to the struggle. In that process I'd partially lost my bearings. Living with Jackie and Ruby, who were reconnecting with their own history through *Roots*, rerooted me in what is real and human about the struggle—both the depths of the injustices and the hopefulness that springs from the warmth and humanity of the oppressed.

It was a good thing I got fortified in this way, because before long I was totally, starkly on my own. The incident that led to my finally getting booted out by the RC was almost comical. To turn around Marc Antony's famous line in *Julius Caesar*, I'd come to praise the RC, not to bury them—but I was perceived as doing the opposite.

One of the central and correct criticisms of the WUO was the lack of accountability to people of color. Our founding politics had centered on solidarity, but once underground we rarely checked in with Third World groups about their strategies and priorities and to see how our own efforts related to theirs. With rectification nearing an end the RC, our new leadership, told those close to them that they were planning an action against "la migra," the Immigration and Naturalization Service (INS), which rounded up and deported "illegal immigrants" in what was the stolen northern half of Mexico. On hearing this, I just knew that the RC had found a way to have dialogue with, or at least to check out the strategy of, key Latino/a groups, such as CASA, that were working for immigrant rights. So to kind of stroke them, like offering up an easy homerun pitch, I asked a question designed to give them a chance to shine: "How does this action fit in with CASA's strategy?"

To my surprise, my question was met with icy stares. Obviously they hadn't considered CASA's strategy, and they took my intended flattery as a challenge. They blasted me for trying to undermine leadership, which, ironically, had been a major charge against dissidents like them in the WUO. I never found out how servile I might have become in order to stay with the "vanguard," because it was too late: I was out on my ear.

My loneliness was doubly grim because I'd just lost my central personal relationship. The problems weren't so much personal as political, as pretty much all the heterosexual couples of the WUO broke up in this tumultuous period. Male supremacy had been a major force for what had gone wrong. While a heterosexual couple doesn't have to be sexist, there is quite a historic weight, a pull-back toward traditional terms, in a form that has been a core institution of patriarchy for millennia. That pull can be counteracted in a number of ways. Support for lesbians and gays and other nontraditional families is one aspect; men working consciously against sexism is another; and perhaps most important is women's collectivity. That mainly hadn't happened, certainly not fully enough, in the WUO. Once the upheavals started, but without yet a vision or ability collectively to build a more progressive, more feminist culture, people's reaction was to break from the old forms by breaking up, generally initiated by the woman. Even though I reluctantly accepted the logic at the time intellectually, I was heartbroken. Then, when I was jettisoned by the RC, I felt utterly and forlornly alone—and without even a baseline self-confidence in my own judgment.

Alone

Here I am, me of all people, watching TV all afternoon. The football that's on isn't even a real game, as it's August and we're watching preseason practice on a local station. But what can I do? Surfacing hasn't been so easy, and the negotiations to dispose of my old legal charges, through a trusted movement lawyer, are taking longer than expected. In the meantime, I can't risk the streets with no disguise and no ID. So I'm laying low by staying in, without even books to read, watching TV. Luckily, it's Denver and the Broncos, and I can get caught up in the excitement of watching them forge their formidable "Orange Crush" defense and gel as a team, in a year that would take them from perennial losers to Super Bowl contenders.

"Alone" doesn't begin to say it. Beyond the intense pain from a breakup of my longtime couple relationship, I didn't even have a community or close friends to fall back on. I was isolated, a completely atomized individual, with no one to work with. And forget about "self-reliance"; my confidence and judgment were in shambles. My nerves, which had always held up well in times of physical danger, were now like a tangled mess of electrical wiring with multiple short circuits.

My first decision was to leave the region. The RC would probably be uneasy about my bumbling around in their area of operations, and I wanted a break from any self-consciousness about favorably impressing them. I left to find refuge with a couple of beloved friends with whom I'd felt great personal rapport throughout my underground years. While never visibly in a Left organization, they had a strong anti-imperialist world view; while not necessarily agreeing with armed struggle, they felt an affinity for our passion, militancy, and humanitarian standards. They were the right people for me to fall back on. When I arrived at their door, I was far from the buoyant, confident activist who had built a friendship with them—quite the contrary, I was a mess—but they welcomed me lovingly and helped nudge me back toward self-reliance.

Before long I had a job, a tiny apartment, and a borrowed three-speed bicycle. The job was perfect for my situation: furniture mover. The work provided physical exercise without the noise and fumes of a factory; plus it paid in cash, with few questions asked. In many ways furniture moving served the same function for men that waitressing did for women: part-time work for aspiring actors, artists, and writers. I felt comfortable with my coworkers culturally and, to the limited degree I expressed myself, politically.

Overall, I was well aware that I was in rough shape emotionally. While I didn't think of it in psychological terms, and in any case probably didn't fully meet the clinical definition, I was depressed. And while I knew nothing about treating that condition, I had spontaneously stumbled into what proved to be a very effective therapy for me at the time: exercise, sunshine, and heart-to-heart talks with my two old friends. The core of my job was physical labor; bicycling was my mode of transportation; and swimming, jogging, and basketball were what I did for recreation. Before long I was in top physical shape, and improving in psychological shape as well.

Politically, while I'd found no organized way to be active, I naturally followed and analyzed what was happening in the world. In the late 1970s, "stagflation" prevailed in the U.S. economy, an unusual combination of slow economic growth and high inflation. There was also a rising awareness and activism around environmental issues, a major upsurge in wildcat strikes, a vicious homophobic campaign against gay and lesbian rights in Miami, raging guerrilla wars against repressive U.S. client regimes in Central America, and a front-line people's war against the racist rule of a 5 percent white minority in "Southern Rhodesia" (now Zimbabwe).

After a few months, I felt together enough to start figuring out what to do with my life. I made a decision that seems paradoxical but turned out to be judicious. Although I had opposed inversion and saw it as emblematic of all that had gone wrong with Weather, I decided to surface. The reason was basic and clear. I couldn't recover from the setbacks and grow again politically, let alone contribute to the struggle, as a lone, uncertain individual. I needed a political community, and to find that I had to go aboveground.

The first question was how. I definitely wanted to minimize the risk of doing prison time. While my arson charge was clearly bogus, the assault charge could result in a year or so in jail even though the officer had received no serious injury. But I knew that the government had a strong interest in dismantling the underground, and that gave me some leverage; I had something to offer—my surfacing—in exchange for their dropping those old charges.

The second question was where. I wanted to avoid the two cities with anti-imperialist organizations closest to the WUO—the PFOC in San Francisco and the May 19th Communist Organization in New York. I didn't want to be once again looking over my shoulder constantly or trying to curry favor; I needed to make sure that my development and positions came from my heart. Reluctant to burden my parents in Boston with my problems, I decided on Denver. I remembered the strong Chicano/a movement there and its positive influence on me. So, once I had saved up enough money from my job, I was on a bus headed toward the Rocky Mountains. I'd been gradually shedding my disguise, and on the last stop before Colorado I got rid of all of my ID, not wanting anything on me that could conceivably lead to anyone still underground.

After a seven-year absence, I was hardly in the forefront of anyone's mind in Denver. I got a room at the YMCA, and the next morning I slipped, unannounced, into the office of Walter Gerash, an attorney I remembered for his work for the Panthers back in 1970. I asked Gerash to negotiate my surfacing in return for the dropping of all charges. He thought there was a good chance, especially because it would be difficult for the DA to try a seven-year-old case. To maximize our legal leverage, my presence in Denver and my determination to surface remained confidential.

While my approach was sound, I had seriously underestimated how long it would take—with the legal system in its late-summer crawl and with the DA stalling, probably to confer with the feds. I went to work at a day labor agency where ID wasn't needed. I moved out of the Y to a rooming house that provided a hot plate and a half-refrigerator, which allowed me to save money by cooking my own meals. I whiled away my "leisure" hours in front of the TV in the common room. Ironically, despite my alienation from macho sports culture, I greatly enjoyed watching the once-lowly Broncos become the Cinderella team of 1977–78, and I developed an anomalous affection for them that would last decades.

After several weeks that felt much longer, the negotiations were resolved. The charges were dropped, and I became legal, aboveground, and "David Gilbert" once again. Several other ex-Weather cadres also surfaced in this period. Most of those who turned themselves in without negotiating from under ended up doing a year or so in prison, being subjected to probation, or both.

Over the course of six years, the Weather Underground had succeeded in dramatically puncturing the intimidating myth of government invincibility, had carried out over twenty armed actions that highlighted and educated about major institutions of oppression, and had written and published, from underground, a book that was a major contribution to articulating the politics of revolutionary anti-imperialism…and then we fell apart due to our own internal weaknesses.

{ A MILE HIGH: ABOVEGROUND IN DENVER }

*O*ur *Men Against Sexism* group has a healthy culture of openness and struggle, so I feel comfortable expressing what I know to be politically incorrect. "There are some traditional 'manly virtues' that I consider positive, like physical strength. I'm a furniture mover, and I like being in shape." Ken, the moving spirit of the group and my best friend, replies gently but firmly, "But there's a male bias in how you define 'strong.' Men may, on average, have greater ability to lift weights, but women have great physical strength in other, often more important ways, such as endurance and in the incredible feat of bearing children. It's fine to enjoy being in good shape, but it's sexist to see men as 'stronger' than women." I hear what Ken's saying, but it doesn't fully sink in emotionally; I'm still enamored of my furniture-moving prowess.

Two weeks later Ken and I are honored and excited to be on an otherwise all-women day-long raft trip on the Colorado River. A local feminist stalwart is a certified guide and annually leads a trip for radical women. Ken and I have grown close to this community through the allied work of our MAS group, especially the childcare we do for women's events, and this year we are invited to come along. The sun is a brilliant yellow, the water a jade green, and cliffs rise impressively along the banks as we raft down the Colorado. People break out a case of beer, and I join in the festivities, even though I hardly ever drink. After a couple of beers, with the motion of the raft and the hot sun beating down, I'm suddenly sick to my stomach and incapacitated. I am dropped off on a shaded islet. Ken volunteers to stay with me; the rest of the party will pick us up on their way back.

In the shade and on solid ground, I start to feel better, and before long we are laughing uproariously as I declaim, "And who was the only one who couldn't handle the physical rigors of the trip? The big, strong furniture mover!" During this weekend of natural beauty and warm camaraderie, I can't begin to imagine that within months I'll become a social outcast, even a bit of a pariah, to most of the women on the raft.

On my own in Denver, I faced a range of pressing needs and desires to rebuild my life and politics: finding a way to make a living; looking for old friends; connecting with the Left; touching base—offering self-criticism and then building solidarity—with the Chicano/a, Black, and Native American struggles, and also with the local women's movement.

To my surprise, I could find only one person that I used to run with in 1970. Mary had led a small, militant collective focused on environmental activism. She had educated me about some of the grave emerging dangers, while I discussed how those depredations related to the nature of imperialism. Back then she had been most interested in what the WUO could offer in the way of militant tactics, since she was contemplating forms of sabotage. We hadn't been very helpful on that level. Now, seven years later, we were happy to see each other, but Mary had health problems, didn't have a collective, and had never related much to the white Left—she didn't think there was much of one in Denver these days.

I hoped she was wrong. I figured my best way to connect was to go to the bookstore that also served as a movement center, RIP, or Radical Information Project. But before I even got there I was jolted by what I read in the *Denver Post*. They ran a series on the Crusade for Justice, depicting them as bullies and thugs. This characterization was given credibility by quotes from "radicals" and "socialists" who decried the Crusade for being anti-white and violent. Those charges from the white Left sounded all too familiar, but what shocked me was that they would be repeated to the corporate press, and for a series that seemed designed to isolate the Crusade from public support and leave them vulnerable to police repression.

So even as I was setting out to reconnect with the Left in a humble way, to learn and rebuild, I had to raise this issue: that it was a problem to give the media ammunition that could be used against the main Chicano/a group in this northern corner of the land that had been ripped off from Mexico. My discussions with various individuals at RIP went nowhere, with one exception. Ken, a new friend who was himself fairly new to Denver, did allow that the white Left could often be racist in its view of

Third World groups. But he also said that he had heard several accounts of Crusade intimidation that made him extremely wary of that organization.

As it turned out, it wasn't my arguments but, inadvertently, the results of my actions that made a breakthrough with Ken. When he heard I was paying a visit to the Crusade at their headquarters, he was sure that I'd get thrown out and, most likely, beaten up because I was white. When he later saw me in one piece and happy about the meeting, he began to consider that it was the white Left's politics, rather than the Crusade's racial attitudes, that was the main source of the friction.

For me, the visit was the warmest and most comfortable moment since my return. They were the only activists (aside from Mary) I knew from 1970 who were still in Denver, and they were still up and running. (Ordinarily, they might have been suspicious of someone who surfaced without doing time—that he had traded information for leniency. But since Walter Gerash, a movement lawyer of great integrity, had handled the negotiations, they had no such doubts.) My self-criticism about the WUO's backsliding on white supremacy came as no surprise to the Crusade people I talked with, but they seemed to still consider us a relatively positive element within the white Left. In any case, they accepted my self-criticism without in any way expressing contempt or disdain.

Naturally I was anxious to hear what had happened with them over the past seven years. A turning point had come during the Native American occupation of Wounded Knee in early 1973—a key moment when the WUO had been shamefully inactive. The Crusade had seen solidarity as its top priority, and had collected supplies and somehow gotten them through the FBI blockade around Wounded Knee. The Denver police had accused the Crusade of running guns to the Indians, although a police raid didn't turn up any weapons. One police raid on the community center, during a youth dance, had resulted in a street battle—tear gas, rocks, fires, police gunfire—in which a young activist, Luis Junior Martinez, was shot dead by the police.

I didn't know if the Crusade ever used coercive tactics within their community, but it was clear that the widespread charges against them for "violence" mainly resulted from their solidarity with Native Americans and their defense of their community center. My impression was that in this era of a receding movement, the Crusade was less active politically. But I was impressed that at a time when most radical organizations of the 1960s had dissolved, they were still here and still had a solid base in their community.

There was no one left from what had been a small Black Panther chapter in Denver. The militants I'd known in 1970 were in prison, or underground, or regrouped in Oakland. One brother had been killed. I was, however, able to find a representative of the revolutionary nationalist All African People's Revolutionary Party (AAPRP), which had been started by Stokely Carmichael, who had taken on the African name Kwame Ture. They didn't have a chapter in Denver, just a couple of members. When I met Rick, I explained who I was and again started with a self-criticism. Rick was gracious about it and, overall, seemed to have a very favorable view of Weather. As we went on to a broader range of discussions, we connected well personally. Over time, Rick and Nadine's house became the place were I felt most at home; it was to become my refuge when I was isolated and under attack by the white Left.

Nadine was Jewish, and while she seemed to me to be too dismissive of white feminists, she had a down-to-earth sense of the real-life conditions of poor and oppressed people. With three beautiful kids and little income, Nadine and Rick lived those survival struggles. She also cautioned me that even for the oppressed, nationalism had its limits. Israel and, to a lesser degree Liberia (where ex-slaves, who migrated from the U.S. in the 1800s, became the ruling class) were painful examples of how the oppressed could become the oppressor. Rick turned me on to the delights of Peter Tosh's music; Nadine treated me like her biological brother.

The third stop on my amends and solidarity track was the women's movement. Since there was a big overlap between the RIP Left and the feminist community, making contact was easy. Compared with the Crusade and the AAPRP, the connection felt less organic because the political history and framework were more divergent. Sabrina seemed surprised that I wanted to meet with her at all. When I started out with a self-criticism for the WUO's dearth of feminist program and macho style, she let out a big "and how!" on the latter point. Sabrina felt that armed struggle was inherently male supremacist, and she didn't see any positive aspects in what we had done. That made me a little uncomfortable, but the point of my visit was not to impose my politics but rather to work on and change my sexism. Given her dislike for the WUO, Sabrina was extremely generous, open-minded, and willing to talk. Some of her suggestions on how to support women's struggles were later put into practice in our Men Against Sexism group.

Long before this first round of solidarity visits was completed, I had found a way to make a living. Here I fell back on my experience as a furniture mover. I also found a cheap but pleasant apartment in a racially mixed neighborhood. Several of my neighbors were very friendly. The one sticking point was that they couldn't understand why I wouldn't get a TV, why I wouldn't even accept their old one for free.

The moving company I ended up with, once again, drew on students and ex-students. The guy who owned it, Jake, had shown a lot of initiative in building it up from scratch—although his lack of capital left me with safety concerns about a few of the rigs. Despite my politics and fugitive past—I was quite open about it—Jake felt comfortable with me as the lead man on a truck. I got along well with my fellow workers, almost all white guys. The one woman at the company, the dispatcher, Bonnie, turned out to be a real gem and became one of my best friends in Denver. Originally from Mississippi, she had left to escape the bigotry she'd encountered after dating a Black man. While never in the organized Left, Bonnie had a deeper sense than many radicals of society's racism, sexism, and class divides—and a willingness to stand up to them in her own, unpretentious way.

Back to Brookline

The evening couldn't have been nicer, a chance to talk, after a long absence, for hours on end. Lydia and I'd been lovers years ago, but comrades for the duration, even when out of touch. While I was still underground, she'd been part of a team defending Black homes from assaults by white mobs, as Boston became the center of open racist violence in the 1970s. We've been catching up on our lives and the state of the world over bagels and coffee in Coolidge Corner, a section of my hometown, Brookline, that borders on Boston.

As we walk to the trolley stop at about ten o'clock to return to our respective homes, we see a ruckus developing. Two white teenage boys are accosting two younger and smaller Black teens—they have book bags and what looks like art supplies—simply for being Black and in the neighborhood. We step in, face the white kids and tell them to cut the BS. But there's already too much static and motion for us to contain. The whites dart around us and the Blacks run. Lydia turns to cool out a group of white girls on the corner who are screaming, "Kill the niggers!" Meanwhile, I see that fifty yards down the road the two white teens have one Black kid (who'd turned to face them to enable his younger brother to get away) down on the ground. I race down there, but as I pull one teen off, the other bolts around me to get in a kick to the head. It alternates like that—seemingly forever but actually for another two or three kicks—as several adult white male bystanders watch the assault without lifting a finger to help me stop it.

The cops drive up, let the white teens flee, and take the Black kid away with them—we hope for the medical attention we demand and not to be booked, but the cops' hostile attitude doesn't bode well. (When we later call the police station, they won't provide any information on the condition of the youth or what happened to him.)

As Lydia and I sort out what happened, I keep reliving those kicks to the head and obsessively going over every aspect of how the events unfolded to see if we could have stopped the attack sooner. It hadn't occurred to me to start throwing punches; now I feel I'd been too passive, that I should have been more aggressive to protect that kid. The moment is doubly upsetting for Lydia. My berating myself, and implicitly her too, for not doing enough reminds her of how Weather trashed activists for not fighting hard enough. The situation is especially infuriating for Lydia because I represented Weather sexism and arrogance in our personal relationship. Despite her anger she's making the effort to explain this to me. I'm still in denial on these issues, and vivid replays of those damaging kicks to the head are looping though my brain. I can't process what she's saying…

Soon after I got settled in Denver, I headed East for a visit with my mom and dad. Needless to say, my parents were thrilled and this reunion was joyous. They even hosted a small gathering for me with old family friends. I enjoyed seeing people after all this time, but there was also a bit of awkwardness, as I perhaps hadn't yet fully decompressed from living underground within a revolutionary organization. While I knew enough not to get into heavy political debates, and certainly not on Palestine/Israel, I nonetheless was thrown off balance and not adequately gracious about the divergences in world views. For example family members were certain that the Vietnamese routinely tortured U.S. POWs, while the U.S. forces of course were humane with theirs.

By the time I'd gone underground, my parents had grown to strongly oppose the Vietnam War; and later, I think, they came to take a certain pride in how early and clearly I had opposed it, and even in the WUO's ability to elude the government without harming any person physically. More broadly, when my father tried to explain why nothing had turned out as he'd hoped and expected with any of his three kids, he would say that the war drove our generation crazy.

As good as it was to be with them again, I felt an edge of uneasiness. My parents obviously hoped that everything would now return to normal: The war is over; our son is back home! But in my heart, I was still fighting imperialism. There was no way I could abide the still massive assault on human life, potential, and dignity involved in "business as usual." The very next night what had promised to be a delightful reunion with Lydia proved to be a graphic and painful reminder of just how pervasive the problems were.

Rebuilding My Life in Denver

About two months after I got to Denver, Rick and Uhuru asked me to run for the community board of directors for the local poverty program. That was quite a surprise, because their analysis was the same as mine: the "War on Poverty" had been designed to co-opt the struggles of the 1960s, to deflect the communities' demands for self-determination with a pittance of government hand-outs that provided a few articulate individuals with jobs and fostered dependency. But the program did fund the community center where Uhuru had a job, which was the base for his community organizing. They were now under government pressure to "integrate" their all-Black board of directors, and Uhuru wanted me to be the white person on the board.

The experience did give me an opportunity to work with some good people and to learn more about community issues, but it also confirmed my already jaundiced view of the "War on Poverty." One of the worst aspects was how the two main centers in the city—ours and the one in the Chicano/Mexicana community—were regularly pitted against each other, competing to win the same funding grants. Uhuru and I worked hard to develop fraternal links, and managed to get an excellent Mexicano organizer hired for a job at our center, but we barely dented the built-in structural problem.

My work on the board put me in touch with police brutality issues. After a couple of especially heinous incidents, a citywide coalition was formed to demand a community review board, better-defined police procedures, and methods to monitor and restrain the police. The coalition provided a good opportunity for activists from the Black and from the Chicana/Mexicano communities to work together (the white Left in Denver wasn't a presence in this work).

What I had never imagined beforehand was that male-to-female transgender activists would be a major component of the coalition. Still fairly ignorant and backward about these realities, I saw them as exotic, if not strange. To me, it seemed that folks should just accept the gender they were "born with" and work from there against stereotypes and for equality. It was only through the discussions that came from working together that I got a sense of how some individuals felt deeply, and as central to their identify, that they belonged to a gender different from the one society had assigned them.

Transgender people of color experienced incessant and cruel abuse from the police. They were regularly stopped, and at times arrested, on any pretext—usually accompanied by taunts, threats, and all too often by gropings or beatings. In the red light districts of the city, the police did their best to make everyday life for the transgendered a constant torment. In spite of this, their representatives, who suffered the worst retaliation for our work, impressed me with their serious, focused, and courageous approach. Overall, our coalition raised consciousness and promoted dialogue among communities, but we did not achieve any structural change to rein in police brutality.

A few months after my arrival, the Native American Longest Walk of 1978 came through Denver. The campaign had started out from San Francisco on February 11, with seventeen marchers, and they were headed all the way to Washington, D.C. Their purpose was to call attention to and defeat eleven bills in Congress that would have annulled treaties protecting Native American sovereignty. By the time they got to Colorado, with spring breaking, they were hundreds strong, and hundreds more of us joined them for the eighty-mile leg from Denver to Pueblo. The bright blue skies, the soaring spirits, and the uproarious welcome we got from the Chicano/a community of Pueblo made for an exhilarating event. By the time the Longest Walk reached D.C. they were three thousand strong; and they won their key demands.

Adams Street

Before a year was out, Ken asked me to go in with him and two other radicals to rent a house on Adams Street. In addition to wanting to live more collectively, Ken felt that the house had the potential to serve as a movement mini-center. It was in a somewhat higher rent district than where I lived, but still cheaper than our four separate apartments. Plus, I'd still be within my district for the poverty program board.

I didn't know the other two people, only that Ken thought highly of them. Flip was the most outspoken gay activist in the Denver Left—radical, energetic, and anti-imperialist. Ginger, from a working-class background, was a feminist and was also open to allying with the Chicano/a movement. She said she'd be comfortable in the otherwise all-male household.

I cherished the privacy of my little apartment as well as my rapport with my neighbors. But my growing friendship with Ken, my favorable impressions of Ginger and Flip, and my desire to become more engaged with the white Left/feminist community tipped the balance. As it turned out, the move led to qualitative changes in my personal and political life.

As busy as each of us was, we tried to have dinner together a few times each week, and we soon got to know one another. Flip amazed me with his openness in describing his early childhood, the depth of his sexual identity, his family's reaction, the problems for and within the gay community, and the obtuseness of most of the Left on these issues—the education he gave me was a real eye-opener. Ginger expressed a healthy frustration with the Left's tendency for lots of meetings and talk that didn't lead to any organizing, and she pushed for projects that put us in closer touch with everyday people. As Ken had envisioned, different activists often stopped by and our dining/living room (which combined could sit close to forty people) became the site of some valuable forums and discussion.

Two seeds that had already started to sprout soon blossomed into my main areas of political work: solidarity with El Comité (in English, "The Committee") and a Men Against Sexism (MAS) group. Audre was the person who provided the keys for both these doors. She was unique, at least for Denver—being both a Maoist and a stalwart feminist, committed to building an independent women's movement. She and I had a lot in common as rare birds who devoted a lot of attention to theory. Our mutual respect and interest in each other's ideas generated a mild flirtation, but with our frequent political friction, no romance developed. I learned a lot from her emphasis on the issue of violence against women, and I appreciated her Maoist reminders that class struggle continues even after the revolution. She seemed interested in my position that the fundamental relations of production could not be reduced to wage-labor and capital; that the economy was also based on subsuming the labor and resources of Third World countries and on the unwaged and underwaged work of women, which meant that those struggles also were fundamental. But I don't think she ever broke from more traditional, labor-centered Marxism. She believed my support for national liberation movements that took Soviet aid was revisionist; I felt the Maoists were sectarian. Surprisingly, given our differences, it was Audre who introduced me to the Chicano/a group, El Comité. She also was the one who a year earlier had urged Ken to form MAS.

Men Against Sexism

When Ken had asked me, not long after we met, to join the MAS, I agonized over my decision. Clearly, I needed collective ways to work on my sexism—but I was wary of joining an all-white group that wasn't anti-imperialist. But here in Denver I had no way to combine the two, so I opted to join MAS while continuing my still isolated efforts to build solidarity with people of color groups.

Other men's groups I had known either self-censored by preimposing a correct line before talking or, racing in the opposite direction, reinforced their sexism, passionately justified as men "expressing our feelings." In MAS, under Ken's leadership, we were encouraged to speak openly about sexist attitudes—no one was jumped on or condemned—but then to struggle with them, to work to get to a better place. While our discussions remained confidential, we regularly consulted with feminist mentors about general issues and the broad direction of our efforts. So when, for example, Carl confessed that he liked *Playboy* magazine, we discussed why that appealed to him and tried to work through the power dynamics of objectifying women. Later we'd check-in with our mentors about the issue, without naming the individual involved. The process felt healthy and helpful to me, including my working through my masculinist distortion of "strong." In retrospect one problem with our politics was that we hewed too closely to the prominent line of the day, as put forth by Andrea Dworkin and Catherine MacKinnon, that pornography was the leading edge of male supremacy. We weren't yet familiar with the critiques that developed among feminists on the dangers of puritanism and of promoting censorship—which could later be used against affirmations of lesbian and gay sexuality.

The main point wasn't some unattainable self-perfection; fighting sexism mandated concrete solidarity with women's struggles. When we asked various women how we could help, the response was a ringing, unanimous chorus: do childcare for our meetings and events! With lots of events, and some of our eight-man group living in Boulder, I got to do lots of childcare, to the point where I developed a relationship to some of these sparkling children, including some personal times out together too.

Solidarity also entailed efforts to educate and organize other males. Our most successful project was a series of skits we did for high school classes. Ken knew some progressive teachers who invited us in—and who must have prepared their students well, because even the boys seemed attentive. The funniest skit had me as guy who thought his wife did nothing all day, on a rare time alone with the kids—while our other members had a ball playing the rambunctious children. Our skits were crafted to cover a range of themes, but I was amazed at the passion one issue evoked: one Black or Latina girl after another spoke out with anger about sexual harassment at their jobs.

El Comité

How strange…me, of all people, passing out leaflets for a Progressive Labor front-group, CAR (Committee Against Racism)! After the 1969 split of SDS, PL made "fighting racism" a top public priority. Naturally they still deny there's a system of white supremacy—to them racism among workers is a matter of bad ideas, not based in white privilege. Similarly, they still oppose independent organizations for people of color. "Fighting racism" is PL's way to unite and lead the (predominantly white) U.S. working class.

What will the comrades in El Comité think when they learn I was here? They can't stand PL because of its rejection of Mexicano/a self-determination. But I'd had no time to consult: I'd only found out about the Ku Klux Klan rally and protest against it through a flier at the bus stop on my way to work. I feel like I'm doing the right thing on this corner in downtown Denver, handing out the (way too rhetorical) CAR leaflet and talking with those who'll stop about opposing the Klan—which in the event doesn't publicly show its face.

Ironically, the only workers at PL's "all for the proletariat" event are myself and three friends from the moving company. We came straight from a job that ran late, so we're still in our work clothes. At the end of the demonstration, I'm surprised to see that the CAR core group scatters, leaving the two most visible speakers, with posters and a megaphone, to walk several blocks back to their car alone. This strikes me as careless, given the Klan's history of violence, so we four movers escort them back to their car. At first taken aback, the CARs seem thrilled to get such staunch support from these anonymous workers.

I met El Comité because of a car accident—Audre's. She broke her leg, which required two weeks in the hospital—leaving her fourteen-year-old son Paul home alone. He was a mature and together kid but still found that prospect unsettling. I moved into their place until his mom came back home.

When Audre returned she told me that the accident had happened on the way home from a talk by Juan Antonio Corretjer, a leader of the Puerto Rican Socialist League. Audre had been interested because she'd heard that, unlike the Crusade, the sponsoring Mexicano/a group was explicitly Marxist. Don Juan Antonio's talk had stressed the anti-colonial nature of Puerto Rico's struggle and supported the armed groups there. Audre saw the affinity with my politics and graciously gave me the contact information of the group that had invited him.

El Comité, with a core of about ten local activists, was affiliated with the statewide Mexicano/a Movement for National Liberation (M-MLN), which in turn was closely allied with the MLN, a Puerto Rican group within the U.S. Most of those in El Comité had a background with the Crusade for Justice and still upheld much of that tradition. But they saw an additional need for a group with more focused politics that explicitly advocated socialism. Also, while still studying the question, they didn't see the spiritual concept of Aztlan as providing a concrete resolution for Mexicano/as within the U.S. and instead leaned toward a reunification of the "Southwest" (which the Mexicans called "El Norte") with the rest of Mexico, striving to build one, socialist country. As a result, they favored the term "Mexicano" over "Chicano." And importantly for me, they stressed solidarity with other national liberation struggles.

The first El Comité representatives I met were Marco and Patricia. Marco, who seemed young for his leadership role, was the brother of Luis Martinez Jr., who had been killed by police in a 1973 raid on a Crusade youth dance. Patricia had a deep history in the Colorado Left, as well as in the Chicano/a movement. As I met others, they all impressed me with their warmth and seriousness. Most of them balanced raising kids and having working-class jobs with organizing. One member, Rafael, delighted in telling coworkers who called Mexicans "wetbacks" that they, as Euro-Americans, were "oceanic wetbacks."

A new and tiny group, El Comité had opted to invite their closest white allies to their weekly meetings. When I arrived, a white couple from Sojourner Truth Organization (STO) had already been attending. I remembered STO's valid critique of Weather's "Hard Times" line and, in any case, was excited to make contact with white leftists who prioritized anti-racism.

Early on Larry and Penny of STO did me an immense favor by introducing me to the work of Samir Amin, whose *Unequal Development* (Monthly Review Press, 1976) is the magisterial work on the post–World War II structure of imperialism. But as happy as I was to meet potential allies, I became disenchanted at my first El Comité meeting. Larry made himself the center of most of the discussions, raising and insisting on points that others didn't consider relevant. He clearly saw himself as much more knowledgeable than the neophytes in El Comité. But, however much Marx and Amin he may have read, his sense of what issues were crucial for the Mexicano/a community was not nearly as good as that of the El Comité organizers. In any case, I found his insistent effort to provide political leadership inappropriate—classic white intervention into a struggle by people of color. I was surprised and uncomfortable, but as a newcomer didn't say anything.

After two more such meetings, El Comité leadership told the three of us that they were changing the structure of the relationship. The weekly meetings would be for members only, to clarify their politics and strategy; they would also hold periodic meetings with us on allied work. The change was a godsend for me.

The new structure also helped me improve my relationship with Sojourner Truth Organization, but my efforts to bring about positive interchange between them and the feminist-centered Left around Adams Street only created friction. The feminists saw Larry and Penny as the prototypical Left heterosexual couple, with the male dominant and heavy into abstract theory. The STOers saw the Adams Street crowd as backward on race and considered my efforts there to be doomed. I felt we were reliving the terribly destructive 1969 split between a male-dominated "anti-imperialist" Left and a white-centered "feminism." But I didn't know of any women-of-color groups (the women in El Comité advanced women's rights but placed primary emphasis on unity for the overriding national liberation struggle) or anti-imperialist/feminist stalwarts such as Naomi or Lydia in Denver.

While STO may have been right about the limits of the Adams Street community, my work there was the only place that provided some solidarity—a small number of whites who would come to EC events and a little bit of fundraising. The tidbits of support I brought to EC were scraps compared to the nutritious banquet they provided me. I learned a tremendous amount from them. They were great examples of being both politically radical and rooted in their community; of being able to study theory and still talk in everyday language; of being committed to their nation and still strong on solidarity with other national liberation struggles. One event in particular made an indelible impression on me, an El Comité–sponsored talk by Ricardo Romero and Priscilla Falcon, two leaders of the M-MLN. I had never been so close up to such a stirring synthesis of humanism and militancy, a lyrical sense of the potential of the children combined with the recognition that we were fighting a ruthless power structure.

A key lesson many of us had drawn from the demise of the WUO was that a white group with little interaction with or accountability to people of color organizations would inevitably drift back to white-centered politics. The prescribed antidote was for whites to operate "under Third World leadership." But what exactly did that mean? There were myriad different interpretations and applications of that concept. Many different errors could be committed in that name: on one pole was the danger of (in effect) picking the leadership—throwing white resources to the particular organization we liked best. Another pole was to act as a free floater among a range of organizations, picking and choosing with no responsibility or accountability to anyone. There were lots of ways to screw up but no formula to guarantee getting it right.

In my view, the terms set by El Comité provided a healthy and fruitful approach. First, our work together was based on extensive political discussions and a high level of unity. Second, I wasn't barred from supporting other progressive groups, such as the Crusade, as long as there wasn't a direct conflict with El Comité's program. Third, while my specific work around El Comité projects was under their direct leadership, I was also encouraged to do a broader range of work, and to use my own political judgment in anti-racist organizing among whites.

My impromptu decision to participate in PL's anti-Klan rally left me anxious as to what El Comité would think. When I saw them next, they spoke first, before I could offer any explanations. "Some of our people saw you at the PL demonstration downtown. As you know, El Comité cannot ally with PL in any way because they deny our most fundamental right: self-determination. If you had gone to that demonstration representing yourself as our ally, that would have been wrong. But from the accounts we got it was clear that you went solely as a white individual opposed to racism. That was your responsibility. We like what you did."

Iran

Outside of El Comité work, I ended up allying with STO and opposing PL in a new and sudden controversy whose seismic waves rippled through the Left—in Denver and around the world. 1974 through 1979 saw a high tide for revolution unprecedented in world history. National liberation struggles waging people's war seized state power in seven different countries in Asia, Africa, and Latin America, while in five other countries regimes that came to power through coups or elections promulgated similar programs. But even amid those upheavals, one revolution burst on the world stage as a total surprise to almost everyone in the West: Iran's Islamic Revolution of 1979.

Iran had been a prime example in my 1967 pamphlet *U.S. Imperialism*, so I was aware of the history. When the democratically elected government of Prime Minister Mossadegh nationalized Iran's oil, the CIA orchestrated an August 1953 coup and installed the Shah (Persian for "king") as the autocratic ruler. Iranian fellow graduate students at the

New School had described to me in angry, painful detail the wholesale jailing, torture, and killing of the opposition by SAVAAK's, Iran's CIA-trained secret police.

But I hadn't been in touch with Iranians students since 1969 and had no idea what was happening in the only places people could still congregate and air their grievances in Iran—the mosques. So I was totally surprised (as was the CIA) when massive street demonstrations erupted in late 1978. By February 1979, the Shah had fled and the religious leader, Ayatollah Ruhollah Khomeini, took power as the head of the Islamic Revolution. While I didn't know anything about the new regime, my immediate concern was our responsibility to block U.S. military intervention.

In Denver the Iranian Student Association and some U.S. Left groups called a public and, as it turned out, well-attended meeting. The Iranians students had a formal unity around nonintervention, but it was clear that beneath the surface there was tremendous tension between the Islamic and the Left students. PL was the most vociferous U.S. Left group, and their speaker made a fiery criticism of the "reactionary, petite-bourgeois Khomeini regime." Someone from STO answered, articulating my position better than I could: "It's not the job of the U.S. Left to tell the Iranian people which government to choose. Rather, our responsibility is to uphold self-determination and staunchly oppose our own country's imperialism. Today the Iranian nation needs our support for their independence. If tomorrow the people have to rise up against a tyrannical regime, we'll support them in that tomorrow."

We had a parallel struggle within MAS. Almost everyone in the group was delighted when U.S. feminist Kate Millett flew into Iran to speak out for women's rights. But Ken and I argued that given the history of destructive Western interventions, and the almost universal Iranian resentment of them, Millett, who in any case wasn't staying to organize or to face the repression, was not doing Iranian women any favors by presenting feminism as a Western initiative.

In retrospect, the rights and wrongs of the debate with PL were not quite as simple as they seemed to me at the time. Yes, we were right to place the primary emphasis on opposing our own country's imperialism and in upholding Iranians' right to choose their own government, and strong emphasis on criticism of the new regime served to undercut that main point. But I was slow in recognizing how serious the dangers were with the emerging new phenomenon of right-wing anti-imperialism. (In 1953, Khomeini had been one of the right-wingers allying with the CIA in building opposition to Mossadegh.) The Khomeini regime did not share essential features of progressive national liberation movements: 1) restructuring the economy in the interests of workers and peasants; 2) promoting greater roles and rights for women; and 3) practicing solidarity with other anti-imperialist struggles. While it would have been wrong to place those problems in the forefront, I should have at least acknowledged those concerns, especially given U.S. imperialism's role in destroying the once-popular secular Left alternative to the Shah.

My Two Worlds Collide

Being a childcare regular meant I almost never attended the events (those to which men were invited) of the women's community, but I usually heard about them later in discussions with friends. A dynamic new form of protest in the late 1970s was "Take Back the Night" marches, where women's collective strength became a counterforce to the sexual harassment and violence that individual women faced daily. Allison and Bev recounted to me how their march down East Colfax Street, the main drag for strip clubs and porno shops, had been greeted with catcalls by a number of Black men out on the street. Many were probably touts who helped hustle prospective customers into the clubs and a few may have been pimps. The women had answered the catcalls with taunts, and Allison and Bev felt a rush of empowerment from the experience.

Their sense of strength after enduring a lifetime of harassment resonated with me. Still, I had mixed feelings about the encounter. Yes, those men and the industry some of them worked for were sexist, but was this very public spat between white women and Black men the best way to empower women and build alliances? Instead of the street people of East Colfax, could the march have targeted the more powerful corporate forces that benefited from exploiting women? (Near the end of my stay in Denver, a small group of us—men and women—did a clandestine spray-painting against some pornography profiteers.)

The next major feminist march, six months later, started with a rally in a park in a Mexicano/a neighborhood. Again, I only heard about the event afterward, but this time from El Comité: "Why didn't the organizers let us know beforehand? Why didn't they coordinate this with any Mexicano groups? The community took the rally as an outside invasion and was very hostile. We believe in women's rights and want to organize our people to work for equality, but this event put us in an awkward position, because it presented feminism as an outside imposition." I gingerly raised this concern with one of the "Take Back the Night" organizers and offered to put her in touch with El Comité, but she felt that women had an independent right to organize other women and that even if the response wasn't good in this first instance, Chicanas would join them over time.

By this time there had already been several incidents when I'd held my tongue. One particularly upsetting moment came during the Longest Walk. A few whites had volunteered to work in the kitchen set up to feed hundreds of marchers. Audrey went to the Native American woman in charge with some criticisms and demands on how to organize the work. The woman, Leah Deer, explained why she didn't agree. Audrey did an about-face and led the three women who had come with her in an angry walkout. I just sat there, the one white person left in the kitchen, quietly chopping onions. Leah Deer, clearly upset, said to her coworkers, "Why is she so sure she knows how to do this better than me? I organized and led the kitchen for the entire Wounded Knee occupation, and we did it well."

While my refusal to join the walkout spoke for itself, I never discussed the incident with Audrey. It was still early in my relationship to this feminist community, and I wasn't sure I had the standing to do so. But this latest incident, in the Mexicano/a neighborhood, raised a conflict I couldn't avoid.

Personally, I felt like the political track I'd been on, with a leg on each rail, was pulling me apart, way beyond any stretch I could manage. Solidarity with El Comité and MAS were my two most fulfilling areas of political work. There shouldn't have been any contradiction, but in practice, in Denver in 1978, it felt like an unbridgeable gap.

The community I lived in was of the white Left/feminist overlap. My politics saw fighting all oppression as central, but identified racism as historically the prime stumbling block to developing successful revolutionary movements in the U.S. My responsibility, as I saw it, was to work on racism within my community. Understandably it was awkward for a man to initiate these, or any sensitive, issues in the feminist community. Nonetheless, we had held a few mixed forums and discussions at Adams Street. Once Audre had even invited the leader of a Maoist communist party, who had touted Enver Hoxha and the Albanian Communist Party as having the correct, revolutionary line in global affairs. Certainly, then, I could initiate a discussion on our relationship to the Black and Mexicano/a communities here in Denver.

Even so, I proceeded with caution. I sought copresenters and asked some of those I was closest too, like Bev and Allison, for advice on the best approach. The response was, "Just go ahead and do what you feel is right." Given the understandable distaste for lectures from male politicos, I decided to limit my remarks to ten minutes before opening up to group discussion. Instead of general political principles, I raised three specific examples of what I considered missteps on race. The first two, from my own history, were met with nods or, at worst, bemused silence. It wasn't until the third, the feminist rally in the Mexicano/a park, that all hell broke loose.

Sexist Dog of the Century

"We're sick and tired of leftist men giving us abstract lectures on politics."

"Oh, shit," I'm thinking, "it's not even two years since the demise of the WUO and I'm about to be all alone again."

The effect of my carefully considered little talk was almost magical. In an instant I was transformed from anti-sexist Male of the Year, who even got invited on the annual feminist raft trip, to Sexist Dog of the Century. My opening didn't lead to the kind of around-the-circle discussion I'd hoped for, and there was almost no engagement with the three examples I raised. Instead there was an outpouring of anger and criticism of a male leftist lecturing women. No one spoke in my defense.

Even with this abject failure, I hadn't yet hit bottom. That came in the following weeks. Those who had disagreed with me didn't keep arguing, instead they stopped talking to me altogether. I went from feeling very much part of a community to feeling like a pariah. Most painfully my closest relationship to kids, to Jeremy and Melinda, withered in the heat of their mom's hostility, as she no longer wanted me to take them out.

One irony of my situation struck me: the proudly democratic-centralist WUO and the explicitly nonhierarchical feminist community could not have been more different in terms of organization and political line. Yet both could be similarly effective in evading political struggle and in using social ostracism as a powerful weapon for suppressing dissent. But of course I wasn't underground anymore. I still had other personal/political friendships that served as a refuge: Rick and Nadine's apartment, alive with their three children and with Peter Tosh's music; my friend Bonnie at the moving company, not in the organized Left but trying to live as an independent woman and an anti-racist; my work with El Comité; and a handful of women who had a strong commitment to forging a whole politics of feminism, anti-racism, and socialism.

Paradoxically, my defeat at the meeting provided the impetus for a consciously anti-racist core in Denver. With those still talking to me, my most telling argument was to contrast the reaction to me with the reception for the guy promoting his pro-Albania party. He had never been in or related to our community. His topic was the political line of a deified male leader on another continent. He had lectured at the front of the room for an hour before taking questions—and in the Q&A had shamelessly claimed that Albanian communism was very supportive of lesbian/gay liberation, without anyone calling him on that blatant lie. In contrast, I lived and worked in our community, focused on specific examples from our practice, and talked for under ten minutes to kick off an open discussion. Yet America's Enver Hoxha was well received while I was blasted for "abstract lectures." The blatant inconsistency exposed a powerful, deep-seated resistance to grappling with our internal racism, and led a few people to see the need for more direct and consistent work in that arena.

Ginger began to do solidarity work with El Comité, which she found to be much more down-to-earth than the white Left. MAS increasingly worked on racism as well as sexism and made more effort to relate to El Comité programs. A few women with strong anti-racist politics, especially Catha (who hadn't been in Denver for most of these conflicts) and Sara, worked on joint study and projects with Ken and me. So, even though my sense of being part of a community—one that had taught me a lot—had shattered, now there was a small set of folks much more consciously working against racism and in solidarity with Third World and people of color struggles.

My critics in turn could point to inconsistency in my practice: I was more willing to criticize white women for racism than people of color for sexism. In fact I did on occasion raise, in a low-key fashion, political issues with El Comité, who proved to be more open to political dialogue than the gathering at Adams Street. But it was still true that my approach in each venue was different. I had felt like I was a part of the white Left/feminist overlap community, yet I was, in contrast, a solidarity worker with El Comité. Also, my political analysis didn't see the two situations as exactly the same. While I believed it essential to confront all forms of oppression, both in program and in internal work, and I supported autonomous women's organizations, I still saw racism as the prime barrier to revolutionary advance in the U.S.

In dealing with El Comité, I always checked in with and responded to the woman in the leadership, who had great politics and judgment, and at times I talked about the central role of women's liberation in various Third World struggles. But I did not do any systematic critique of El

Comité on these or any other issues. As for the old pattern of the ivory tower male politico, I honestly felt I was learning a tremendous amount from both sets of relationships. Despite my current and difficult differences with many in the community, they had, over the past year, provided helpful challenges to my sexism. And, naturally, I found the work with El Comité to be invaluable. But one's character is never permanently set in stone as a "good guy" or "bad guy." There was a real danger of my growing to fit the stereotype if I didn't develop a more collective work situation. Being so isolated politically, I was doing precious little to organize in any community or to confront state power.

Long before the turning point of that meeting, I had been exploring going back underground. I had considered "inversion," the surfacing of the WUO, a major mistake and setback, and I was especially critical that we hadn't done more to support the armed clandestine organizations that had fought harder and taken much heavier casualties. At the same time, ego played a major role in my restlessness; I was eager to find post-WUO redemption by "fighting on the highest level." This journey also had a very compelling personal aspect, which eventually had the spectacular result of the birth of my son.

I couldn't tell those I worked with that I was going back under, but to be responsible I gave a month or two's notice that I'd be leaving, to move to another city. As that date approached, there were already some modest advances in political work—but that improved qualitatively after I left. Ken, based in MAS and with some allied women, led in building a solidarity group with El Comité, called the "San Patricio Corps." The name came from a group of Irish-American soldiers who went over to the Mexican side during the U.S. war of conquest of 1846–48.

My last political debate in Denver happened in the same spot as my first—the RIP Bookstore. Then, it was with someone I'd just met, about the white Left's public attacks on the Crusade for Justice. This time it was a chance encounter with my former good friend/adversary Audrey, and was about Vietnam's recent invasion of Cambodia. This time I lost decisively; in fact I was left speechless.

From Audrey's Maoist point of view, the pro-Chinese Khmer Rouge (KR) of Cambodia was revolutionary, while the Soviet-aligned Vietnamese Communist Party (VCP) was revisionist. From my national liberation perspective, I had supported both against the U.S. invasion. I had seen some charges of KR brutality in the corporate press, but it was so standard for the West to discredit revolutionary forces with disinformation about atrocities that, like pretty much everyone else on the Left, I paid those accounts no mind.

While I supported the new government in each country, I had a lot more knowledge of and respect for the VCP, with its decades of effective struggle against Japanese, then French, and then the U.S. invaders, successes clearly based on deep and strong roots among their people. I knew little about the KR, which had been a relatively small and untested organization until 1970, when the U.S. had engineered a coup to overthrow the popular Prince Sihanouk, because he wouldn't give the green light for U.S. military incursions. The coup brought Gen. Lon Nol to power, and resulted in a quick and total collapse of legitimate authority in Cambodia. In the relative blink of an eye, by April 1975 the KR captured the capital, Phnom Penh. Now in early 1979, to the shock of everyone on the Left, Vietnam had invaded Cambodia.

Audre challenged me to condemn the invasion, but I balked. She pointed to the history of Vietnam acting as a dominant and at times oppressive nation among the three of Indochina (Laos, Cambodia, Vietnam). While I couldn't formulate, even for myself, any clear political rationale, I just had more affinity for and trust in the VCP than the KR. Audre fired back, "The whole time you've been here you've vociferously argued that the highest, most inviolate political principle is self-determination of nations. How, then, can you possibly condone Vietnam's invading and taking over Cambodia?" Although still unwilling to concede, I had no answer.

It wasn't until a year or two later—I was back underground and no longer in touch with Denver—that the grisly reality became apparent: KR responsibility for the deaths of over a million (later estimates put it at 1.7 million) of their own people. Genocide is the one situation—both in international law and in humane morality—that overrides the principle of self-determination. The Khmer Rouge horror must serve as a lesson—if Stalin wasn't enough—to the Left that we can't automatically endorse every group that employs Left rhetoric and fights against imperialism.

The Vietnamese invasion was undoubtedly motivated in part by their national interests—but it stopped the genocide in progress. It was amazing, if not amusing, to see how the corporate media, which had expressed such concern about Cambodian lives when that served to discredit a "Left" regime, now did not deem it worthy of their attention when those lives were being saved by the Vietnamese. Imperialism performed dizzying political somersaults in order to remain consistently inhumane. The U.S., which had first brought about the collapse of legitimate authority in Cambodia and then condemned the triumphant KR as radicals in power, now supported them in order to undermine the main revolutionary force in the region, the Vietnamese. The U.S. insisted that the UN recognize the ousted genocidal regime as the legitimate representatives of the Cambodian people and gave material aid to KR guerrilla resistance.

But the revelations of the scope of the horrors in Cambodia, and then the U.S. diplomatic gymnastics to support the genocidal KR, were yet to come. At that moment in early 1979, I was standing tongue-tied in the RIP Bookstore…and on the verge of leaving the community, battles, and organizing in Denver to fight imperialism on another level—but whether to be more or less effective remained to be seen.

{ BACK UNDER }

"**N**o, you don't have to worry about that high deposit we have posted. I can see that your credit is good. We only have that sign up to keep the niggers away."

I'm a bit taken aback by his blunt language, and have to bite my lip not to respond. But then I get some satisfaction, picturing the look on his face if he ever learns who used his rental car. I simply reply, "Yes, I can understand why you would do that."

I was headed underground once again. The first time, in the spring of 1970, we were reeling from the townhouse disaster but we had a developed organization with extensive support among students and youth. Now, in the spring of 1979, I was making a less pressured, more deliberate choice, but with virtually no organization and with little popular support. In both cases, inspired by guerrilla movements around the world, there was disproportionate emphasis, too much ego, about armed struggle being "the highest level." Although there was now much less of a mass movement to build off and to encourage, I felt I had learned essential lessons about prioritizing struggles of people of color and working under direct Third World political leadership. On another but crucially important level, there was a powerful personal dimension to my current journey.

The ebbing of the anti-imperialist movement was a sobering reality, but I remembered that the conventional wisdom in 1970 was that the WUO wouldn't last for six months, yet we'd gone on to operate successfully for six years. Besides, my immediate priority this time wasn't movement-building but rather direct material aid to internal national liberation struggles. Throughout history the striving of Black and other people of color had tilled the soil to create the receptive furrows for all other forms of progressive protest in the U.S. But those groundbreaking plows had been blunted, and at times broken, by brutal repression. White revolutionaries had a responsibility to help in the face of those attacks. If people of color movements could become resurgent, then so too could a broader range of justice movements following their lead.

The civil rights movement had been inspired by the flowering of independence struggles in Africa. Now a new wave of national liberation abroad seemed to hold the potential to help rejuvenate struggles within the borders of the U.S. As I headed back under in 1979, Zimbabwe had just won a ten-year people's war to oust a white settler regime; the Sandinistas were on the verge of overthrowing the brutal Somoza dictatorship in Nicaragua; and guerrilla wars were being waged in a number of Third World countries.

Internally, the withering government attacks had wreaked havoc. But several Black revolutionary nationalist organizations were still active. Most called themselves "New Afrikan"—Africans as an oppressed nation within America. The Puerto Rican armed clandestine organization FALN (*Fuerzas Armadas de Liberación Nacional*) was carrying out bold attacks within the U.S., and there were four or five such groups on the island where support for the *independistas* was strong. The Mexicano/a, Native American, and Asian-American communities also had promising revolutionary currents working to rebuild.

My hope that military action could breach the dam and get the waters of protest flowing again was a reversion to a kind of foco theory; but it didn't seem completely unreasonable, given the deep reservoir from the still recent mass struggles and with the global rivers of national liberation still surging. Then on November 2, 1979, it happened, a dramatic action that seemed to embody all that potential: Assata Shakur, often referred to in the media as "the soul of the Black Liberation Army" (BLA), was liberated from prison.

Having long admired Assata, I was thrilled. Shakur (her government or "legal" name was Joanne Chesimard) had joined the BPP as a college student, and then in the face of the lethal repression gone underground. Soon she was charged with every bank robbery in which a Black woman was involved. On May 2, 1973, police stopped a car on the New Jersey Turnpike and a shoot-out ensued. Zayd Shakur, whom I'd met while doing Panther 21 support work, was killed, as was a New Jersey state trooper, Werner Foerster. Sundiata Acoli got away but was captured a day or so later. Assata was wounded and arrested at the scene.

What ensued was a tornado of abuse and trials, vividly recounted in her book, *Assata: A Memoir*. Though she was cleared in every one of the five or six cases that had been pending against her before the stop on the NJ Turnpike, and forensic evidence in this case showed that Assata had never fired a gun and had been shot with her hands in the air, an all-white jury found her guilty of killing trooper Foerster. Assata, who now had a young daughter, was sentenced to life plus thirty-three years.

Part of what made her escape so exhilarating was that no one was hurt. The BLA unit involved forced a guard to open a gate and then commandeered a prison van in such an organized and authoritative way that no shots were fired and most of the prison had no idea what was happening until it was all over.

As it happened, just three days later, a large number of people marched from Harlem to the United Nations to demand human rights and self-determination for Black people in the U.S. While this protest had been planned long before, Assata's break-out infused it with new spirit and energy, and an inspiring statement from her was warmly received by the protesters. A very positive aspect of this event was that for the first time in quite a while, almost all the various New Afrikan groups worked together. To me, during this first week in November 1979 it really looked like a resurgent New Afrikan Independence Movement (NAIM), with a coalition of political groups and an allied clandestine capacity, was coming together.

My first months under, not yet animated by that spectacular event, were in many ways dreary and difficult. Making two major under/over life changes in less than two years was hard. Not being in an organization meant fewer resources and a lot less help in making decisions. I was still earning my living as a furniture mover; the flexible hours and the ebb and flow of workers made for both invisibility and anonymity, and I was back in New York, living on the Upper West Side of Manhattan near Columbia University, where I had graduated thirteen years earlier. Neither choice would have been viable were I being hunted, and possibly both would have to change in the future, but for now these arrangements were OK.

Politically I was trying to implement the lessons from the collapse of the WUO, particularly the importance of operating under Third World leadership and the responsibility to use white privilege to provide material aid. There was no group I admired more than the BLA, but in the context of clandestinity the forms and formats for solidarity were quite different from, for example, my relationship with El Comité in Denver. Now, I wasn't having regular political discussions with a range of people, but rather occasional clandestine meetings with a single contact. Sometimes we talked politics but more often the focus was on immediate tasks.

Underground, without any organization, I was now taking no responsibility for anti-racist organizing among white people, and I had no contact with other people of color struggles or even with other New Afrikan groups. Other white revolutionaries had a more developed history and higher level of alliance with this BLA unit, but initially I didn't even know about them, and we never had a collective relationship. They probably had serious questions as to how reliable I would be, given that I had been a stalwart of the now-discredited WUO.

A top political priority for this unit was their concern about a plague of serial killings of young Black males in the Atlanta area. The death toll was up into the twenties, with no cases solved. Many in the Black community there thought these deaths were a wave of terror perpetrated by the Ku Klux Klan, perhaps in collaboration with some elements of the police. There were rumors that some of the youths had been ordered into what looked like a sheriff's squad car. The BLA wanted to send cadres down to Atlanta to investigate and try to solve these murders. (The perception of racist violence was later defused when an eccentric Black man, Wayne Williams, was arrested and convicted for several of these killings, based on questionable forensic evidence later shown to be invalid. While the rate of such murders slowed after his arrest, they didn't stop—although media attention to them did.)

This armed clandestine organization was concerned about the dual legacy of the destruction of the Panthers and then the influx of drugs into the ghettos. In their view, the underground had a responsibility to support community programs that worked against drug addiction, and also to support efforts to raise revolutionary nationalist consciousness among the youth. Internationally, they felt an especially strong bond with the recent victory for majority rule in Zimbabwe and were eager to support the struggle against apartheid in South Africa. They also expressed strong solidarity with the recently arrested Puerto Rican militants and with all political prisoners.

Accomplishing any of these goals required some fundraising. What the law defined as "robbery," we considered "expropriation"—taking back a miniscule percentage of the trillions of dollars that businesses and the government had looted from the oppressed. And, revolutionaries were not going to be awarded grants from the Rockefeller or Ford Foundation. The first wave of the BLA had taken its heaviest casualties during high-risk fundraising activities. We hoped a face of white respectability would greatly reduce the risk of confrontation and thereby the danger of gunfire.

My work was a classic example of using white privilege to provide material aid. I could readily rent cars, thus averting the need to steal them. And with my white face and middle-class style, I could defuse the hostility that often greeted Black men in white neighborhoods. For example, when a businessman became suspicious of a group of Blacks, I was there to complain about how "my workers" were goofing off. The irony was twofold: the men were far from "goofing off," and "my workers" were in fact my political leadership.

Socialism?

I was able to have a little bit of contact with aboveground activists and to pursue some studies. An economics professor doing solidarity work with Third World revolutionary movements helped me understand the incredible obstacles to building a viable and more equitable economy after liberation. Her real-world experience combined with my related study brought home just how overwhelming the obstacles could be. Most of the countries that achieved liberation after 1975 were immediately beset by brutal, U.S.-sponsored guerrilla opposition—for example, the "contras" in Nicaragua, the UNITA in Angola, and the MNR in Mozambique. These organizations were terrorist in the true sense of the word, because they targeted civilians, especially health workers and educators trying to improve the lives of the impoverished in the countryside.

Meanwhile, these small countries were being drained of their wealth through unequal exchange in a world market where prices on raw materials from the Third World were artificially low while the prices on advanced machinery and technology were artificially high. These problems were compounded when the U.S. imposed a boycott. Now if one key component broke—say the drive shaft on a tractor—there was no replacement part and the whole machine was rendered useless.

The legacy of underdevelopment also took a human toll. With a largely uneducated population, very few people had the technical and administrative skills crucial to building a modern economy, which left the grave danger that this narrow sector could develop into a new elite. Even the revolutionary party, with its base in the peasantry and working class, was usually led by people from a petit-bourgeois background that had afforded them some access to education.

The scope and depth of these problems didn't render the situation hopeless—the great strengths of these revolutions had been in the mobilization of the impoverished majority, liberating tremendous energy and creativity. And there was a potential to change the balance of forces in the world as more countries became liberated. But the sustaining of major advances for the majority and the laying of a foundation for building socialism were far from automatic. The structure and pervasiveness of the world market militated against such success. Some theorists, like Samir Amin, thought that Third World countries could attain more leverage by forming regional blocks (e.g. Africa, South America)—but it was almost impossible to achieve such unity in practice. (This set of formidable obstacles later became the subject of a May 1986 essay and study guide on "National Liberation and Socialism," which I wrote jointly with solidarity activist and chair of Revolution in Africa Action Committee, Judy Jensen.)

Such studies aside, my lack of collectivity and the task orientation in my work were frustrating. But the example of the dramatic freeing of Assata sold me on the value of well-organized and highly skilled clandestine operations. At the same time, I was going through changes in my personal life that were more than exciting and also incredibly demanding.

Dancing Feet

Kathy's contractions are getting stronger. I'm out in the street hailing a taxi, my emotions a charged combination of anxious and thrilled. For some reason what's going through my mind are all those scenes from TV and the movies where the expectant dad is totally bumbling and useless. I'm determined to be focused and calm.

When the cabbie pulls over to the curb and sees that Kathy is ready-to-burst-big, his eyes get wide enough to match. I give him the address and tell him the best route: "Go down Riverside Drive, which is a divided street with favorable light patterns and not too much traffic." The nervous cabbie quickly turns into the wrong side of the divided street, driving downtown with the uptown traffic heading right at us. Now it is a struggle to stay calm. As firmly and clearly as I can, I tell him, "OK, there's a cross-over at the next corner. Take it across the divide and then take a left to head downtown." And we're on our way.

A big part of my coming to New York was to get back together with Kathy. We had a long-term, deep bond of love, along with our share of past difficulties and mutual hurts. The soundtrack for my solo and roundabout trip from Denver to New York was "Reunited" by Peaches and Herb.

The reunion was indeed sweet, but the lack of organization and community also meant a challenging new context for our relationship. One way we tried not to get locked into the traditional couple mindset was to have separate places, even though we spent most nights together. Given New York City rents and our modest budget, I rented a room in someone else's apartment. Mainly we tried to treat each other with respect and talk out differences. We almost never bickered, if anything erring on the side of compromise. On a rare occasion when we got to compare notes with another politically conscious couple, and they asked how issues got resolved, each of us said that the other was the one who prevailed 60 percent of the time.

But one issue eclipsed all the others. Kathy dropped a bombshell: she wanted to have a baby. I was most reluctant to do so. My worries and fears look ridiculous today, with our son now a wonderful young man, the greatest joy in my life and, for whatever genetics are worth, my best contribution to society. But the reasons to worry were totally real. Living underground is a precarious existence, and there was always the risk of a bust that would suddenly leave the child parentless.

Our diverging sentiments also reflected gender differences. With us now in our mid-thirties, a woman's "biological clock" was on the horizon for her. As for me, despite all my earlier vanity about fatherhood, I still suffered the common male fear of being tied down. Even underground, I had spent time and bonded with children, but it's a hell of a lot easier to be the buoyant "uncle," arriving once a week for fun and games, than to have awesome parental responsibility, twenty-four hours a day, seven days a week.

Most people in the world had no choice but to have their children in the most precarious of conditions—poverty, lack of medical care, civil wars and violent repression. There was no way for us to now wait for ideal conditions. But there were ways we could mitigate the dangers for the child, by modifying what risks we faced, by agreeing we'd never have both parents at the same risky scene, and by lining up willing and able "godparents." After we had lots of discussion and worked on some practical steps to best protect the child, Kathy—most thankfully and wonderfully—carried the day on this issue.

Her pregnancy entailed amazing physical changes, but also lots of preparation. Kathy, much more than I, studied what foods *not* to eat— even a cup of coffee was out—and equally importantly how to fulfill her now much higher nutritional requirements. Many forms of exercise were fine, and Kathy remained physically active. There were baby clothes and cribs to buy (on our budget, everything was secondhand), and a host of other concerns: knowing what inoculations the baby would need and when; whether, if the baby was a boy, to circumcise him; and the challenge of picking a name, since no particular choice clicked into place.

Our most valuable decision was to join a natural birth class at a birthing center, with provisions for a midwife to handle the actual delivery. The mothers and their partners (often the baby's father but sometimes a lesbian coparent or a close friend) took the classes and practiced the breathing and relaxation techniques together.

We made a few friends in the class, particularly James and Nina, who both exuded an easygoing warmth. James was originally from Kenya; Nina was a white American. Kathy and I couldn't reveal that we were underground, but we did share many values and sentiments. The first time we went swimming together, I saw that James had scars all over his body. Shocked, I asked, "How did you get those?" He replied matter-of-factly, "The British caught me working for the independence movement in Kenya, the 'Mau Mau,' when I was eleven. They tied me to the back of a jeep and then drove it down a dirt road—hence all the scars. After that they threw me into a pit with a grating on top, which served as my jail cell. An international agency intervened to get children released and deported; that's how I came to the U.S." James, who had far less education than I, could speak four different languages, which was standard for East Africa. The birth class led to a lasting friendship, and the two resulting "babies" are still good friends today.

When I was nineteen, the first two contemporaries I knew who became fathers had told me that they lost interest in their wives sexually as their bodies swelled. My reaction was the opposite. As the pregnancy proceeded, Kathy looked more and more attractive to me. Naturally there's a strong emotional bond of creating and nurturing life together, but even on a physical level her body became more luscious—what could be sexier?—as the pregnancy progressed.

Of course it's easy for me to romanticize pregnancy—which can become extremely taxing and uncomfortable for the woman. Pregnancy raises the body temperature a whole degree, and our baby was due in the sweltering heat of August. But Kathy, happy about being pregnant, rarely complained and remained emotionally focused and physically active the whole time.

Before long we found out that our baby (we made a point not to learn the sex before birth) lay in the wrong position, with the head up rather than down in the uterus. Feet-first, or breech, births are doubly dangerous: for the baby because the head is inside the birth canal longer and the umbilical cord can get wrapped around the neck and cut off oxygen; for the mother because of a chance of greater tearing and bleeding. When the baby is turned feet down, doctors routinely schedule Cesarean sections, which are, in any case, more convenient and profitable for the doctor. Concerned about the toll of anesthetics and surgery on the mother and baby, we didn't want to make the C-section automatic; we wanted to go for a vaginal birth if it could be done safely. We kept trying holistic methods to turn the baby; at the same time we had a back-up plan with a supportive obstetrician who told us she was willing to try for the natural birth, but only in a hospital.

The night the contractions came on strong, we called Nina, who had given birth just five weeks earlier, and she said she'd meet us at the birthing center. When we arrived—after a shaky start down the wrong side of Riverside Drive—the midwife could tell that the baby still hadn't turned. We now had to head back uptown to the hospital, but this time, with Nina driving, the trip was less harrowing.

At the hospital they sent us down to X-ray, to see if Kathy's pelvic structure could accommodate a breech birth, or whether we had to go straight to a C-section. The hour was now late enough that we were dealing with the graveyard shift. They were wonderful! The X-ray technician, a middle-aged Black man with tortoise-shell glasses, could see our anxiety, and casually assured us that everything would be OK.

And so it was. We were sent up to a small prebirth room, where a nurse and a young resident each came in intervals to check on us. We'd learned breathing techniques for each stage of the labor, and that's what we concentrated on. I'm not a take-charge kind of guy, and Kathy, despite all the pain, was focused and coherent throughout. I wasn't so much her "coach," as some trainings would have it, as her partner, sounding-board, and shoulder to lean on.

By 6:00 a.m., Kathy had been in labor for close to twelve hours. Timing the contractions as I'd been taught in class, I thought the birth was imminent. We called in the young resident, who checked the dilation of the cervix and said, no, the birth was still a couple of hours away; but that in any case the obstetrician, who had been called and awakened an hour earlier, was on her way. A few minutes later, I saw two little feet pop out of her. The nurse, who was with us at that moment, exclaimed, "Look, the baby's dancing into the world!" Then everything moved into high gear as they wheeled Kathy into the delivery room, with me by her side, just as the obstetrician came rushing in. At 6:17, with a big push and gushes of blood, our child was born. The nurses and doctor worked at lightning speed to get the baby's head free, and then to untangle the umbilical cord from around the neck and then to cut it. Seeing signs of stress, they pumped the baby's lungs to clear out blood and other debris. "Look!" said the doctor, "a boy—and we think he's completely healthy. We'll have to do some tests to be sure, because of the difficult birth." Wow!

Before long our baby was at his mother's breast, and soon after that both fell asleep. They had done the exhausting work, but I was on the adrenaline rush of a lifetime—out the door and off into the city. I walked the streets in the early morning sunlight; then called the few friends I could, to give them the good news; then did some (unnecessary) shopping for additional baby accessories. I don't remember any of the specifics, just the feeling of elation. It wasn't until eleven that night, a Thursday that I wound down and realized that I hadn't been to sleep since Tuesday night.

In one way we were totally unprepared for the birth—we hadn't come up with a name. That wasn't from a lack of working on it. This deficiency was much more on me than on Kathy, because I was firmly against naming a child after anyone else—whether a beloved family member or a revered revolutionary. My somewhat stubborn view was that every person is unique and should be unencumbered by any expectation to be like anyone else. I loved the traditions in some Native American and African tribes of picking names from nature or from events at the time of the birth. We found some beautiful names, but they weren't from our experience or culture. Then we focused on the unique aspect of this birth, which the nurse had articulated so well: the first signs of this baby were his feet dancing into the world. We starting looking into how to say "Dancing Feet" in various languages. Our first try was from our own cultural background, but the term in Yiddish had much too harsh a sound. Then we tracked down how to say it in Swahili, a kind of lingua franca for East Africa, with the much more pleasing sound of "Chesa." As an added plus, James told us that when folks partied in Kenya they often shouted, "Chesa!"—sort of like "Dance!" or "Get Down!" in English.

Coming up with this name took over two months and was finalized as the three of us took a lovely hike, with the baby held against my chest in a Snugli, through the exquisite autumn colors of a New England woods. "Baby Boy" was now Chesa. There was something else special about his birth—the date. On August 21, nine years earlier, the eloquent and inspiring prisoners' rights activist and BPP field marshal, George Jackson, had been killed at San Quentin prison. Given the date and the great admiration for him, I had to make an exception to my general rule, as we gave the baby the middle name of "Jackson." Such a unique name as Chesa was problematical for being under in that it might be remembered in scenes we were just passing through, so at the tender age of three months the baby also had a pseudonym, the closest sound-alike, "Jason" or "Jase."

After a few months, when his neck was strong enough to support his head, Chesa graduated to a little backpack. While not nearly as warm and cozy as the Snugli, it enabled him to look out over my shoulder at the wider world. At six months—even though I knew it was far too early for him to focus in on such fine detail—he joined me on a trip to the Metropolitan Museum of Art. Much to my surprise, he eagerly responded to the paintings, pointing and cooing at them over my shoulder. Like me, he was a big Monet fan.

Whether admiring Monets, or playing in a park, or bopping onto a bus and enjoying the array of new faces, our mutual delight in being together was totally evident. Total strangers, almost always women, would compliment me on what a great dad I was and say how much they enjoyed seeing us together. I soaked up the effusive praise and couldn't help crowing about it to Kathy, who brought me back from the clouds to more solid ground. "You know I've never once received such a compliment, even though I'm just as good a parent as you, and with Chesa a lot more. It's just taken for granted that mothers will do all that and more, but considered special and admirable for a father." In 1980 it was still unusual for men to do a major share of childcare and to be out, alone, with an infant. Kathy's observation wasn't said as a put-down of my parenting—she fully encouraged and loved my time and rapport with our child—but was meant as a reminder of social realities and perhaps also to help prevent me from getting too swelled a head.

And in fact, Kathy was doing much more than half of the parenting. Totally committed to breast-feeding, because it is so much healthier for both child and mother and such an intimate bond, we had agreed that she would spend more time with the baby the first year, while I would put in more hours earning our living. Then the next year, after Chesa was weaned, we would switch those roles.

We never got to implement that second year.

Back Above, the Hard Way

Despite my self-image, I wasn't such a terrific father in all ways. Yes, as I had long envisioned (actually, even more than I had imagined), I was exuberant with my son, fully expressing my affection and always encouraging his wonder at the world. I read about and took all the steps to baby-proof the apartments, such as covering any electrical sockets he could reach. At the same time, without guidance and support from an extended family,

I was oblivious to other common hazards. For example, he had two bad falls that I should have anticipated and averted. Fortunately, his resiliency made up for my inattention.

The mundane daily miscues were only a minor reflection of deeper structural problems and should have been a warning that my situation was becoming increasingly untenable. Underground work demands clarity and careful attention to detail. My isolation and lack of collectivity, the task orientation of my assignments, and my lack of strategic overview all combined to take a toll on how well I functioned. As the months went by, the strain of handling family, job, and the political work—and the stress that meant for my family—became more telling.

As it became clear that we should surface, I was initially reluctant. I had turned my life upside down to surface in 1977, and then to come back under in 1979; I didn't want to deal with a third such major disruption less than two years later. Politically, I was still taken with the brilliant success of the underground in freeing Assata. While frustrated about not being in a collective and not having more political dialogue and overview, I was anxious, given the failures of the WUO, to demonstrate that I could be useful and dependable; and hopeful that a better political relationship would be built on my proving myself in practice.

Despite my reluctance, by March 1981, I came to see that the situation just wasn't viable for my family and that we had to work out a way to surface. The unit I was relating to was understanding of that need. Still, our making a careful and responsible transition, as well as dealing with legal issues and negotiations, would take some time. But the basic decision was made in principle, and we planned to complete the process and surface by the time of Chesa's first birthday.

A lot of things happened in August, but surfacing wasn't one of them. In that month Chesa said his first words and took his first steps—exciting advances in the life of any child. It's awesome that kids somehow accomplish these two different, most amazing milestones of human development at pretty much the same time. Once he could walk, he'd refuse to revert to his more stable and still faster crawl, even when we played at chasing each other. And he always had something in his hands. The psychological theory I'd read said that walking was such a scary new step that the child held onto familiar objects for a sense of security. But the exuberant look on Chesa's face suggested a different explanation to me: the child was relishing the new-found ability to carry things as he moved, in a way reprising why bipedalism had been such an advance for our species ages ago.

Our own first steps toward surfacing were not going nearly as well, as we weren't making the determined effort needed to quickly hack our way through the political, psychological, and legal thickets involved. So we took a short excursion, Chesa's first backpacking trip, high into the mountains. Two friends and I carried Kathy's share of the gear, while she had the most precious cargo on her back. Chesa was never so much at home, in his element, as he was outdoors in the woods. We still have a picture of him in the mountain air with a smile that could illuminate the world.

As always, the political and personal were closely interwoven. The ways I was out of sync politically impinged on my sensitivity to family needs; the difficulties for my family in turn made it harder for me to function well politically. From my considerable underground experience, I knew it was unwise to give high-risk assignments to someone who didn't have a full understanding of the politics and strategy involved. Yet in effect I was doing that to myself because, in the franticness of trying to help one last time before I surfaced, I didn't get a full picture of my own role even on the tactical level. Another, and still shocking, example of being way out of kilter is that despite our earlier firm guidelines, both parents ended up in a danger zone. Finally, my own lack of focus played a role—one, as I later learned, of several mistakes—in the disaster that unfolded on October 20, 1981.

{ BUSTED }

"*The government that dropped napalm in Vietnam, that provides the cluster bombs used against civilians in Lebanon, and that trains torturers in El Salvador calls us 'terrorists.' The rulers who have grown rich on generations of slave labor and slave wages...label us as 'criminals.' The police forces of Amerika who have murdered 2,000 [people of color] over the past five years and who flood the communities with drugs say that we 'have no respect for human lives.'*

"We are neither terrorists nor criminals. It is precisely because of our love of life, because we revel in the human spirit, that we became freedom fighters against this racist and deadly imperialist system." (From my statement in court, September 13, 1982.)

Everything, just everything, goes wrong on October 20, 1981. First of all, for my immediate family: we were supposed to have surfaced two months earlier, and instead, inexcusably, both parents have ended up on the same dangerous operation. Now, in the distance, there's the ominous sound of gunshots—despite this BLA unit's consistent practice of taking control quickly and decisively to prevent gunfire, which can lead to unnecessary casualties and draw police. Then, a confused switch point with, as it turns out, a rare moment of a resident looking out her rear window. A little later, a light turns red, and during that half-minute delay police cars block off a turnpike entrance. A stop, a shoot-out, a chase, a crash, the $1,580,000 taken from the Brink's truck eventually recovered by the police...The grim toll for the day includes a Brink's guard and two policemen killed, three others wounded, and four revolutionaries arrested. A cascade of busts and other losses follow in the days and months ahead, including BLA militant Mtayari Shabaka Sundiata, killed by the police on October 23.

In my twenty years as an activist I had never experienced the force and fury of the state in such a close-up, immediate, and personal way. Amid the assaults came the distress of learning that people had been killed. The beatings and threats, surprisingly, didn't shake me; there is an inner calm in knowing that, no matter what, talking is not an option. After hours of questions, fists and a shotgun barrel, I was taken out of interrogation to get fingerprinted, and I caught a glimpse of Kathy. We exchanged a longing look, a shared anguish about our toddler son. Late that night we were taken to a makeshift arraignment, in a completely charged and hostile atmosphere. A codefendant, Samuel Brown was brought in, unable to sit up, moaning in pain, and with his pants falling down.

Trial by Trial

The physical test at the point of capture was nothing compared to the emotional pressures, duress, and difficulties that followed for the next two years, until the completion of the trial. The state has you in its grasp, ready to put you away for life; the media and local community are screaming for your blood; much of the Left denounces you for your violent actions; your family has had the fabric of their lives ripped apart by your cavalier decisions; loved ones are urging you to mount a traditional, legalistic defense; the other defendants themselves have differing approaches, with little opportunity to communicate, on how to build political support and fight the case in court.

My main focus during that initial period was on staying in one piece psychically, first through a challenging week in Rockland County Jail (RCJ), and then through ten weeks in isolation. The sheriffs who ran RCJ considered themselves in a state of war with us. Sam Brown and I were on different floors, and the two women, Kathy and Judy Clark, were isolated on a separate, female wing. When I was taken off the floor to be fingerprinted again, I was jumped, knocked down, and kicked by four correctional officers (COs). I later found out that Brown was assaulted a few times by the same goon squad. One of the leading members later spoke proudly to us of being a born-again Christian and tried to convert us.

The first unknown for me was how other prisoners would react. On the one hand, I knew that most didn't like the police; on the other, our case was notorious and considered heinous in the community. The COs did their best to inflame other inmates against us, but establishing rapport with the other eight men on my floor proved to be no problem. When supporters left me money for commissary, I naturally shared with those who had nothing. With the atmosphere on the floor so peaceful, the COs regularly brought along their lapdog inmate—big, young, and evidently stupid—to threaten me from the other side of the bars that enclosed our floor. The one time I ran into him without bars separating us, he immediately apologized, saying he hoped I understood.

After a couple of days, I relaxed a bit too much. Even though I knew it wasn't wise to go to sleep before we were all locked in, I was exhausted from the ordeals of the past few days and went to bed with the cell gates open and the other inmates out on the gallery. I hadn't yet fallen asleep when I heard a new arrestee brought up to the floor. He knew some of the guys and, after they told him who I was, said, "Well come on, let's go fuck him up." I decided that it was best to pretend I was asleep to at least have the element of surprise by springing out of bed when they came into my cell. But I heard another voice answer the new jack: "Nah, he seems like a pretty good guy." I'm not sure what saved me from that beating—my personality, my generosity with commissary, the good heart of my fellow prisoners? I'd guess that the biggest factor was that the more experienced guys in Rockland County Jail knew that my case would be highly respected by state prisoners, who were mostly Black, and they didn't want an unnecessary jailhouse beef to follow them upstate. By week's end, it was clear that the COs' efforts to turn other inmates against us had failed.

Isolation

They're marching me, handcuffed, to a barber's chair. After a couple of weeks in isolation, they have to give me a haircut, especially with court appearances imminent. I count seven COs in a circle around me, as the inmate barber walks in. He's blond and blue-eyed, with the look of an experienced con. I'm nervous. I've read a lot about white supremacist gangs in prison. Is this haircut a set-up? Am I about to get stabbed in the neck with a scissors?

Now he's trimming the side of my head. With the electric razor blocking the view of his lips and its buzz covering the sound, he whispers into my ear: "You know, don't you, that guys in here all support you; we love you for standing up to the cops. You gotta be careful, though—don't talk to anybody about your case. The unit they're holding you on is filled with rats." While my face doesn't betray any emotions to the COs, I couldn't be more pleased—not only that the barber expressed his solidarity but also that he provided such a good example of how to function in a cool way to communicate under these most repressive conditions.

After about a week at RCJ, they shipped us out to federal prisons. The two women were sent to Manhattan Correctional Center (MCC) in the city, while Brown and I went to the Federal Correctional Institution at Otisville, New York. Since we hadn't been charged with any federal crimes, the legality of these transfers was dubious, but Rockland's position was that their jail was not secure enough for the likes of us. The first thing the feds did upon my arrival was to take pictures of all my bruises, which meant pretty much every inch of my body. The feds didn't want legal liability for my earlier beatings. Now, instead of being on a floor with eight other prisoners, I was alone in a cell in a Special Housing Unit (SHU), "the box," in lockdown twenty-three hours a day, with no contact with other prisoners.

The first day the guy in the next cell did try to talk to me, despite the difficulty of the solid door and thick walls, but a CO spotted him, and he was given a disciplinary write-up and moved out. Then the administration took all the other inmates off that wing, leaving just Brown and me with a few empty cells in between us. Once when I was being escorted to a medical check-up, we walked by an indoor recreation area. The heavily tattooed, muscular white prisoner lifting weights inside saw me and went to the glass to hold up pictures from a "girlie" magazine for my view. Such meat rack displays were not my thing, but I knew he felt he was doing me a favor and taking a risk to do so. I gave him a friendly nod, and he tried to tell me something in pantomime, but I couldn't figure it out before I was whisked away. It wasn't until two weeks later with the barber's whispered words that I realized that he was probably also trying to warn me about snitches—sound warnings but unnecessary in practice, since the isolation cell blocked me from any social interaction with other prisoners.

Solitary confinement can be extremely boring, especially when I didn't yet have defined work on my case and hadn't had a chance yet to develop other personal projects. Outside supporters sent me books, and I tore through the 1,200 pages of *Shogun*, a book I never would have taken the time to read on the outside. I did mental exercises to keep track of time and to stay sharp. Pacing the cell and doing push-ups—and after a while, an occasional hour of outside recreation—were of limited benefit in terms of physical fitness, but did a lot to burn off nervous tension. And a number of political supporters bravely corresponded with me. In my letters, I quipped, "President Reagan, who has killed thousands of people in order to steal trillions from the poor to give to the rich, is revered as a great statesman; we, who are accused of killing three people in an armed robbery of $1.6 million from the rich to give to the poor, are reviled as heinous criminals."

The only visits we were allowed were either immediate family or lawyers, and the procedures to set them up were cumbersome. My mom and dad, now in their seventies, made the physically demanding and emotionally arduous journey from Boston to Otisville. They were calmer than I had expected and, as always, very loving. They said they knew me well enough to be sure that whatever I did came from humanitarian motives, but that nonetheless they could in no way condone actions that led to deaths. They hoped I understood that what I did was terribly wrong; they still loved me and supported me personally. We agreed that they would not spend their retirement savings on lawyers; they did want to help support their grandchild, Chesa, who, naturally, they found to be absolutely delightful. They had met the other grandparents, the Boudins, and liked and admired them. As we hugged goodbye, I felt incredibly blessed to have them for parents.

While the atmosphere at Otisville didn't feel as embattled as at Rockland, the conditions of solitary confinement were more repressive. I was on a "two-man hold," which meant I couldn't leave the cell for anything—even the shower I got three times a week, or the occasional rec period—without at least two COs to watch me. Before they would open the door, I had to stick my arms out, behind my back, through a slot to be cuffed. Then they would open the door and put chains on my ankles. I was subject to frequent pat frisks and strip searches, even going to and coming from rec where I had no contact with anyone. One CO turned a pat frisk into a sexual groping. I turned and warned him in no uncertain terms never to do that again. The excessive searches and less than one hour per day for recreation led me to suspect that the prison was not affording me legal minimum standards. I demanded and got limited access to the law library, which led to my getting a little more outdoors rec (as I remember it, now up to three hours a week) in a small yard, and then access to that haircut.

My most immediate worry was Brown's terrible physical and mental condition. Although we were separated by a few empty cells, Brown, who had done time before, alerted me to how we could talk to each other through the vents—although such conversations had to be brief since a CO came by our cells every fifteen minutes. I'd never met Brown before the bust, so I didn't have any baseline for comparison, but it was clear that he had seriously deteriorated. He moaned about the pain in his neck and the side effects from the painkillers they were giving him. Mainly he ranted incoherently, and my best efforts on the vents didn't do much to help him. The authorities could see that he was falling apart, and COs would stop by his cell to taunt him. Whenever I heard that, I would yell out insults at the COs. My usual style, even with cops, is to be polite and soft-spoken, but this was an effort to get them to leave the vulnerable Brown alone and mess with me instead. It didn't work; like buzzards they kept circling the most defenseless body. Then the visits to taunt Brown abated as the COs began to take him out for doctor's visits. I could hardly complain about that: I'd been demanding medical care for Brown both directly to prison personnel and by getting outside supporters to call the federal Bureau of

Prisons. While I was suspicious about the excursions off the unit, Brown confirmed to me that he was seeing a doctor, although he couldn't give me a coherent account of diagnosis or treatment.

Because I felt Brown was suffering a breakdown in spirit and sanity, I sent word to the outside that getting support to him should be our most urgent priority. He wasn't getting family visits, so that meant a lawyer, both as someone to talk to and to demand better treatment. But October 20 had led to a cascade of serious busts and crises, and our extremely limited legal resources had been stretched far beyond the breaking point. What little we had was tied up in a chance for a significant legal victory. Mississippi State Police and the FBI had used tanks and a helicopter to arrest a mother and a household of children around our case because of her prominent role in the aboveground and legal Republic of New Afrika. Our few legal people got them released, which exposed some of the government's overkill in political cases. At the same time, some of the outside decision-makers didn't credit my assessment of Brown because I had no previous prison experience. They assumed—perhaps this was wishful thinking—that the jailwise Brown was putting on a crazy act as a way to fend off harassment.

At this point there was basically just one lawyer seeing the four of us in custody and dealing with the host of contentious pretrial issues. Susan Tipograph was a feminist and anti-racist attorney who had done work with the white anti-imperialist political group supporting those captured, the May 19th Communist Organization. Tipograph showed great courage and determination in walking into the criminal justice furnace that engulfed us. When she arranged to visit Brown and me at Otisville, the administration told her that they wouldn't allow a joint visit, but that she could see us one at a time, in turn. She called me out first to get my assessment of Brown's condition, in order to be better prepared to work with him. After using up half the allotted time, we ended our visit. I was returned to my cell but Brown was never brought out to see her; the administration reneged on the deal. Later that night Brown was yelling at me on the vents, feeling betrayed. The COs had told him, "The lawyer came but she only made time to see the white guy." The same COs later told Brown, "The white girls at MCC fingered you as the trigger man." This was one of several police ploys designed to create a Black/white split among the defendants. None of the others had worked. But Brown—in intense pain, isolated, almost delirious—was especially vulnerable. I was on the vents, every chance we got, trying to calm him down.

The COs woke me at four one morning. "Come with us." "Where are we going?" "We can't tell you—security; just do what you're told." "I want to call my lawyer." "No, no calls. Let's go." They provided some breakfast, but no coffee, and then handed me over to the Rockland County sheriffs, who chained me hand and foot. The cuffs were so tight that my hands swelled up (it was six months before the numbness in my thumbs went away). I was transported in a convoy of sheriffs' cars, with sirens screaming, racing down the highway at eighty-five miles per hour. The whole time a sheriff held a shotgun at my head, talking about how he'd love to blow me away. I didn't think he'd pull the trigger intentionally, but a bump or a skid would have done it for him.

They brought me to a courtroom packed with law enforcement personnel, heavily armed and bristling with hostility. I couldn't find one friendly face; the defense had not been notified of this "hearing." The judge, having recently ruled that Attorney Tipograph could not represent more than one defendant, told me that if I didn't have an attorney the court would now appoint one. The atmosphere was intimidating but clearly orchestrated, so I figured they needed to scare me into something that they couldn't legally impose.

Objecting that this hearing took place without notice, I refused to accept a court-appointed lawyer. While having almost no knowledge of the law, I felt that if the court imposed a lawyer on me so suddenly, over my objections, they risked any subsequent conviction getting overturned. My hunch may have been right; the judge sputtered and grumbled but gave me two months to find a lawyer. In the meantime he assigned a Legal Aid attorney to look out for my interests. Then the chains were clamped back on, I was pushed into a sheriff's car, and the convoy sped off with the shotgun at my head. The sheriffs, who all wore parkas, rolled the windows down. It was freezing cold, but I made up my mind not to shiver, and I never did. After an hour the sheriffs got cold and rolled the windows up. The only damage done was to the suit the state had provided me for court, now spattered with meltwater and mud the tires had spun up from the slushy roads. My solitary cell felt like a refuge when that day was finally over.

The most wrenching aspect of my situation was the separation from my son. He had been at daycare at the time of the bust. It had to be a fourteen-month-old child's worst nightmare, that his parents would never return for him. After we were long overdue, Nina picked him up; then, when she saw our pictures on TV, she knew what had happened. The Boudin's were prominently featured in the news stories, and Nina brought Chesa to them. So, I knew that at least he was in loving hands, but of course I had no way to fully comprehend the trauma for him or the strain for the Boudins. About to turn seventy, they now were caring for a toddler and at the same time trying to put together Kathy's legal defense.

I understood that it would take a while to set up a visit for me with Chesa. His first visit was with Kathy at MCC, a much shorter trip. The feds insisted that for "security" reasons mother and child could not touch. This was a special restriction; the norm at MCC was contact visits. Kathy offered to remove the baby's diaper in front of the guards, so that there could be no issue of his being used to smuggle anything in, but the administration was adamant: no contact. Needless to say, the visit turned into a disaster. Prohibiting the child from touching his mother was a form of torture, and within minutes he was wailing. After that, we all agreed there'd be no more trips to either of his parents until we won the right to contact visits.

The ban on mother and child touching was the cruelest of a host of unusual conditions that went beyond any legitimate security concerns. The government was using isolation and deprivation to try to break us down, to render us incapable of mounting an effective defense politically or legally. Kathy's father, Leonard Boudin, was a renowned civil liberties attorney who had won a number of landmark cases, even at the height of the McCarthy era, and had represented such people as Paul Robeson,

Rockwell Kent, and Dr. Benjamin Spock. Leonard hired lawyers to challenge the conditions at MCC (any success there could then be applied to me and Brown at Otisville) as unprecedented and undoubtedly unconstitutional for pretrial detainees. I knew about the suit but had no idea of when or how it would be resolved.

On January 7, 1982, COs woke me at four in the morning and chained me for transport. This time we weren't going to court but rather to Woodbourne, a New York State prison. At the time, I was mystified about the reasons for the move but it later became clear. The federal court was scheduled to hand down its decision in Kathy's conditions suit that day. Since Rockland County and the feds knew that what they'd been doing was illegal, they colluded and in effect kidnapped us out of the federal court's jurisdiction just hours before its decision in our favor was rendered. Now to pursue litigation against the continuing isolation and restrictions, we'd have to start all over again, in New York State courts.

When I arrived at Woodbourne the COs seemed more matter-of-fact, not personally enraged against me, as they walked me up to a small, isolated section of the prison, where I was alone in a row of three cells. At about seven in the morning I was surprised to hear women's voices. Were there female COs around? But the voices sounded familiar. Was I engaging in wishful hearing? Finally I couldn't resist and gave a shout, and I got a surprised but delighted response. The voices did indeed belong to Kathy and Judy, who were on the other side, in a set of cells back to back with my row. We now had at least voice contact!

Climbing Mountains

From the foyer of our special housing unit, waiting to be ushered into our little visiting room, we can see them slowly making their way down the hall—Leonard and Jean Boudin, with Chesa! My first instinct is to run up to my son, lift him high in the air, clasp him to my chest, kiss him. But Bill Ayers, who works in a preschool daycare center, has prepared Kathy and me for this first visit. For a one-and-a-half-year-old, the three-month gap is a long time. Initially he may not be sure who we are. We need to take it slow, give him time to get reacquainted.

Bill was right. I can see Chesa's uncertainty as he holds on to Leonard while they walk through this unfamiliar territory. When Chesa sees our beaming faces, his shows a mixed expression—a spark of recognition combined with an uncomfortable uncertainty. He quickly retreats and hides behind Leonard's leg. Then he slowly peeks out; a tentative smile is beginning to form. Kathy and I walk up slowly, then kneel to be at his level. Chesa takes his own cautious step forward; then, a hesitant hug seamlessly segues into long, full-hearted ones. Our bond is back intact!

By the end of the three hours we feel completely close, suffused with love. Just as Bill prepared Kathy and me not to rush Chesa, his grandparents must have prepared him well, since he knows the visit has to end and seems to take that in stride.

The move to Woodbourne Correctional Facility put me in more than just voice contact with Judy and Kathy. After breakfast we were allowed to sit at our respective ends of the short hall that connected our two sides and talk, if at a distance, face-to-face. Two COs, one male and one female, were present at all times, and there was a sergeant whose main job was to supervise our unit. We were in what had been Woodbourne's SHU, or "box," cut off from the rest of the prison. There was even a small, eighteen-by-twelve-foot outside rec area, walled-in with mesh wire over the top. With greater personal contact with COs, I came to see that while their job was to keep us locked up, they were also human beings, with a great range in terms of personality and sense of decency. It's also where I learned the value of knowing prisoners' rights law, a defense against unwarranted hassles.

While it was great to be together, this brand new situation raised a couple of thorny questions. Firstly, where was Sam Brown and how was he being treated? Secondly, what could we do about being kidnapped out of the federal court's jurisdiction, into a different venue but still under illegal isolation and restrictions?

The second dilemma was resolved with the help of the lawyers who had done the suit against the feds. It was at that time unprecedented to put pretrial detainees into a New York State prison for convicted felons, not to mention holding women in a men's facility. If we sued, we'd probably win, but they'd just move us to a new jurisdiction. We'd be jumping from horse to horse on the same merry-go-round. Besides, we wanted to devote our energy and focus to fighting the criminal charges. So, with the leverage of a possible suit, the lawyers negotiated improved conditions for us within our still isolated unit. The concession that meant the most to us was that we now got contact visits, especially important for Kathy and me with Chesa, and for Judy and her daughter.

Most immediate were our worries about Brown. I learned that in response to my alarms people had found an outside doctor to review his medical records. Two vertebrae in his neck were fractured, causing him intense pain and leaving him in fear of becoming paralyzed if he didn't get surgery. X-rays taken upon arrest didn't show any fracture; his neck had been broken while in custody.

By now his debilitating pain and fear of paralysis had gone on for eleven weeks. We asked our outside political supporters, as beleaguered as they were, to make Brown's condition their first priority. Then two of us went on a juice-only hunger strike to demand medical care for him. The staff and administration at Woodbourne got nervous when we started refusing food, although we did our best to reassure them that our protest was not directed against them. Brown got his long-needed operation four days later. We were pretty sure our hunger strike was not the reason—it hadn't gone on long enough—but we were definitely relieved. (It was only months later that we figured out what had accomplished his getting this long overdue medical treatment.)

Within a week, Brown was with us in the Woodbourne SHU. While his surgery had been a success, he was still a wreck psychologically. But he seemed to enjoy having some company, being able to talk to Judy and Kathy when we were out in the hallway, and more extensively with me on the men's side. He was very voluble, and his stories were fantastic. At various times he told me that he'd been the first architect to introduce solar panels to Harlem, of his prowess as a star athlete, about his key role in the Selma march for voting rights, and later of his heroics in Vietnam—as I calculated it, in the same time frame as Selma. Clearly here was a man frantically trying to pump back up an ego that had been deflated by multiple punctures.

Privately, Brown tried to convince me that the "niggers" involved in October 20 were just trying to use me; that they were no good; that I shouldn't protect them but rather do whatever I needed to get myself off the hook. Later, Brown erupted into all-out hysteria when the radio reported that two men wanted in our case had just been captured. Screaming, "What's wrong with them? Didn't I tell them to get out of town?" he started pounding the walls and then ran into his cell (our doors were open at this hour) and started sobbing. I headed toward him in hopes of placing a soothing arm on his shoulder, to be someone to talk to, but the CO on our unit ordered me to stay away from Brown, so I had to try to comfort him and talk him down from ten feet away.

His outburst made me wonder if he'd given up information that had led to the arrest and was now distressed due to a guilty conscience. But Brown wasn't capable of frank discussions, and I had no way to sort the situation out. I asked the main New Afrikan organization supporting us to find him a Black lawyer for both legal and emotional support. The attorney they found was a staunch nationalist and not afraid to stand up to the government, but he had little experience in BPP or BLA cases. After visiting once he gave Woodbourne an order that no lawyer other than himself be permitted to see Brown. Perhaps he was concerned that government lawyers would try to sneak in or that, understandably, our all-white cultural milieu would be difficult for the traumatized Brown. The problem was that this lawyer was busy and didn't make it back up to Woodbourne again while we were there. The order meant that Brown couldn't join our legal meetings, leaving him feeling excluded and unprotected—and often alone on the unit with the COs.

The main Black organization building support for the defendants was the New Afrikan People's Organization (NAPO), the branch of the Republic of New Afrika that focused on support for Prisoners of War and Political Prisoners (POW/PPs). Their most visible spokesperson was Ahmed Obafemi, a calm and intelligent veteran of the struggle. The main white organization was May 19th, initially one of the groups that had split from PFOC after the disastrous Hard Times Conference. These two groups were the core of the Coalition to Defend the October 20th Freedom Fighters. They showed great courage and determination in entering the hurricane howling around us at the time, with the local community wanting our blood and much of the Left condemning us as criminals. Despite insults and threats, they showed up for all our court appearances in Rockland County, often carrying signs supporting "The October 20th Freedom Fighters."

My main contact with the coalition was with May 19th people. They defined themselves in opposition to the opportunism that had led to the 1976 collapse of the WUO, yet they reminded me a lot of us in our early days—fiercely extolling anti-racism and militancy, while insufferably arrogant and sectarian to those who didn't fully agree with them. One big difference was that their leadership was almost all women and predominantly lesbian. As we were all to learn over the next two years, female leadership is not an automatic structural guarantee against hierarchy and commandism.

The terms set for the coalition were "unconditional support for the freedom fighters." Not long after the bust, Bob Feldman, an old friend from Columbia SDS, wrote to me. He and his partner, Jan Cannavan, were longtime supporters of the Irish Republican political party Sinn Fein. Based on that model, Bob argued—and I agreed—that the basis for support should be a lot broader; that many people who disagreed with the action might still defend us as political prisoners—as people who, whatever mistakes had been made, had been motivated by and fighting for a legitimate cause. The narrowness of the coalition's terms became most apparent in Denver, where old friends of mine started a branch. Most did not consider themselves revolutionary and definitely didn't endorse armed struggle, but still wanted to support us as people motivated by anti-racism. I found it unreasonable to browbeat them about endorsing the Brink's expropriation, but my arguments in this regard fell on deaf ears.

In truth, I myself didn't extend "unconditional support" to myself or my comrades, since I felt we needed to analyze our mistakes. Over the years I'd followed many cases where revolutionaries were busted on charges of armed struggle. I believed there were two fundamental yet very difficult responsibilities in such a situation: in the face of the firestorm of repression and criticism, to continue to uphold the basic principles of fighting against racism and imperialism, and at the same time to engage in self-criticism so that the broader movement could learn from the setback. Each task is extremely difficult under the circumstances; doing both at the same time can feel impossibly contradictory. It's a given that the same establishment that consistently refuses to prosecute or even renounce the government's attacks against a peaceful movement will vehemently discredit armed resistance as "criminal" and "terrorist." At the same time most of the Left will also condemn such actions, usually arguing that any armed struggle provides a pretext for government repression of the broader, legal movement. Also, much of the predominantly white Left opposed revolutionary Black nationalism.

A common criticism of us was that there was nothing political about a robbery. To me that was a shuck since almost all revolutions have used expropriations to obtain funds. The highly political purposes of the BLA should have been obvious, given that this same grouping was also accused of breaking Assata Shakur out of prison. Also, those still at large had put out a communiqué from the "Revolutionary Armed Task Force" stating the need for resources to stop a "Black Holocaust" and to help rebuild nationalist programs for ghetto youth. (As it turned out, their account of how funds were used was not fully forthright.) I would quip that the same leftists who loved Robin Hood of old couldn't abide modern revolutionaries recouping some of the wealth that had been plundered from New Afrikans.

Some of my friends sincerely couldn't understand why I would "advocate" a Republic of New Afrika. The idea of the breaking apart of the

United States, with a separate Black nation located in the five "black belt" states in the South, seemed completely outlandish. As I explained, *I* didn't advocate that or any other specific solution for Black people; that was their determination to make. But I felt completely comfortable supporting the RNA, as a principled organization making a legitimate demand. Solidarity with them was a way to highlight the New Afrikan right to be an independent nation; and the idea of secession, while radical, was not as "outlandish" as the way the "United" States had been put together—conquering and subsuming whole nations of Native Americans, New Afrikans, Mexicans, Puerto Ricans, Hawaiians. In any case, the important point here for white radicals wasn't the practicality of any particular solution to racism, but rather the politics of solidarity—respect and support for principled Black challenges to the white supremacist basis of America.

At the same time there was obviously, even if I came to grips with it slowly, a lot to analyze critically about our actions: four people had been killed, three wounded, many revolutionaries busted; clandestine networks had crumbled, and the movement as a whole had suffered a major setback. These human and political consequences were very serious. Kathy was a positive influence on me to look more critically at what had happened, an approach in keeping with my long-held views on the responsibilities of PPs.

Even when under fierce attack from the state and media, we need to both fight back and analyze our mistakes. We have to consider criticisms from the movement; and even when criticized from the Right, by forces that seek only to discredit us, we have to examine the content because unprincipled people can seize on real weaknesses to use in their polemics. As revolutionaries, our commitment isn't to our own status but rather to advancing the struggle. Indeed, if we can draw out useful lessons, our personal sacrifices are not completely in vain.

Even though I didn't have an overview of the politics and strategy involved in "Brink's," as it came to be called, it seemed to me that there had to have been serious mistakes on many levels, but my initial attempts to get such discussions going with May 19th people gained no traction.

Nonetheless, I greatly appreciated their fierce commitment to basic principles and their willingness to support us. It was May 19th that found a lawyer willing to defend me, the extraordinary Lynne Stewart—completely unflappable and down to earth, she was like a sturdy tree for me to hold onto while being buffeted by hurricane winds. I also appreciated her political history. Lynne had been a school librarian in Ocean Hill-Brownsville and became a staunch ally of the struggle there for community control of schools that I had found so inspiring in 1968. After losing her school job, she studied law as a way to contribute to efforts for social justice. (More recently, in 2001, Lynne was disbarred and prosecuted for the offense of not abiding by government restrictions in her aggressive representation of a radical Islamic client. In 2010 she was sentenced to ten years in prison.)

Figuring out legal strategy was as complicated as, and interwoven with, political stance. While in isolation at Otisville, I'd simply assumed that we'd use a traditional Left political/legal defense: affirming our politics and the right to resist illegitimate authority while still contesting the prosecution's charges every step of the way. Versions of that approach had been employed effectively in many Panther cases, by the American Indian Movement after the siege at Wounded Knee, by a few GIs accused of "fragging" officers, and in a couple of anti-war "conspiracy" cases. But when I got to Woodbourne, to my surprise, that option didn't seem to be on the table. Two different, more polarized choices were put forward: one was to mount a straight legal defense; the other was to refuse to recognize the legitimacy of the government's courts to try us at all, and to engage in the proceedings as little as possible.

In this tough situation, the divergent positions reflected differences in both political and legal analysis. Was the action so terribly flawed that, instead of defending it in any way, we should just do our best legally to minimize our losses? Or were the October 20th Freedom Fighters leading exemplars of struggle to be extolled? Given the nature of the events and the intensity of the local community's hatred for us, how much could be gained from a legalistic approach? And what would it take to get our political positions heard?

The two strategies, while very different, weren't necessarily antagonistic, given that none of us would consider taking steps to hurt or undermine other defendants. Each pole had some outside support and legal resources behind it. I didn't fully agree with either, but had neither the means nor the inclination to go it alone—leaving me with a difficult choice to make. Having followed many earlier political cases, I was well aware of the pitfalls of how a PP could respond: compromising one's position in order to garner crucially needed outside support, or, alternatively, reacting to the frustrations of the situation in an individualistic and sectarian way.

May 19th was a staunch proponent of our refusing to recognize the legitimacy of the courts. They had been inspired by recent Puerto Rican POWs, who had set a sterling example of noncollaboration. Of course that position had been based on the reality, recognized by the UN Decolonization Committee, that Puerto Rico was held as a colony of the U.S., which therefore had no legitimate jurisdiction. The stance toward the colonial courts was combined with a political campaign demanding the prisoners' release. To me, there was much that was applicable in that example. The New Afrikans were fighting against a form of colonialism, and we, as white allies, were fulfilling our obligations under international law to fight against racist and repressive regimes. The only legitimate proceedings, therefore, would be in an international court. Still, I was wary of promoting the idea that revolutionaries must, on principle, refuse to participate in criminal proceedings. Such a dogma would announce to the authors of COINTELPRO that they could get away with any frame-up, no matter how crude, anytime they wanted. At this point, with Brown incoherent and with no direct communication with Sekou Odinga, I couldn't consult with any New Afrikan defendants. (Subsequently, Sekou led in a political defense for the related federal trial.)

Grappling with these issues, I wouldn't commit to either approach for almost a year. By the summer of 1982 we were back at a heavily beefed up Rockland County Jail, and had been joined by New Afrikan freedom fighter Kuwasi Balagoon, who had been captured in the Bronx in January. His sense of the values and the problems of each approach was similar to mine, but it took me longer to make up my mind. Given how heavily the legal dice were loaded and how totally demonized we were in the media, the freedom fighters position had a two-sided advantage: it took the focus away from the grim forensic details while leaving the media little to say about our defense apart from our political stand. By being completely unambiguous, we could at least make it clear that we saw ourselves as people fighting for a just cause. It wasn't until the very eve of our first pretrial hearing that I finally decided to join Judy and Kuwasi, announcing in the September 13, 1982, court statement (quoted in the epigraph for this chapter) my position that the court had no right to try us.

While all this was being decided, there was a far more pressing and ultimately much more important decision to be made: who could care for and raise Chesa. The Boudins' efforts were both loving and heroic, but there was no way that grandparents entering their seventies would have the energy for the long-term care of such a young child. One of the teachers from the daycare center where Bill worked moved in to help them, but only for a few months. The godparents we had lined up before Chesa's birth didn't have the resources; and with the incredible furor about the case, they both would have lost their jobs. Then, wonderfully, Bernardine Dohrn and Bill Ayers stepped into the formidable breach and offered to take him. Honestly (and in retrospect, quite foolishly) they would not have been my first choice because the breakup of the WUO had been so frustrating and difficult for us all. But that was in the abstract; in the real crisis for our child, their open arms meant the world. Kathy and I had the opportunity for extensive discussions of the options and, with admiration for how child-centered they'd made their lives, agreed that Bernardine and Bill would be best for Chesa. He soon joined their family, with their two other sons, now our extended family.

Amid the chaos around our legal case, political stance, and fights for better prison conditions, I asked the lawyers to work on protection against the state's trying to take custody of Chesa. (This fear was not completely unfounded; in two subsequent cases, the FBI took charge of political prisoners' kids for almost a year.) We drew up guardianship papers, which also affirmed Kathy and my parental commitment to Chesa, and they were supplemented by affidavits from all four grandparents stating that they wanted Bill and Bernardine to be his guardians.

In those six high-stress months at Woodbourne, we were dealing with a heady mix of emotional challenges and life-altering decisions. Sometimes, at least with folks beyond our immediate circles, separate aspects could get tangled up together. At one point a lawyer involved with our families seemed to be saying to me that my access to my son could depend on my renouncing the action. I nearly went ballistic in what was by far my angriest moment of the whole ordeal. While it took some time and a lot of anxiety to sort it out, that apparent threat proved to be only a phantom. On the real ground of Chesa's overlapping families, there was basic clarity: We all wanted him to feel part of and centered in his new home, and at the same time to have a full and loving relationship with his imprisoned parents. While the principles were clear enough, none of us had any idea of the mountains of work that would be involved…or of the pinnacles of fulfillment we would reach.

The Rock Is a Hard Place

Here comes the first physical test of our stance of noncollaboration with any procedures that criminalize us: the line-up. Sekou, Kuwasi, Judy, and I have vowed not to cooperate. The CO calls out: "Gilbert!" I briefly wonder why they are starting with me. Do they assume, in a simplistic reversal of our politics, that the white male will be the least resolute? Whatever their reasoning, it's on, and I know what I have to do. Chained-up, I go limp. A sheriff sneers, "Oh, passive resistance is it?" and two of the biggest COs start dragging me down the hall. There are no punches or kicks; I guess any visible damage could invalidate the line-up. Instead of the usual standing line-up, this one will be done sitting down. It's amazing how hard it is to force a body, even one in chains, into a position it resists, and after twenty minutes the winded cops trying to seat me on the bench are replaced by another four-man team. I laugh to myself that this should be filmed as a "tag-team match" for "pro wrestling" on TV. The second group gets tired and the first team comes back in. They finally succeed in tying me to the back of the bench with the five loops around my chest so tight that I can barely breathe, and I feel on the edge of suffocation. That sensation and helplessness are a lot scarier than any of the beatings. They've constricted my chest way beyond what was needed to hold me in place, I guess as a way to punish me.

They're not ready for the lineup yet. A Bronx police officer who is a makeup technician walks in. The prosecution thinks I may have changed my appearance while in jail, so they're having the specialist, while two officers hold my head in place, apply make-up to make me look more like the descriptions they have of the suspect. "Is that legal?" I wonder, but legal niceties are hardly the point on either side. When the Bronx officer leaves to get more supplies, the other cops immediately break into derisive ridicule. "Did you see his hand movements? Obviously a fag." "Queer as a three-dollar bill." "They shouldn't allow faggots on the force." The patter stops as he returns. I wonder if he has any idea how much his fellow officers revile him, but whatever views this cop may have on homophobia, he's clearly anxious to show he shares their hatred of me and to do the best job possible.

The other five men for the lineup are all white, but otherwise no one looks much like me. Blankets are placed over us so that my ropes and chains don't show. Despite the fact that I'm the only one with my head drooped down on my shoulder, refusing to cooperate—and gasping for breath—only two of the six witnesses identify me.

The tag-team wrestling match and the suffocation line-up takes the entire morning, for me alone, and the quality of the line-up is in doubt. The encounter feels like a moral victory to us; still, it is but a small, symbolic act compared to the reality of being captured and in their hands.

By the summer of 1982, we were moved from Woodbourne back to Rockland County Jail. They had beefed up security in major ways, with physical modifications and additional personnel. Holding us there would save them the cost of frequent transports, with their caravan of armed sheriffs, for pretrial hearings and forensic procedures. This time we were segregated from other inmates, with a gallery nine cells long for Kathy and Judy in one section of the jail and one for the male defendants in another section. As tense and contested as RCJ could be, the situation provided me a welcome opportunity to get to know Kuwasi and Sekou. Also, I could finally get some help in assessing and working with Brown.

Kuwasi exuded an incredible *joie de vivre*. He also wrote great poetry. "Back in the day" he had done recitations in cafés as a lead-in for the group that became the Last Poets. He took his name from the Yoruba: Kuwasi means "born on Sunday" and Balagoon, "warlord." Kuwasi was one of the Panther 21 who went underground before they were rounded up. Some months later, he was arrested and convicted for expropriations in New Jersey. By October 20, 1981, Kuwasi already had two daring prison escapes under his belt. Both times he had gotten away cleanly and was secure; both times he risked his own freedom to try to free others.

Kuwasi and I ended up spending a lot of time together, isolated from other prisoners—so we were lucky that we got along so well. We rarely got on each other's nerves, and when we did we could talk it out pretty easily. We had lots of time for political discussions. On one occasion, telling old "war stories," we discovered that our paths had crossed in 1968. During the Columbia strike right-wing students had surrounded the main building to stop supplies, hoping to starve the occupation out. People in Harlem had organized a solidarity march that broke through the blockade to bring the strikers food. Kuwasi, who had been discharged from the army in 1967 and was a tenant organizer in Harlem in 1968, had joined the solidarity march to Columbia.

Sekou Odinga had picked his name to honor two different leaders of independence struggles in Africa. He was being held primarily by the feds and was with us for only a couple of months at RCJ. Sekou too had been one of the Panther 21 and had made a dramatic escape, jumping out of a fourth-floor window as the police moved in. Months later he ended up with the BPP International Section in Algeria. His leaving the safety there to come back to the U.S. spoke volumes about his commitment to the freedom struggle.

Sekou hadn't been at the Nanuet Mall (where "Brink's" began) on October 20, but the police were able to trace leads from that debacle to the registration of a car, which he and Mtayari Sundiata were driving in three days later. A vehicle and foot chase ensued. Mtayari was shot in the back and killed as he tried to scale a fence. Sekou was captured. There are pictures of a perfectly healthy Sekou, walking on his own power as he was taken into the police station. A few hours later he was in the hospital and on intravenous tubes for three months. As soon as they had IDed him, the torture began. They put cigarettes out on his body, held his head down to near drowning in a urine-filled toilet, ground off his toenails, and inflicted systematic blows that wrecked his pancreas. Sekou never wavered. Sekou never talked.

Kuwasi, a playful "uncle" to a number of children, didn't have any of his own. Sekou had several, and talked about them often. Both expressed a lot of empathy with my love for and concern about Chesa. Kuwasi was an anarchist, Sekou a devout Muslim. They clearly went back a long way together, and despite their differences there was a lot of mutual affection. I was surprised by the range of ideologies, since I'd assumed that everyone in the BLA adhered to the Marxism-Leninism of most of the national liberation struggles. Many cadres did see themselves in that tradition, and overall historical materialism was a major mode of analysis; but Kuwasi and Sekou showed me that there could be a unity in fighting for the independence of New Afrika even while having different visions of the ultimate shape of that society. The political discussions among us—with mutually respectful anarchist, Muslim, and Marxist-Leninist perspectives—were incredibly lively and rich, with alliances and oppositions shifting according to the particular issue—women's liberation, drugs, form of organization, lesbian and gay struggles, the role of religion, class formation, and economic model. Still, we always felt a rock-solid unity in siding with the oppressed against U.S. imperialism.

While the time we had for in-depth discussions on the gallery was a gift, we missed being able to talk with the women—hearing their ideas on these issues, running our thoughts past them. We only got to speak with Kathy and Judy at legal meetings, which included politics, but did not afford the time for such wide-ranging and extensive discussions.

When Brown was at RCJ, he was still a mess. Sekou and Kuwasi tried to counsel and comfort him, but despite his obvious respect for them they didn't make any progress. Since Brown didn't leave our floor for the hour of outdoor rec, the three of us could readily consult about him. The combination of the circumstances of Kuwasi's arrest and Brown's hysterical reaction to the news that Chui and Jamal had been busted made it obvious that he had talked and implicated others. This was a serious betrayal. But he hadn't volunteered information to make a deal; rather, he had broken under torture. While Sekou provided the positive example for standing up under such duress, not everyone could do that. Brown needed nurture and understanding to regain his sanity. He was obviously broken, visibly trembling in front of the COs and police, but we hoped that with discussion he could come to grips with what had happened. Such openness would enable him to debrief the defense in order to avoid further surprises and to eventually forgive himself and rebuild as a politically conscious person.

I don't know if this approach could have worked over time. One day we returned from rec and Brown was gone. At first we feared the feds had grabbed him to apply more pressure. But legal inquiries ascertained that he had signed himself over to the feds for protective custody. Since he thought he was deceiving us, he was terrified we would "find out" he had talked and attack him. But of course we had known for quite a while, and if we had wanted to hurt him there had been plenty of opportunities. In my view, the tragedy was that Brown's bravado didn't allow him to admit that he had broken and talked. Without facing that, he couldn't rebuild and remained crippled by self-hatred. That dishonesty and fear left the FBI's hooks still deeply embedded in him. Since they broke him, the government never had to offer him anything for the information he gave up. Just like three others of us, Brown got the maximum sentence of seventy-five years to life—but he ended up doing his time in protective custody, with his personality shattered.

A major theme for me throughout the pretrial period was the need for us, collectively, to do a self-criticism with useful lessons for the broader movements. Soon after my return to RCJ, but before being brought together with Sekou and Kuwasi, I decided that if it was so hard to generate collective discussions, I would start the process with myself. While I couldn't assess the whole action, let alone the full politics and strategy behind it, I could talk about my own mistakes, which played a pivotal role in the setback.

During my ten years in clandestinity my greatest fear wasn't for my personal safety; far worse was the danger of making a mistake that would lead to others getting busted and the organization crippled. Maybe my years of grappling with the issue helped me now look into the dragon's mouth of how I had contributed to such devastating losses. Also, unfortunately, it wasn't by any means all on me; several other serious mistakes had gone into the setback.

I prepared a short self-criticism, as concrete as possible on what I thought I'd done wrong. My request and understanding was that this potentially incriminating statement would exist in written form for only a day—just long enough for outside people to make the minimal, cryptic notes needed for subsequent discussion. A month later the police recovered it in the pocketbook of someone they arrested as allegedly part of the related federal conspiracy case. In response to my shocked inquiry, I was told that a May 19th leader (I don't know if my statement was ever shown to or discussed by New Afrikan revolutionaries) was trying to find the time to visit me in order to struggle with me about my racism—because what I had presented as a self-criticism was in reality an underhanded attack on the Third World leadership of October 20th.

In truth, my effort did of course imply that leadership too must have made major mistakes, and my intent was to promote self-examination at all levels. But that didn't seem devious or racist to me, especially since I had started with myself. And even if comrades had legitimate criticisms, they didn't have to hold onto that piece of paper like an exhibit in an indictment of me. That approach seemed to be, as so often happens with sectarianism and competition, another example of elevating internal differences above our common struggle against the state. Beyond concern about how the prosecution might use the statement, I admittedly also was embarrassed that my errors were the only ones publicly revealed, which could make it look to the outside movement like I was *the* screw-up causing the whole debacle.

Time and events brought about a greater openness to analysis and self-criticism. With Tyrone Rison, who described himself as part of the action core group, and Peter Middleton, a key supporter, becoming snitches, and with clandestine infrastructure tumbling down so quickly, it became obvious that there had been major cracks in the political and strategic foundation. As time went on, May 19th moved from "unconditional support" to encouraging the type of analysis I'd been pushing for. Judy Clark and I wrote a self-criticism of our role as white allies. One of the fundamental problems we discussed was "interventionism," in which the offering of white resources played an inappropriately big role in deciding strategic differences within the NAIM (New Afrikan Independence Movement). We also talked about having abdicated our responsibility to organize other white people against racism and toward revolution. But what we wrote was far too rhetorical and far too shaped by May 19th's new line about our job to build socialism within the white oppressor nation. I don't know whether our statement ever got circulated or discussed, but I never got any feedback on it.

The qualitative advance came when Sekou and Kuwasi joined us at RCJ. What was most amazing, given both the political losses and the dire life consequences for each of us, was the complete absence of recriminations. They could have blamed my mistakes for landing them in jail facing life sentences; I could have blamed the New Afrikan unit for leading me into this abyss. Instead, we shared the openness and warmth of comrades who have dedicated themselves to the struggle for social justice.

Kuwasi and Sekou were happy to see each other and anxious to sort out what had gone wrong. The recent informants and Brown's breakdown were especially disconcerting. To my surprise, they invited me to sit in on their discussions of what had happened in the BLA and even welcomed my questions and input.

In looking at Rison and Brown, they realized that each had been recruited based on his militancy—Rison as a Vietnam vet, Brown as a strong fighter in prison—but both lacked political depth. In fact, there had been far too little political discussion. Rison had once told them about how he and his buddies in Vietnam murdered a local woman who had lured and then killed a GI in their unit. When I asked if he told the story with regret for having brutalized her, they said no—kicking themselves now for not having challenged him. He told it simply as an old war story. Overall they concluded that far more than militant posturing, it took a solid political understanding and a profound commitment to the oppressed to be able to hold up against the full fury of the state. The three of us and Judy wrote up and published an analysis of how this major weakness had resulted in snitches and the damage that they had done.

Another issue was drugs. The BPP and especially the Panther 21 had a history of opposing the influx of drugs into the ghettos as a form of chemical genocide. Yet some members of this unit had rationalized the personal use of cocaine. Sekou, based on his religious principles, was opposed. Kuwasi, in many ways a free spirit, thought limited personal use was OK as long as it didn't get in the way of the struggle. What was striking was that Rison and Middleton, the snitches, had been among the heaviest users. Drugs were not, as slanders in the media charged, the main purpose for the expropriations. The lion's share of the funds went to the struggle. But those into cocaine were the ones who had pushed hardest to do robberies, apparently hoping that with more funds around a few thousand going to "recreational purposes" wouldn't be missed.

Sekou had opposed the Brink's action, feeling that there were a number of pitfalls, and he wasn't part of it. That difference was one of several layers of dynamics internal to the NAIM that I hadn't known about. I'd pictured the BLA as a centralized organization like the WUO, but now I saw that they functioned more as a set of distinct units fighting for a common purpose. Also, the BLA was part of the broader NAIM, and evidently not all the organizations in it agreed that the level of consciousness in the nation could sustain armed struggle in the 1980s. In addition, I was now learning of significant political disagreements even within this unit. Apparently some had been resolved, at least in part, by who had access to white resources that could help facilitate such actions.

These discussions fostered a fuller understanding of what I had done wrong. In my alacrity to ally, I'd made a serious interventionist error in that my support played an inappropriate role in resolving debates that needed to be struggled out politically within the NAIM. It's not always wrong to ally with one particular group, but that should be done only on the basis of full political discussions and with a companion effort to be broadly supportive of all revolutionary tendencies within the oppressed nation. Our practical work can't be a decisive factor in their internal struggles. My ignorance of these debates was no excuse but rather another form of the error. How could I—with so much experience that taught that clandestine work can only be built on the basis of full political and strategic understanding—have allied on such a high-risk tactical level with so little knowledge of the political context?

The answer lay in my own form of corruption. Drugs and money had no allure for me, but ego did. Especially after the collapse of the WUO, I was anxious to reestablish myself as a "revolutionary on the highest level," as "the most anti-racist white activist." What better way to validate myself in this way then to work closely with the most revolutionary Black group going? If the political and strategic terms weren't clear to me, I would quietly make myself useful until trust and a higher level relationship developed. Not only is this a terribly wrong way to build solidarity, but also the "exceptional white person" mentality usually undermines any serious effort to organize other people against racism—a fundamental aspect of developing solidarity and working toward revolution. When some friends told me that this unit of the BLA had "used" me as a resource, my reply was that I had used them as well, to be my source of validation.

The recognition, under these difficult life circumstances, of my corruption of ego did not prove shattering to my core beliefs and commitments. I had observed many times how movement leaders, who started with the most idealistic motives and who had taken great personal risks, later got blindsided by their egos. While it's much easier to see such behavior in others, why should I be exempt? Each of us is raised in this society. I couldn't expect to simply anoint myself a "good guy" and miraculously be 100 percent pure from then on. What was required instead—the essential challenge of being a revolutionary—was an honest, ongoing process that involved both serious introspection and constructive collective discussions. It's not like we're adrift on a featureless, turbulent sea. We're deeply rooted in the solid ground of the needs and aspirations of the oppressed. Whenever I start feeling full of myself or sense that I'm taking a direction that's not right, I need to grapple with that and, if possible, get help. "How does or doesn't this particular path advance the interests of the oppressed?" "What self-interests do I have here and how do they complement or conflict with the goals of the struggle?"

Another reason that such a heavy self-realization did not derail me was the example of Kuwasi and Sekou, two freedom fighters with a staunch commitment going back through the Panther 21 case. They didn't bemoan their current fate but instead expressed love for New Afrikans and for all oppressed people.

Daily Life

We're watching world news as the camera brings viewers right into the middle of a poignant moment in Poland. Lech Walesa, the leader of the public opposition to the Communist regime, is being placed into the back seat of a police car. The announcer explains that the authorities would be holding Walesa overnight to question him about his alleged ties with the underground resistance. As the car door slams shut, Walesa turns to the camera and says, "Tell the world they are violating my human rights." The scene is moving—and the coverage highly hypocritical. Kuwasi immediately talks back to the TV: "Yeah, they make one guy being held one night in Poland a headline item, but they never even report that right here in New York people are being held for a lot longer time for the same thing." Most Americans have no idea that in this country people are jailed for months, even years at a time, with no trial, without even any criminal charges. The jail time isn't a "sentence" but rather legal coercion to compel a potential witness to talk to a grand jury. At this time about thirty people in New York are being detained, indefinitely, for refusing to talk to grand juries investigating underground resistance.

Day-to-day life at RCJ was not as tense as it had been that first week after the bust, but there were many conflicts and problems. One big issue was that visitors and prisoners were separated by plexiglass. We couldn't touch and could only talk through phones. Chesa was better prepared than a year ago, but dividers, the inability to touch, drive kids and parents crazy. I did my best to entertain him with my ape imitations and the like. He wouldn't be deterred—even when a sheriff brandished a shotgun at him in a shameless attempt to scare a two-year-old. Amazingly, Chesa managed to be loving and all there for us; but the stress took a toll and got expressed in anger and frustration after the visits.

The same lawyers the Boudins had hired regarding conditions at MCC now brought a suit against the plexiglass partitions. It was success-ful; NY state case law was much better than federal law on this issue. The plexiglass came down and, even in our constricted space, the visits together were more joyous. When Kuwasi was down for visits at the same time, Chesa loved crawling on his back, getting tossed in the air, sitting on his lap. The COs constantly told the regular inmates that we were causing problems for them, that every new restriction in the jail was due to high security around us. But in reality our lawsuit brought contact visits for everyone, and we also achieved some more minor reforms, such as getting fruit juice into the diet.

For most of my year at RCJ, Sekou was being held by the feds and Kuwasi was my sole companion on our isolated floor. For our daily hour of recreation, we engaged in one-on-one basketball, long-distance races, dashes, and even a risibly clumsy effort to learn soccer. On our gallery, we did a lot of reading, letter-writing, and political discussions, broken up by card games, pushups, and sit-ups. One big advantage to our isolation was the television. On the other galleries the TV was on and blasting at full volume from seven in the morning to ten at night. We turned ours on for an average of one hour a day, as there were only three programs we watched: the news, the *National Geographic* nature show, and, for entertainment, a new situation comedy, *Cheers*, as we cheered Diane's efforts to bring feminist consciousness to a sports bar frequented by an amusing cast of characters.

Watching the news could be instructive. Once the lead story was an armored car robbery in the Bronx, where the guards had been immediately gunned down. The agent-in-charge of the FBI's New York office, Kenneth Walton (if I remember correctly), was asked if this robbery could be related to the Brink's case in Rockland County. Walton didn't hesitate, and his analysis was crisp: "No, because the modus operandi is so different. The Black Liberation Army never came out shooting like that." So, as we suspected, they knew that their standard line—repeated in every mass media discussion of the Brink's case—that "the robbers just came out shooting" was a lie, which was just one of several pieces of disinformation designed to discredit the defendants politically.

Shining the spotlight on Poland while keeping the public in the dark about U.S. grand juries was just one small example of the media's colossal double standard. We decided that the word "hypocrisy" wasn't nearly adequate, and we coined the term "chutzpocrisy," which later got escalated to "mega-chutzpocrisy."

We knew we'd be in a different jail when it came time for trial. Kathy's lawyers had won a change of venue motion with a thorough showing of overwhelming prejudice against us in Rockland County. Of course the court didn't move the trial one county south, to Westchester, a bit more representative, but rather further upstate to Orange County, even whiter than Rockland and with an unusually high number of people with jobs in law enforcement.

During the year at RCJ, I made one brief trip down to MCC for a pretrial hearing in the related federal case, where I was listed as an "unindicted codefendant." As our case had developed, the authorities had split us between a state and a federal case. Anyone they felt they could tie physically to the events of October 20 would be tried in the state because under New York's felony murder law all participants in the robbery could be sentenced to seventy-five years to life for the three deaths that resulted. Those they couldn't tie to the scene were tried under federal conspiracy laws (RICO), with twenty years for each act attributed to the group. Thus, while I was listed in the federal indictment, my trial would be in the state.

This hearing had a very straightforward legal purpose. Two of the defendants, Jamal Joseph and Chui Ferguson, had been busted solely on the basis of wiretaps. The only grounds to get the warrant to do those taps had been statements made by Sam Brown. If that information had been obtained by coercion, the wiretap was illegal and the indictment of those two invalid. I had been called by the defense because I had been around Brown at the time and could describe his out-of-his-mind pain and the way he trembled in the presence of COs and police.

For the lunch break after my morning on the stand, I was pleasantly surprised to be placed in the same holding pen as the male defendants. Sekou introduced me to the others, and there were big hugs all around. The mood was buoyant, first with the warmth of comrades meeting, but also because people felt the hearing had gone really well. "You know we were nervous about calling you because it went against the general rule of never putting a codefendant on the stand. But Sekou assured us you'd do a good job, and you did. It was great."

My testimony was completely consistent with the documentary evidence, which was conclusive. The defense brought medical records that proved that Brown had been living with a broken neck for eleven weeks and didn't get surgery until he gave up information to the FBI. The facts and the law were clear, yet when the court ruling came down the wiretaps and resulting arrests were allowed to stand. Then, as now, torture was "legal."

As the federal trial moved toward jury selection, the assistant U.S. attorney, Stacey Moritz, made a motion to have an anonymous jury. At the time, this was an unprecedented step for this type of trial, as there had never been a BLA or WUO case with even allegations of threats against a juror. Telling jurors that their names had to be kept secret to protect them against such dangerous defendants created a powerful pressure for a conviction. Moritz supported her motion with a sworn affidavit saying that I had been caught coming out of a legal visit at RCJ with a blueprint of the Orange County Jail, to which we would soon be moved. The obvious implication was that we were working on an escape, which would put us in a position to retaliate against jurors.

It was a lie. There was no incident at all, never any time when anything was confiscated from me after any kind of visit. We immediately demanded a meeting with the RCJ administration. In response to our lawyers' questions, they admitted that they had no record of any such incident. We asked them to say so publicly, but despite their admission to us they wouldn't say anything to the courts or the media. Our outside people then went to John Castellucci, the main reporter on our case for the local newspaper, and said, in essence, "Look, we know you don't like us but here's a chance for a real scoop. You can prove that an assistant U.S. attorney perjured herself in order to undermine Fifth Amendment rights. All you have to do is make a Freedom of Information Law request to RCJ, asking for a copy of any disciplinary report against Gilbert and any 'Unusual Incident Report.' They are required by law to have both these written records if any such alleged contraband was found." Castellucci, who made a career of crediting ridiculous, scurrilous rumors about us, did not pursue this particular hot tip. The prosecutions got their anonymous, conviction-prone juries for the federal case, and for our state trial that followed as well.

Facing Life

"Mr. Gilbert, do you understand now?"

"Yes, Judge Ritter, I understand you. You know, the planta-
tion owners used to sit on their verandas, sipping mint juleps,
complaining about how lazy the slaves were. The U.S. govern-
ment, which broke virtually every treaty it ever signed with Native
American nations, coined the term 'Indian giver.' The same people
who stole the northern half of Mexico claim that all Mexicans are
thieves. In that tradition, your ruling makes perfect sense to me."

Our first court session in Orange County opened with a bang, as four of
our coalition supporters were beaten and arrested. While that was upsetting
in itself, the way it unfolded indicated that the judge may well have been
complicit in a preplanned provocation to intimidate our people. This June
2, 1983, session was our first appearance in front of Judge David Ritter, who
would be presiding over our upcoming trial. As with all our previous hearings, those attending had to wait in long lines and pass through a gauntlet
of intimidating security overkill—snipers on the roof, detailed ID checks,
metal detectors. Family and friends of the police were ushered to one side,
our supporters to the other, a separation that was standard and reasonable.

This first hearing in Orange County added a new twist, however, as
the sheriffs assigned specific seats to specific individuals. Ahmed Obafemi,
who had been very visible as NAPO's main public spokesperson around
our case, was seated right by the aisle. When the judge entered, and our
people did not rise to honor him, the sheriffs immediately pounced on
Ahmed, hitting him with clubs. When three nearby friends tried to
protect him, all four were dragged out and arrested. Standing or not
standing is purely an expression of opinion, completely protected by the
First Amendment, and it was well established that our people didn't rise
for the judge; no notice had been given that this was now considered a
punishable offense. Ahmed had been placed quite deliberately where he
could be jumped without warning.

Naturally, we reacted vociferously:

> **MR. GILBERT:** We cannot proceed until it is established that our people will not be attacked and the people who were attacked are released and brought back.
>
> **THE COURT:** Mr. Gilbert, you are going to leave me no choice but to remove you…
>
> **MR GILBERT:** The man was sitting down. He was singled out as a Black activist and the goons went and clubbed him for sitting down.
>
> **THE COURT:** Will you remove Mr. Gilbert, please.
>
> (From the transcripts, page 8)

Judy and Kuwasi raised the same objections and were escorted out with me. This was the first of many times when we were removed or when we ourselves walked out of the courtroom. When we returned later that day, the judge demanded that we pledge not to be disruptive. My reply was my "mint julep" statement, which concluded, "Now you, sir, ask me if I'm going to be disruptive when you presided over an assault and battery, a racist assault and battery."

The hearing had been set to resolve two issues for the impending trial, counsel and severance. Kuwasi, Judy and I had put in motions to go *pro se*, to represent ourselves, which we considered the best way to get across our position that we were freedom fighters involved in a just and necessary struggle. In our view, Kuwasi was a Prisoner of War (POW) from the NAIM; Judy and I, captured as white anti-racist allies, were political prisoners (PPs).

While we didn't recognize the court's right to try us, we planned to participate in the proceedings to the extent that we could bring out what we saw as the basic issues: the white supremacy that formed the foundation of U.S. society, oppressed peoples' right to fight to achieve self-determination, the U.S. government's record (COINTELPRO was only one of many examples) of violent suppression of legal dissent, and the obligation under international law to oppose racist and repressive regimes. The most likely places to get some of these issues out would be during the initial questioning (*voir dire*) of prospective jurors and during opening and closing statements. We felt we could best do so by speaking for ourselves.

Given that we were educated and articulate, and despite our alleged "disruption," our motion was granted. We wanted to keep our current lawyers as legal advisers, but Judy's attorney, Tipograph, and mine, Stewart, were also representing clients in the related federal conspiracy case. Although we had been captured and indicted first, the federal prosecutors, for their own tactical reasons, pushed their trial ahead of ours. We asked for a delay until Tipograph and Stewart were free, but Judge Ritter wouldn't grant it. Trial would start in July, with Attorney Judy Holmes as the one legal adviser for all three of us.

The second issue was severance. Kathy, on her father's advice, was pursuing a legal defense. Obviously, trying her with three codefendants proclaiming themselves freedom fighters, especially given the close bond between her and me, would be prejudicial. The fifth defendant in the trial was Sam Brown, and none of us wanted to go to trial alongside someone so terrified of and prone to manipulation by the police. But Judge Ritter was adamant: no severance. (In addition to being pro-prosecution, he was probably concerned about the costs, with all the inflated "security" expenses, of two separate trials.)

This time, however, the state got tripped up in its own machinations. In an earlier proceeding, I had been temporarily represented by a public defender against my wishes. That same public defender, Peter Branti, was now representing Sam Brown, who had broken with his movement lawyer. Potentially there was a blatant conflict of interest, if I had earlier confided anything to Branti that would now be useful for Brown's defense but which could hurt me. Judge Ritter applied all kinds of pressure on me to release Branti from confidentiality. I adamantly refused. The court had no choice but to grant severance—or what amounted to the same thing, give Brown time to find a new attorney. Given the necessity for a second trial, there was no excuse for forcing Kathy to be tried amid our freedom fighters approach. The severance was a big relief. The three of us, going to trial immediately, could present our political stand as directly as possible. After that Kathy (although at this point still with Brown as a codefendant) would have a chance to present a real legal defense.

We got to question our first, and last, prospective juror on July 20. With my name first on the indictment, the judge had me lead off. They had to allow questions about the impact of pretrial publicity, and the juror himself offered that he had heard we were "terrorists," so I asked him to define the word. He came back with, "A person who uses violence to achieve their goals or objectives." When I asked whether pilots who dropped napalm on villages or cops who shot unarmed Black youth were terrorists, the court wouldn't allow the questions. I knew I'd be blocked from presenting positive examples of armed resistance, such as Nat Turner or John Brown, so I tried another tack. "Well then, was George Washington a terrorist?" Guess what, he wasn't. I then asked if the juror was saying that it was all right for white people to fight for independence, but not for Black people to do so? The juror didn't get to answer, as the judge quickly intervened and stopped my line of questioning.

Judy and Kuwasi followed, each asking questions useful for drawing out racial prejudice: Did the juror ever invite his Black friends home for dinner? Did he or anyone in his family have any relationship to the Ku Klux Klan? Had he ever spent time in Harlem or in the central ward of Newark? Each time the court blocked the questions, even though prevailing law recognized the need for searching inquiries about racial prejudice. We withdrew from *voir dire* and from the room. The judge took over the inquiries, each time with a single yes or no question about racial bias. The reader will be glad to learn that not a single potential juror in Orange County was the least bit prejudiced.

When it came to opening statements we asked to change the order so that Kuwasi would lead off. Politically he was the best one to describe the basis of our actions in the struggle for New Afrikan Independence, with Judy and I following as allies to that struggle. Tactically, we knew we would get muzzled before long; if we could only get part of one speech out, his was the most important.

Kuwasi, the least likely of the three of us to ad lib in court, was by far the best writer. His August 8, 1983, opening statement, reprinted in *Kuwasi Balagoon: A Soldier's Story* (Montreal: Kersplebedeb, 2003) was, in my opinion, a brilliant presentation of the history of racism in the U.S., the formation of a New Afrikan nation within the U.S., and the right to self-determination.

The court cut him off about halfway through. Once Kuwasi was censored, Judy and I walked out too, never presenting any of our prepared openings.

Looking back at my own series of court statements, they seem to become progressively more rhetorical and hardened as time went on. My sentencing speech in particular spilled over from healthy defiance to crass insensitivity. Trying to show that life sentences didn't deter revolutionaries, I declared that the issues that motivated us to fight—the depth of racism in the U.S. and the millions of people killed each year by the economies and wars imposed by imperialism—were much larger than three lives. I meant the three of us facing life in prison. (Because I included Mtayari, who was killed three days later, I thought of the this confrontation as having cost four lives.) But when I said "three lives," I caught a glimpse of a woman in the court who flinched as if I had struck her. Only later did it dawn on me that she was a relative of one of the men killed on October 20, thinking, feeling, that those three lives were the ones I was dismissing so cavalierly.

How could I have become so insensitive? I, at one time a pacifist, had come to ally with national liberation movements under fire. Not only were New Afrikans engaged in a just struggle, but it was a war that had been forced upon them by the murderous assaults on legal dissent, while so much of the white Left looked on passively. The BLA never shot anyone who wasn't an armed professional and always took great care to avoid civilian casualties—a far cry from government forces who killed civilians on a grand scale and later came up with the dehumanizing euphemism of "collateral damage."

Yet, even in a just war, as the Vietnamese had showed us, we need to feel the pain and tragedy of losses on the other side. And in this particular encounter our own mistakes and failings had led to unnecessary casualties. Even though the government's aggression was the source of the conflict, these particular individuals working as enforcers of the rule of capital didn't at all see themselves in a warfare situation. If I had been more of a revolutionary, more fully rooted in humanism and less anxious to show my mettle, I would have expressed, in addition to my commitment to the struggle, sadness and regrets about the lives lost and the families shattered.

We became more embattled as the two years of court confrontations progressed. Three basic issues led to our being removed or, more often, our walking out. One was the treatment of our supporters, such as the attack on Ahmed. The worst incident was life-threatening. A carload of people, two adults and three children, barely avoided a serious accident when the front wheel came loose as they were returning home from a visit with us. When they took the car to a mechanic, he said that someone had removed a cotter pin. Since there was no problem on the way up, it had to have been done in the jail's parking lot.

Our major frustration in terms of the conduct of the trial was the way we were consistently blocked from discussing racism. We weren't allowed to conduct a searching inquiry of potential jurors for bias; we were stopped every time we tried to present the situation of New Afrikans and other people of color within the U.S.; discussion of relevant international law was forbidden; and we were blocked from bringing up COINTELPRO and other well-documented illegal government programs that had driven previously nonviolent activists into underground resistance.

Our most telling obstacle was our inability to have the legal meetings needed to prepare our defense. When the court was in session, the only time we could meet was at night. Orange County Jail, which had previously allowed nighttime legal meetings, changed the rules to prohibit them. We, inexperienced *pro se* defendants, now had to go through the week with no way to evaluate what happened one day or to prepare for the next.

We persistently raised this problem in court. In response, the judge authorized the release of the names and phone numbers of everyone we called from the jail. His rationale was to show that we had adequate opportunity for legal advice via phone calls—but the vast majority of our calls were personal, and what legal calls there had been could readily be spotlighted without publishing names and numbers. Given the cotter pin incident and other threats to our supporters, which we had described to the judge for the record in court, this public release of personal information was a chilling effort at intimidation. The lack of meetings and preparation, more than any other issue, occasioned our walkouts and boycotts.

We spent most of the trial in holding pens underneath the courtroom, in three separate cells, surrounded by law enforcement personnel. There was no one in the courtroom representing us, and the proceedings were piped in via a speaker. We were told that at any point we could return to the courtroom as long as we promised not to be "disruptive"—in other words, insist on talking about forbidden topics. The drone of the speaker, amid the buzz of a swarm of hostile guards, as the link to the pomp and pretense of the court was all a bit surreal. Going to the bathroom became truly bizarre. I (or Kuwasi or Judy) would be chained hand and foot and taken to a large room with a toilet on a raised platform in the middle to pee while still chained and closely watched by five guards.

At one point I could make out from the speaker some testimony by an FBI lab technician, who said that glass particles had been found in my clothing that could only have come from the windshield of the Brink's truck. I was astonished because the prosecution knew full well that I'd never been within a mile of the truck. For a moment I had an impulse to go back upstairs to contest this fraudulent "evidence." But what could I say to refute this highly credentialed FBI technician? And what good would it do?

We talked back and forth, trying to figure out why they would resort to a fabrication when it's so easy to get a conviction for felony murder—all they had to do was show some role in the robbery. Perhaps they were worried that a jury might balk at felony murder, at giving full legal responsibility and punishment to a nonshooter—perhaps especially one who was white. Was that what led them to now insinuate that I could have been a shooter?

Such tactics dovetailed with a systematic media campaign to dehumanize us. The Black comrades were always portrayed as thugs—despite the reality that Kuwasi's and Sekou's histories were fully and deeply political. The media didn't mention that they had been part of the Panther 21 case—who could have more justification for moving into clandestine forms of struggle? The white defendants, who had attended elite universities, weren't depicted as thugs but instead as psychopaths—a standard method going back at least to John Brown of discrediting whites "crazy" enough to throw their lot in with people of color. These portrayals were visually reinforced with the artists' sketches of us in court (no cameras were allowed). Even the COs commented that in person we didn't look anything like those newspaper portraits.

The atmosphere at Orange County Jail was a bit less hostile than it had been at RCJ, but the food was even worse. Kuwasi and I were alone on one unit with Kathy and Judy on another, but this time our floors were back to back, so we at least had voice contact, as well as legal meetings, and thus a little more sense of community. Kuwasi and I used our rec hour for handball—a new sport for us and, since we were evenly matched, a lot of fun. When we were in the yard, armed guards regularly circled above us on the flat roof. Our trial had occasioned an orgy of spending on security—with all kinds of new equipment and personnel. I mentioned to Kuwasi that with the rapid hiring and minimal screening of these newly armed COs, one of them could just lose it, pull out his gun and shoot us—as COs at RCJ had threatened to do a couple of times. Sadly, later one of these neophytes did snap and use his gun to commit suicide.

Heading up the River

Our visiting is kept separate from other prisoners and families. Thankfully there are no plexiglass partitions, although the conditions for us are especially onerous. When a seventy-nine-year-old family friend brings Chesa to visit, she is subjected to a strip search before entering a visiting area filled with tables that looked like McDonalds. The large room is empty except for Kathy and me in the middle—and about six COs. Orange County Jail is adamant: absolutely no toys or children's books are allowed; Chesa can't have even a piece of paper and a crayon, nor is he allowed to move around the room. All he is permitted to do is sit facing us across the table, while the COs circle us at a radius of about ten feet. Such harsh restrictions on a three-year-old should result in tears and a refusal to ever come back again, but Chesa surprises us all. He looks straight up at the COs and says, "Hey, you guards, why are you bothering us? I want to be with my mom and dad." The COs look embarrassed, at least for a moment, and seem a little less menacing. Then Chesa initiates a game we can play together, acting out fantasy stories: We are a family in the woods looking for a magic herb; or we are cooking a special meal, collecting an array of delectable ingredients. This visit is the first of several at OCJ that greatly strengthen our family bond.

The prosecution presented seven or eight days worth of forensic and witness testimony while we stayed in the pens below. For our defense, we had asked for two witnesses. The first was Geronimo Pratt, a highly respected Panther who at that point had done twelve years on a life sentence in California. He had been convicted of a murder that occurred while he was four hundred miles away, under FBI surveillance, at a Panther meeting. (The FBI refused to release the records, and Geronimo ended up doing twenty-seven years before he got the conviction overturned.) The judge refused our request on the grounds that Geronimo's testimony was not germane. Our second request, for Sekou Odinga, was granted; as a defendant in the related federal conspiracy case he was by definition relevant.

Our one-day defense happened on September 12, 1983, with Sekou on the stand and Kuwasi asking the questions. Since the court had to allow matters that directly related to the events, Sekou was able to describe some of the BLA's standards—the commitment to fight oppression along with the great care to avoid unnecessary casualties. Another aim was to articulate the broad legitimacy and goals of the Black Liberation Movement.

Here the judge was more restrictive; but the thoughtful exchange between these two longtime and unbowed Panther veterans spoke volumes.

Still, conviction was a foregone conclusion; the surprise was that the jury deliberated for hours rather than minutes. Was that just a question of the time it took to go over all the details on the verdict sheet? Or, I wondered, could that one juror that we got to *voir dire* about racism have taken up some time to raise questions or qualms?

Sentencing took place on October 6, 1983: my birthday, as it happened, the day I turned thirty-nine. While I was never sentimental about my birthday, I had noticed that thirty-nine could be a fateful year for those who fought injustice: Malcolm X, Che Guevara, and Martin Luther King Jr. had each been murdered at that age. Of course I hadn't played nearly their roles, nor was I paying the supreme price. The seventy-five years-to-life sentence—and in New York State one has to do every minute of the minimum—condemned each of us to die in prison, but I was brash and optimistic enough to believe there would be radical political changes, freeing many POW/PPs, in our lifetimes.

After sentencing, everything suddenly started moving at a rapid pace. Kuwasi, Judy and I were swept out of the jail that same morning. Each of us was placed in a sheriff's car, surrounded by a heavily armed caravan with a helicopter flying overhead, and taken to the state prison system's reception centers (Downstate for men, Bedford Hills for women). I was suddenly out of my cocoon—very restrictive but quiet and close to my codefendants—and into the din of a large cohort of men. A CO went through the minimal personal property one had at the jails—virtually none of it was allowed in now—accompanied in my case by a running, highly derogatory commentary. We were seated in a row of barbers' chairs to have heads shaved and any beards removed, then covered with a smelly de-licing fluid, and then sent to a row of showers. There were long lines for each of these procedures, but the COs moved me to the front of each one. I heard one inmate whisper, "That guy must be a senator's son or something." But my VIP treatment didn't reflect wealth and influence; rather the Department of Correctional Services wanted me and Kuwasi out of reception and into more secure Max A facilities as soon as possible. Downstate was so incredibly regimented that I found it hard to keep track of all the rules. We were marched to chow in double file and complete silence. The food was somewhat more palatable than county jail and more plentiful, but we had less than ten minutes to chow down and file out.

Despite this initial culture shock, some guys who had served time before assured me that "upstate" life was a lot less regimented; there was more leeway for socializing, exercise and programs. The way these veterans made an effort to reach out to me was also a sign that my case and what I stood for would win me some respect and friendship upstate.

Early on the morning of October 13 I was taken out, without explanation, and chained hand and foot. After a wait, I was put on a bus with just a few prisoners in the front, and marched to the back. To my delight, in these most undelightful circumstances, there was Kuwasi, head shaved and also in chains. I'd known he too was at Downstate, but we had been put in different units and had never seen each other. While the average stay at Downstate was six months, we were moved out within a week.

The bus headed out, traveling about ninety miles northeast of Albany to arrive at Comstock. The walls, the fences, the exercise pens all looked forbidding. Two COs went into the prison and came back out shaking their heads. My designation for Comstock had just been cancelled. I wondered if it could have been because the COs had heard me tell Kuwasi that a family friend had a house nearby. But he, more experienced than I, thought it more probable that an incident inside had led to the prison getting locked down.

The bus headed out for a long drive west, past Syracuse to Auburn, a little town at the top of the Finger Lakes. The COs ordered me off the bus—Auburn prison was where I'd landed. Kuwasi stayed put—he was being sent to the only Max A even farther west—the notorious Attica. Despite the order to "move it!" Kuwasi and I hugged, awkwardly since we were both chained, and wished each other the best. We didn't know if we would ever see any of our other codefendants or each other ever again. Escorted by COs but completely alone, I hobbled off the bus to face an unimaginably different and challenging new life.

{ AFTERWORD }

Five Pages on Twenty-Eight Years

Prisons are an insult to the human spirit and a shameful waste of human potential—but life goes on. People can be creative and daring in finding ways to assert themselves, in good ways and bad.

I've been very fortunate to have a lot of love in my life and solid outside support, as well as respect from my fellow prisoners. These strengths have helped me fend off the several flurries of harassment from the administration or officers I experienced due to my case and politics. My situation, in contrast to how prison is depicted on TV, has not been defined by a constant threat of violence. So far, I have never had a fight with another prisoner, have never been assaulted by staff, have never been sent to the box. While I have been kept in the most restrictive of New York's prisons, often with stringent limits on what jobs they permit me to get, I have not faced the near total isolation of the "supermaxes" such as California's Pelican Bay and the federal prison in Florence, Colorado. Like all prisoners I deal with a major loss of control over many aspects of my life, arbitrary authority, and physical separation from loved ones and activities. And it's painful to see daily injustice; my scattered efforts for prisoners' rights have produced extremely meager results.

In addition to many loving relationships with family and friends, I have been able to stay engaged politically with the world and our movements. This ability was built on an earlier generation of prisoners' struggles that won access to a range of literature and correspondence. I've written many essays and book reviews over the years, some of which were collected in a book, *No Surrender* (Montreal: Abraham Guillen Press, 2004). I've also tried my best to carry on that dual responsibility of upholding basic principles while being open about errors and flaws.

The world has changed considerably in twenty-eight years, yet the fundamental issues of humanity and justice remain. The national liberation struggles that lit up the globe in the decades after World War II brought significant changes but generally have not freed the oppressed from want and have not made them masters of their own destiny. National liberation no longer seems to me to be an adequate form of struggle in itself to build socialism and to spearhead world revolution. The setbacks and limitations have resulted from imperialism's fierce military, economic and cultural attacks. Under such intense pressures some internal weaknesses cracked open, of elitism and corruption, of inadequate efforts around class transformation and women's liberation. These defeats created opportunities for right-wing forms of anti-imperialism, often groups initially fostered by the CIA as counter-forces to the Left. The government and media's floodlights on these often brutal conflicts create the challenge for us to still concentrate our efforts on the main source of the problems, imperialism, without at all embracing reactionary opponents.

Within the U.S. we've seen a proliferation of organizational approaches. While I'm in no position to evaluate them, I've been encouraged by the creative efforts to be both democratic and effective, and in developing both independent people of color and multiracial forms. I still believe that for whites building solidarity is key for developing transformative politics. From inside the criminal justice system I've seen, in even more detail and with greater intensity, how central and deep racism is in the U.S. Also, the environment, always an important issue, has become an urgent matter for the very survival of our species and thousands of others.

In my view the most basic divide is still between imperialism and the oppressed majority of humankind in, and from, Africa, Asia, Oceana, and Latin America. We can expect the fiercest clashes there and the most advanced politics. For white radicals, internationalism and responding to leadership from the Global South and from communities of color within the U.S. are crucial for achieving qualitative change, including around the environment. At the same time it is essential that we consistently and full-heartedly fight all forms of oppression—race, class, gender, sexuality, disability—in society and in ourselves.

One surprising benefit of prison has been the opportunity to meet, although under these unfortunate circumstances, several ex–Black Panthers who are political prisoners in New York State. Naturally each individual is different, but all of them have been special and valued friends, with useful analyses of what's happening in the world, thoughtful reflections on history, and a still-burning passion for qualitative social change.

My dad died on September 21, 1986, at the age of eighty-two, my mom on January 24, 2000, just shy of her eighty-seventh birthday. Our relationship had been sustained through visits and phone calls. They both knew that I loved them; they both faced death without having me by their sides.

The sorrow of my absence for my parents and the difficulties for my son growing up with a mom and dad in prison led me to think and feel more fully about those killed during the Brink's robbery and shoot-out—what it meant for wives to carry on without husbands, for children to grow up without fathers. Three men were killed that day and others were wounded. Three days later one of our comrades was killed. Families were suddenly and painfully fractured. For a number of years I was not able to publicly express my regrets about this terrible toll and my role and responsibility in what happened. I got hung up in feeling that nothing I said would be adequate; I also felt paralyzed by the hypocrisy and disproportion of the dominant society, which never expresses remorse about its wholesale, massive violence, mainly against unarmed civilians. There hasn't been any accountability even for the government's illegal and lethal campaign against the Panthers, the context for the formation of a Black Liberation Army.

As my son approached college age, he became the strongest advocate for my expressing my sorrow and regrets in a direct and forthright manner—and I've done so publicly on a number of occasions. The colossal social violence of imperialism does not grant those of us who fight it a free pass to become callous ourselves. Especially in fighting for a just cause, we need to take the greatest care to respect life and to minimize violence as we struggle to end violence. There is no contradiction: I full-heartedly continue my commitment to the oppressed; I deeply regret the loss of lives and the pain for those families caused by our actions on October 20, 1981.

Kuwasi Balagoon, my codefendant, died on December 13, 1986, at the age of thirty-nine. The surprising diagnosis was AIDS. I turned my intense grief into a near-obsessive study of the AIDS epidemic. At that point DOCS (Department of Correctional Services) was downplaying the problem, but I knew that a high percentage of NYS prisoners had been injection drug users. A tidal wave of an epidemic was forming.

I also studied the response by gay activists and learned that peer education—by trusted members of the community—was the most effective way to promote support and prevention. In the spring of 1987, two other of Kuwasi's friends, Mujahid Farid and Papo Nieves, and I proposed what was evidently the first comprehensive peer education project on AIDS in a prison. We initially faced incredible bureaucratic hostility and obstacles, but eventually got at least part of our program going.

For the next thirteen years my main passion and work was on AIDS in prison. I believe that the extensive outreach we carried out combined with the intensive one-on-one counseling—to the degree we were permitted to do so—saved many prisoners' lives and lives in the communities to which they eventually returned. In addition, I provided counseling and support for scores of prisoners with AIDS, and I was able to intervene in time to get life-saving medications to about twenty AIDS patients who were being improperly denied. During these years I also tutored hundreds of prisoners academically, many of whom went on to achieve their high school equivalency diplomas.

Sam Green and Bill Siegel's documentary film on the Weather Underground was released in 2003. Since then, about two hundred of today's activists have written me as a result of the film and video (and in a few cases, my book). These people express being drawn to our deep commitment to revolutionary change and our passionate solidarity with the oppressed. I've been buoyed by and learned a lot from these dialogs.

Kathy Boudin spent twenty-two years in prison; her contributions to her community there are worth a book in itself. She was one of the key organizers for what became the model for a successful AIDS counseling and education (ACE) program in prison. She earned a master's degree, did extensive academic tutoring, and facilitated a parenting center that helped mothers in prison stay positively involved in their children's lives. Kathy was finally granted parole in 2003 and shines on the outside: working with women with AIDS, helping children of prisoners go to college, initiating programs to prepare people to parole successfully. At this point, DOCS does not allow us to have visits or even phone calls, but we do correspond and maintain a strong bond through family and friends.

As a child, Chesa Boudin amazed me by his ability to both be engaged and loving during our visits and yet to live fully in his outside family and life—but it wasn't easy for him. Working through the difficult stresses took a lot of spunk on his part, world-class parenting by Bill and Bernardine, and the love and support Kathy and I could offer from prison. Now a young man, his accomplishments are impressive, including his becoming a Rhodes scholar; his extensive world travel and work experiences; and his being translator, author, coauthor, or coeditor of four books. Having already earned two master's degrees, he completed law school in 2011. But what's far more important and fulfilling for me is that he is such a caring and thoughtful person, loving and supportive to family and friends and with deep empathy for people throughout the world.

The book ends here; the struggle of course continues…with love and for the unity of humankind.

One love,
David Gilbert, May 2011

{GLOSSARY OF ACRONYMS}

AAPRP	All-African People's Revolutionary Party
AIM	American Indian Movement
ANC	African National Congress
BLA	Black Liberation Army
BOP	Bureau of Prisons (federal)
BPP	Black Panther Party
CAR	Committee Against Racism
CC	Central Committee
CFJ	Crusade for Justice
CIA	Central Intelligence Agency
CO	Corrections Officer
COINTELPRO	Counter Intelligence Program
CORE	Congress of Racial Equality
CS-I, -II	Cadre schools
DOCS	Department of Corrections Services (NY)
FBI	Federal Bureau of Investigation
FNLA	National Liberation Front of Angola
FOIA	Freedom of Information Act
FPA	Foreign Policy Association
ICV	Independent Committee on Vietnam
IRA	Irish Republican Army
ITT	International Telephone and Telegraph (originally)
KKK	Ku Klux Klan
KR	Khmer Rouge
LBJ	Lyndon Baines Johnson (president)
LGBT	Lesbian/Gay/Bisexual/Transgender
M2M	May 2nd Movement
MAS	Men Against Sexism
MCC	Manhattan Correctional Center
MDS	Movement for a Democratic Society
M-L	Marxist-Leninist
MLN	Movement for National Liberation
MPLA	Popular Movement for the Liberation of Angola

NAACP	National Association for the Advancement of Colored People
NAIM	New Afrikan Independence Movement
NAPO	New Afrikan People's Organization
NC	National Council; also National Convention
PAC	Pan-African Congress
PAS	Port Authority Statement
PF	Prairie Fire
PFOC	Prairie Fire Organizing Committee
PL	Progressive Labor
POW	Prisoner of War
PP	Political Prisoner
RAM	Revolutionary Action Movement
RC	Revolutionary Committee
RCJ	Rockland County Jail
RICO	Racketeering Influenced and Corrupt Organizations Act
RIP	Radical Information Project
RNA	Republic of New Afrika
ROTC	Reserve Officers Training Corps
RYM	Revolutionary Youth Movement
SDS	Students for a Democratic Society
SHU	Special Housing Unit (the box, solitary)
SNCC	Student Nonviolent Coordinating Committee; later, "National"
SRU	Students for a Restructured University
SWP	Socialist Workers Party
STO	Sojourner Truth Organization
TDA	The Day After
UFT	United Federation of Teachers
VCP	Vietnamese Communist Party
WITCH	Women's International Terrorist Conspiracy from Hell
WUO	Weather Underground Organization

{ ACKNOWLEDGMENTS }

The most difficult part of the book to write is the acknowledgments. I can't come close to adequately thanking the many people who provided me invaluable help and support in many ways. And an "Acknowledgments" that even suggested that quantity and quality of assistance would leave the reader wondering why my book is so very far from the Nobel Prize for Literature level. Still, there is a joy in recalling thank-yous, so I'll do my best.

Terry Bisson, the talented author, generously served as my editor, making a consistent effort to liven-up my writing. Even more importantly, Terry shepherded this project through all the steps to publication and was warm and encouraging throughout the process. Naomi Jaffe did a thorough reading of the draft and offered both detailed commentary and penetrating political perspective. She also read and made helpful suggestions on my re-writes of various sections and has provided astute advice on every aspect of this project. As a number of people have commented to me, "We should all be so lucky as to have the kind of friend Naomi is to you." Dan Berger, in my opinion the foremost historian of the struggles touched on in this book, contributed a careful vetting and valuable comments on my manuscript. He also did a Herculean amount of fact-checking, although he couldn't possibly, nor did I ask him to, check every detail. I am fully responsible for all the errors that come with the fallability of memory.

A number of family, friends and correspondents read all or part of the manuscript and offered, some generously despite political differences with some of my interpretations, helpful comments and suggestions. My thanks are mixed with an apology in that the disorganized way in which I work meant that I didn't fully incorporate many of the good ideas and thoughtful criticisms. Still, their efforts made a big difference: elana levy, Claude Marks, Ken Yale, Callie Williams, Sharon Martinas, Roxanne Dunbar-Ortiz, Jess Ross, Chris Chanlett, Chesa Boudin, Eleanor Stein, Jeff Jones, Bernardine Dohrn, Bob Feldman, Mindy Stone, B. Loewe, Laura Foner, Vic Dedaj, Papo Torres, Judy Jensen, Simona Sharoni, John Mage, Lenny Weinglass, Moe Stavnezer, Olga Palo. In addition to reading and comments, Walidah Imarisha and Laura Whitehorn contributed, each in her own way, with their enthusiasm and in moving the project forward.

Many people have engaged me in stimulating and useful dialog on the history; here, I will only take space to acknowledge a few, with some of the more extensive exchanges: Molly McClure, Ari Clemenzi, Ty Jarrett, Vicky Daza, Herman Bell, Marilyn Buck, Seth Hayes, Jalil Muntaqim, Nuh Washington, Donna Willmott, Rob McBride, Vicki Legion, Matt Meyer, Meg Starr, Cathy Wilkerson, Becky Thompson, Karl Kersplebedeb, Victor Wallis, Leslie Pickering, Dana Barrett, Ron Grele, Chris Taaffe, Michael Smith, Janet Stavnezer, Marshall Hyman, Helen Hudson, Sara Falconer, Amy Schwartz, karen emily suurtamm, Rick Ayers, Barbara Zeller, Susie Day. Particular recognition goes to Sam Green and Bill Siegel, whose documentary did so much to revive interest in the Weather Underground.

No person is an island, and none of us could be functional, let alone productive, without a lot of support and engagement from others. This reality is several orders of magnitude higher for a prisoner. I've been blessed with a bounty of love and support from the outside, and also from many fellow prisoners, beyond anything I could have imagined—people who give me books and publications, healthful foods within the stringent limits of what's allowed, stimulating political dialog, and lots of love. It would take pages to list all the names, so I won't try to do so, but I hope that each and every individual involved feels my deep personal gratitude. Within that, there is a small grouping, Friends of David Gilbert (FODG), which has spearheaded work around my legal status, my case, and my prison conditions. A particular thanks in terms of this project goes to FODG West who, without my asking for it, raised money to get the effort to publish this book off the ground. And a broader, heartfelt thanks to the many activists and friends who support the range of prisoners whose incarcerations came out of the struggles for social justice.

Finally, a special lifetime thank-you to Chesa, Kathy, Bernardine, and Bill.

ABOUT PM

PM Press was founded at the end of 2007 by a small collection of folks with decades of publishing, media, and organizing experience. PM Press co-conspirators have published and distributed hundreds of books, pamphlets, CDs, and DVDs. Members of PM have founded enduring book fairs, spearheaded victorious tenant organizing campaigns, and worked closely with bookstores, academic conferences, and even rock bands to deliver political and challenging ideas to all walks of life. We're old enough to know what we're doing and young enough to know what's at stake.

We seek to create radical and stimulating fiction and non-fiction books, pamphlets, t-shirts, visual and audio materials to entertain, educate, and inspire you. We aim to distribute these through every available channel with every available technology, whether that means you are seeing anarchist classics at our bookfair stalls; reading our latest vegan cookbook at the café; downloading geeky fiction e-books; or digging new music and timely videos from our website.

PM Press is always on the lookout for talented and skilled volunteers, artists, activists and writers to work with. If you have a great idea for a project or can contribute in some way, please get in touch.

PM Press
PO Box 23912
Oakland CA 94623
510-658-3906
www.pmpress.org

FRIENDS OF PM

These are indisputably momentous times—the financial system is melting down globally and the Empire is stumbling. Now more than ever there is a vital need for radical ideas.

In the three years since its founding—and on a mere shoestring—PM Press has risen to the formidable challenge of publishing and distributing knowledge and entertainment for the struggles ahead. With over 150 releases to date, we have published an impressive and stimulating array of literature, art, music, politics, and culture. Using every available medium, we've succeeded in connecting those hungry for ideas and information to those putting them into practice.

Friends of PM allows you to directly help impact, amplify, and revitalize the discourse and actions of radical writers, filmmakers, and artists. It provides us with a stable foundation from which we can build upon our early successes and provides a much-needed subsidy for the materials that can't necessarily pay their own way. You can help make that happen—and receive every new title automatically delivered to your door once a month—by joining as a Friend of PM Press. And, we'll throw in a free T-Shirt when you sign up.

Here are your options:

- $25 a month: Get all books and pamphlets plus 50% discount on all webstore purchases
- $25 a month: Get all CDs and DVDs plus 50% discount on all webstore purchases
- $40 a month: Get all PM Press releases plus 50% discount on all webstore purchases
- $100 a month: Superstar—Everything plus PM merchandise, free downloads, and 50% discount on all webstore purchases

For those who can't afford $25 or more a month, we're introducing **Sustainer Rates** at $15, $10 and $5. Sustainers get a free PM Press t-shirt and a 50% discount on all purchases from our website.

Your Visa or Mastercard will be billed once a month, until you tell us to stop. Or until our efforts succeed in bringing the revolution around. Or the financial meltdown of Capital makes plastic redundant. Whichever comes first.

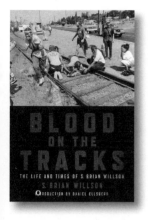

Blood on the Tracks
The Life and Times of S. Brian Willson
S. Brian Willson
ISBN: 978-1-60486-421-2 • $20.00

"We are not worth more, they are not worth less." This is the mantra of S. Brian Willson and the theme that runs throughout his compelling psycho-historical memoir. Willson's story begins in small-town, rural America, where he grew up as a "Commie-hating, baseball-loving Baptist," moves through life-changing experiences in Viet Nam, Nicaragua, and elsewhere, and culminates with his commitment to a localized, sustainable lifestyle. Willson provides numerous examples of the types of personal, risktaking, nonviolent actions he and others have taken in attempts to educate and effect political change: tax refusal, fasting, and obstruction tactics. It was such actions that thrust Brian Willson into the public eye in the mid-'80s, first as a participant in a high-profile, water-only "Veterans Fast for Life" against the Contra war being waged by his government in Nicaragua. Then, on a fateful day in September 1987, the world watched in horror as Willson was run over by a U.S. government munitions train during a nonviolent blocking action in which he expected to be removed from the tracks and arrested.

Losing his legs only strengthened Willson's identity with millions of unnamed victims of U.S. policy around the world. He provides details of his travels to countries in Latin America and the Middle East and bears witness to the harm done to poor people as well as to the environment by the steam-roller of U.S. imperialism. These heart-rending accounts are offered side by side with inspirational stories of nonviolent struggle and the survival of resilient communities.

Throughout his personal journey Willson struggles with the question, "Why was it so easy for me, a 'good' man, to follow orders to travel 9,000 miles from home to participate in killing people who clearly were not a threat to me or any of my fellow citizens?" He eventually comes to the realization that the "American Way of Life" is AWOL from humanity, and that the only way to recover our humanity is by changing our consciousness, one individual at a time, while striving for collective cultural changes toward "less and local." Thus, Willson offers up his personal story as a metaphorical map for anyone who feels the need to be liberated from the American Way of Life—a guidebook for anyone called by conscience to question continued obedience to vertical power structures while longing to reconnect with the human archetypes of cooperation, equity, mutual respect, and empathy.

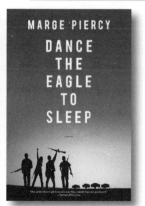

Dance the Eagle to Sleep
A Novel
Marge Piercy
ISBN: 978-1-60486-456-4 • $17.95

Originally published in 1970, Marge Piercy's second novel follows the lives of four teenagers, in a near future society, as they rebel against a military draft and "the system." The occupation of Franklin High School begins, and with it, the open rebellion of America's youth against their channeled, unrewarding lives and the self-serving, plastic society that directs them.

From the disillusionment and alienation of the young at the center of the revolt, to their attempts to build a visionary new society, the nationwide following they gain and the brutally complete repression that inevitably follows, this is a future fiction without a drop of fantasy.

As driving, violent, and nuanced today as it was 40 years ago, this anniversary edition includes a new introduction by the author reflecting unapologetically on the novel and the times from which it emerged.

Let Freedom Ring
A Collection of Documents from the Movements to Free U.S. Political Prisoners
Edited by Matt Meyer
ISBN: 978-1-60486-035-1 • $37.95

Let Freedom Ring presents a two-decade sweep of essays, analyses, histories, interviews, resolutions, People's Tribunal verdicts, and poems by and about the scores of U.S. political prisoners and the campaigns to safeguard their rights and secure their freedom. In addition to an extensive section on the campaign to free death-row journalist Mumia Abu-Jamal, represented here are the radical movements that have most challenged the U.S. empire from within: Black Panthers and other Black liberation fighters, Puerto Rican independentistas, Indigenous sovereignty activists, white anti-imperialists, environmental and animal rights militants, Arab and Muslim activists, Iraq war resisters, and others. Contributors in and out of prison detail the repressive methods--from long-term isolation to sensory deprivation to politically inspired parole denial--used to attack these freedom fighters, some still caged after 30+ years. This invaluable resource guide offers inspiring stories of the creative, and sometimes winning, strategies to bring them home.

Contributors include: Mumia Abu-Jamal, Dan Berger, Dhoruba Bin-Wahad, Bob Lederer, Terry Bisson, Laura Whitehorn, Safiya Bukhari, The San Francisco 8, Angela Davis, Bo Brown, Bill Dunne, Jalil Muntaqim, Susie Day, Luis Nieves Falcón, Ninotchka Rosca, Meg Starr, Assata Shakur, Jill Soffiyah Elijah, Jan Susler, Chrystos, Jose Lopez, Leonard Peltier, Marilyn Buck, Oscar López Rivera, Sundiata Acoli, Ramona Africa, Linda Thurston, Desmond Tutu, Mairead Corrigan Maguire and many more.

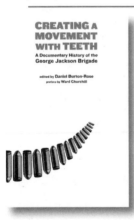

Creating a Movement with Teeth
A Documentary History of the George Jackson Brigade
Edited by Daniel Burton-Rose
ISBN: 978-1-60486-223-2 • $24.95

Bursting into existence in the Pacific Northwest in 1975, the George Jackson Brigade claimed 14 pipe bombings against corporate and state targets, as many bank robberies, and the daring rescue of a jailed member. Combining veterans of the prisoners' women's, gay, and black liberation movements, this organization was also ideologically diverse, consisting of both communists and anarchists. Concomitant with the Brigade's extensive armed work were prolific public communications. In more than a dozen communiqués and a substantial political statement, they sought to explain their intentions to the public while defying the law enforcement agencies that pursued them.

Collected in one volume for the first time, *Creating a Movement with Teeth* makes available this body of propaganda and mediations on praxis. In addition, the collection assembles corporate media profiles of the organization's members and alternative press articles in which partisans thrash out the heated debates sparked in the progressive community by the eruption of an armed group in their midst. *Creating a Movement with Teeth* illuminates a forgotten chapter of the radical social movements of the 1970s in which diverse interests combined forces in a potent rejection of business as usual in the United States.

On the Ground
An Illustrated Anecdotal History of the
Sixties Underground Press in the U.S.
Edited by Sean Stewart
ISBN: 978-1-60486-455-7 • $20.00

In four short years (1965–1969), the underground press grew from five small newspapers in as many cities in the U.S. to over 500 newspapers—with millions of readers—all over the world. Completely circumventing (and subverting) establishment media by utilizing their own news service and freely sharing content amongst each other, the underground press, at its height, became the unifying institution for the counterculture of the 1960s.

Frustrated with the lack of any mainstream media criticism of the Vietnam War, empowered by the victories of the Civil Rights era, emboldened by the anti-colonial movements in the third world and with heads full of acid, a generation set out to change the world. The underground press was there documenting, participating in, and providing the resources that would guarantee the growth of this emergent youth culture. Combining bold visuals, innovative layouts, and eschewing any pretense toward objectivity, the newspapers were wildly diverse and wonderfully vibrant.

Neither meant to be an official nor comprehensive history, *On the Ground* focuses on the anecdotal detail that brings the history alive. Comprised of stories told by the people involved with the production and distribution of the newspapers—John Sinclair, Art Kunkin, Paul Krassner, Emory Douglas, John Wilcock, Bill Ayers, Spain Rodriguez, Trina Robbins, Al Goldstein, Harvey Wasserman and more—and featuring over 50 full-color scans taken from a broad range of newspapers—*Basta Ya, Berkeley Barb, Berkeley Tribe, Chicago Seed, Helix, It Ain't Me Babe, Los Angeles Free Press, Osawatomie, Rat Subterranean News, San Francisco Express Times, San Francisco Oracle, Screw: The Sex Review, The Black Panther, The East Village Other, The Realist,* and many more—the book provides a true window into the spirit of the times, giving the reader a feeling for the energy on the ground.

Resistance Behind Bars
The Struggles of Incarcerated Women
Victoria Law
ISBN: 978-1-60486-018-4 • $20.00

In 1974, women imprisoned at New York's maximum-security prison at Bedford Hills staged what is known as the August Rebellion. Protesting the brutal beating of a fellow prisoner, the women fought off guards, holding seven of them hostage, and took over sections of the prison.

While many have heard of the 1971 Attica prison uprising, the August Rebellion remains relatively unknown even in activist circles. *Resistance Behind Bars* is determined to challenge and change such oversights. As it examines daily struggles against appalling prison conditions and injustices, *Resistance* documents both collective organizing and individual resistance among women incarcerated in the U.S. Emphasizing women's agency in resisting the conditions of their confinement through forming peer education groups, clandestinely arranging ways for children to visit mothers in distant prisons and raising public awareness about their lives, *Resistance* seeks to spark further discussion and research into the lives of incarcerated women and galvanize much-needed outside support for their struggles.

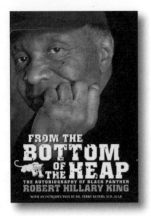

From the Bottom of the Heap
The Autobiography of Black Panther Robert Hillary King
Robert Hillary King
ISBN: 978-1-60486-039-9 • $24.95

In 1970, a jury convicted Robert Hillary King of a crime he did not commit and sentenced him to 35 years in prison. He became a member of the Black Panther Party while in Angola State Penitentiary, successfully organizing prisoners to improve conditions. In return, prison authorities beat him, starved him, and gave him life without parole after framing him for a second crime. He was thrown into solitary confinement, where he remained in a six by nine foot cell for 29 years as one of the Angola 3. In 2001, the state grudgingly acknowledged his innocence and set him free. This is his story.

It begins at the beginning: born black, born poor, born in Louisiana in1942, King journeyed to Chicago as a hobo at the age of 15. He married and had a child, and briefly pursued a semi-pro boxing career to help provide for his family. Just a teenager when he entered the Louisiana penal system for the first time, King tells of his attempts to break out of this system, and his persistent pursuit of justice where there is none.

Yet this remains a story of inspiration and courage, and the triumph of the human spirit. The conditions in Angola almost defy description, yet King never gave up his humanity, or the work towards justice for all prisoners that he continues to do today. *From the Bottom of the Heap*, so simply and humbly told, strips bare the economic and social injustices inherent in our society, while continuing to be a powerful literary testimony to our own strength and capacity to overcome.

Lucasville
The Untold Story of a Prison Uprising, 2nd ed.
Staughton Lynd
ISBN: 978-1-60486-224-9 • $20.00

Lucasville tells the story of one of the longest prison uprisings in United States history. At the maximum security Southern Ohio Correctional Facility in Lucasville, Ohio, prisoners seized a major area of the prison on Easter Sunday, 1993. More than 400 prisoners held L block for eleven days. Nine prisoners alleged to have been informants, or "snitches," and one hostage correctional officer, were murdered. There was a negotiated surrender. Thereafter, almost wholly on the basis of testimony by prisoner informants who received deals in exchange, five spokespersons or leaders were tried and sentenced to death, and more than a dozen others received long sentences.

Lucasville examines both the causes of the disturbance, what happened during the eleven days, and the fairness of the trials. Particular emphasis is placed on the inter-racial character of the action, as evidenced in the slogans that were found painted on walls after the surrender: "Black and White Together," "Convict Unity," and "Convict Race."

An eloquent Foreword by Mumia Abu-Jamal underlines these themes. He states, as does the book, that the men later sentenced to death "sought to minimize violence, and indeed, according to substantial evidence, saved the lives of several men, prisoner and guard alike." Of the five men, three black and two white, who were sentenced to death, Mumia declares: "They rose above their status as prisoners, and became, for a few days in April 1993, what rebels in Attica had demanded a generation before them: men. As such, they did not betray each other; they did not dishonor each other; they reached beyond their prison "tribes" to reach commonality."